Dr Lin Berwick (MBE) is a writer, lecturer, broadcaster and freelance journalist, despite being totally blind, having Cerebral Palsy Quadriplegia, partial deafness and being a permanent wheelchair user. She has previously published four books, mostly on the subjects of disability. She was cared for by her mother, Alma, and her father, George, until she met and married her husband, Ralph, who loved and cared for her for almost twenty-five years until he died. Lin's passion is classical music – she loves going to concerts, socialising with friends and eating out.

I wish to dedicate this book with love to my brother, George, who features in the book as George Philip Berwick for his on-going support and interest.

Dr Lin Berwick (MBE)

NOBODY DOES IT BETTER THAN ME: THE STORY OF ALMA

AUSTIN MACAULEY PUBLISHERS™

LONDON • CAMBRIDGE • NEW YORK • SHARJAH

A CIP catalogue record for this title is available from the British Library.

ISBN 9781035821570 (Paperback)
ISBN 9781035821587 (ePub e-book)

www.austinmacauley.com

First Published 2023
Austin Macauley Publishers Ltd®
1 Canada Square
Canary Wharf
London
E14 5AA

I would like to acknowledge my cousin, Kevin Herridge, for his help in providing archive notes regarding Alma's family home.

To Mary Spain for her reading and editing help.

To Stephen Karl Cottage for his dedication as my wonderfully creative amanuensis in setting down my story with such enthusiasm and skill.

I would also like to acknowledge Access to Work that provides Stephen Cottage as my support worker, for without the government provision, I could not possibly carry out this work at all.

Chapter 1

Alma Evelyn Herridge was a woman who had been through the rigours and hardships of coping with life in the East End of London – she'd certainly been put through the mill, emotionally and physically. She came from an ordinary working-class family in Canning Town. Her mother, Violet, had twelve children, two of whom died in early infancy and the other ten survived – eight boys and two girls in total. She was hard-working and extremely poor. Living at 18, South Molton Road, which was, according to *The New Survey of London Life and Labour vol.4*, 'a road where the inhabitants were living below Charles Booth's poverty line.'

The family lived in an upper flat with four rooms and a wash house – the flat roofs were liable to leak as they were made of felt or tarpaulin, with sand or earth on the top, coated with pitch. Violet's girls, Alma Evelyn and Violet Ann, were the ones that supported her by doing all the housework and cleaning. Alma told how she had to iron forty-eight shirts every week for her father and brothers. Needless to say, she was an excellent ironer!

Alma learned to be a really good cook – nothing fancy, just good wholesome English cooking. Her cakes and pastries were to die for. Alma's education was basic because she left school at thirteen. She was a product of the war years, working in 1939 in the munitions factories and making seat covers for the Jeeps whilst also machining the tarpaulins that went over the tops of lorries. It was a time of long hours and hard graft.

In 1940, a bomb was dropped on the Anderson Shelter at the bottom of Alma's parents' garden. Alma was always terrified when the sirens sounded. She either hid under the stairs or table, or ran to the bottom of the garden to the air raid shelter. Her reluctance to go in the shelter was legendary – most times she had to be pushed. She had a fear of being closed in and an even greater fear of what might happen – her one dread was that her family would not survive.

This particular day, 16 October 1940, there were too many family members to fit in the one shelter so some of them went to another close by. Alma could hear the German planes approaching.

The next thing that she was aware of was the screeching sound of the bombs dropping. Then, she was unconscious. She woke periodically, aware that dirt and dust was falling into her ears and eyes and mouth—in the distance she could hear voices—some were crying, others were desperately clawing at the rubble. Inside the Anderson Shelter, it was mayhem. Alma's father, who sat with his back to the entry hatch when the bomb struck, was killed instantly – his body falling across his daughter, Alma. The youngest child, Violet Ann, aged sixteen, lay dead at his feet. Her mother, Violet, lay crying and injured.

It took hours to get them free as the bomb struck their house in two, leaving one half standing with the dresser and its plates still intact, and the other half had fallen on top of the Anderson Shelter – this is why it took several hours for the rescuers to free the people inside. Violet's youngest son, Norman, who was six-years-old at the time, was clawing at the rubble and desperately crying. Rescuers took Alma and her mother, Violet, to a local psychiatric hospital that was decommissioned as a hospital designated for war victims. Norman was inconsolable and was only helped when he was able to see his mother almost a week later.

Violet was grief-stricken for her husband and child yet had to cope with the intense pain from her injuries of a fractured pelvis and fractured legs along with extensive bruising. Alma's legs had been crushed by the weight that had fallen on her and doctors said that she would never walk again. She was in the hospital for some three-months, having physiotherapy to try and help the nerves to recover. She had both legs in plaster from her toes to her thighs. She would lie in bed saying, "This is not going to beat me – I will walk again!"

All the time trying to move and straighten her legs at every opportunity. Doctors told her that she must try and wriggle her toes in order to gain movement. She strained with every sinew. One day she got the tiniest movement in her big toe – she called for the doctor and of course, when she tried to show him, she failed, but still she would not give up. As the weeks progressed, Alma was gaining strength. Eventually, movement did occur, starting the process of much physiotherapy and heat-treatment to try and get things moving.

Some three months later she was allowed to leave hospital, using crutches but where to go was the problem. After all, there was no house! It was a case of bed-down wherever you could! Firstly, Violet and Alma stayed in the home of one of her sons, Harry. Everybody was living on rations so to have extra members brought into your family put the whole process under a terrible strain. The war, with all its problems, still dogged Alma wherever she went and whilst she was staying at the home of Harry, her brother, an incendiary device dropped down the chimney during an air-raid, landing alight in the hearth. This was shovelled into a bucket of sand and disposed of quickly.

Some weeks later, Alma got off a train at Heathway Station in Dagenham, only to see German planes flying very low to the extent that one could see the pilots with their machine guns firing all around at the people coming out of the station. One elderly man shouted to Alma, "Get down you silly cow!" Throwing her to the ground and landing on top of her. On other occasions, she would go to the underground and stay there until the all-clear was sounded. Alma really felt that the Germans were out to get her! But amazingly, she survived!

Alma used to do shift work at the munitions factory and sometimes would be around when her brothers, Norman and Lenny, were in the playground at the nearby school. Lenny was a weak child, always crying and snivelling. He frequently needed someone to fight his corner in the playground. He looked to Alma in this regard. She was always "sorting out" the bullies and defending the younger ones – even then, she had a great compassion for the underdog which would stand her in good stead for the future. The East End of London was a target for the German war planes because of the docks. There were fires burning all over London.

Eventually, Violet found it too stressful and evacuated the boys, some of them went to an elderly couple in Leicester where they spent many happy years. They were taught good socialisation skills and manners, were well-fed, and cared for. But in the end, Violet said that, despite the risk, she wanted her children back home. They remained back home with her until the end of the war although they did have a temporary move to Pitsea in Essex after yet another air-raid.

Country life was strange to the Herridge family. They had only been used to a poverty stricken City life. They knew what it was like to go hungry and frequently lived on bread, margarine, and sugar. Their answer to everything was to swear (the "F" word being the most prevalent) and fight.

Alma's brothers could not complete a sentence without the "F" word in the middle, at the beginning, and at the end! That remained until Norman died at the age of eighty-four, in 2018.

Going back to Alma and her life at the time – although she loved the quietness of the countryside she was ever-fearful of the planes coming over the horizon. Once she got back on her feet, even though she still had a plaster-cast, she decided to work in the local pub behind the bar, serving pints. This was a case of history repeating itself because her mother, Violet, worked at The Ship public house in the East End from a child until she was married. She used to tell the story of how the pints would be lined-up along the bar in readiness for the ship-workers and dockers coming in from their early shift at five in the morning to have beer and breakfast – they would literally throw their pennies at the staff behind the bar, picking up their pints as they went.

So Alma, when she visited the pub at Pitsea, was at home behind the bar as it had been part of her very early childhood. George, and his father and brothers, were staying with their grandmother at Pound Lane in Pitsea. They would frequently visit the pub. George became very smitten with Alma but he was painfully shy.

Alma was an extremely good-looking woman. She had dark brown hair which she curled – a particular curl lay across her forehead in a very attractive manner. She had dark brown "come-to-bed-eyes" with beautiful skin and a fine, striking face which was devoid of make-up, giving over to her natural radiance. Her teeth were beautifully white and even. She knew how to flash a smile – her face absolutely lit up when she smiled. People were drawn to her. It was no wonder that George found himself mesmerised by her.

He was not usually the type of man who surrounded himself with beautiful women.

The thought of asking her out filled him with dread and he would go red in the face and feel very awkward and frequently disappeared. Eventually, he plucked up courage and offered to walk Alma home in blackout conditions down the country lanes. Alma was terrified about that journey so was only too pleased to have someone accompany her. As the weeks and months went by, George walked Alma to and from the pub, particularly in the winter evenings.

Eventually, the inevitable happened – they became lovers and prepared for their future lives together. Everything was said when the end of the war comes, we can be together. However, George got his call-up papers for the Army in 1942, so it was decided that he would marry Alma by special licence. As can be imagined, it was a rushed affair – everybody clubbed together saving bits of their rations to make for a good wedding reception. It took most of the rations to make a wedding cake but Violet achieved it. The happy couple went back home to George's grandparents where there was an amusing incident when Alma's wedding dress got caught on one of the rose bushes – George was so intent on doing things right that he picked Alma up and carried her over the threshold only to find that he was further impeded by the rosebush. George did no more, took hold of the rosebush, and yanked it out of the ground, carrying Alma and the rosebush inside!

They just had forty-eight hours of married life before he was sent to Italy, driving trucks for the war effort. He had never been away from home and never really socialised with anyone and had little or no social graces yet he was a friendly fellow and teamed-up with a man by the name of Harry Brett. Their friendship endured for many years until Harry's death. Harry's wife became great friends with Alma and in later years the children of both families were close and great friends.

But for that union of friendship in adversity, George would never have coped. He was always intensely shy. Family weddings or parties of any kind were a nightmare to him. Alma's large family teased him mercilessly, revelling in his embarrassment. He would use whatever excuse that he could to escape these occasions of frivolity – he just wanted to sit quietly in a corner and watch, eat, and get merry.

Chapter 2

Whilst George was away in the Army, it was decided that Alma would live in her mother's home in Canning Town. Finding a new form of employment was difficult after Alma's injuries sustained during the war. She couldn't cope with heavy lifting so she took a number of jobs, none of them financially lucrative and some, down-right horrible – all set in a backdrop of labour-intensive work and people-centred activity as there was none of the automation that one would see today. One of the first jobs that Alma had was working in the Knight's Castille soap factory. It was not defined quite what her role was but she hated it because she experienced the constant odour of the animal bones that were boiled to make the soap. She told of how it turned her stomach and she couldn't wait to leave.

Her next move was working for Tate and Lyle Sugar in Canning Town – her role was sealing-up the bags of sugar as they came off the conveyer belt and then helping to stack the bags in quantities of two-dozen or so. It was physically hard work and she was exhausted by the end of each day but she loved the camaraderie of the people that she became friends with on the line.

The sugar refinery was a very dusty environment – clouds of sugar seemed to hang in the air and although she wore an apron and a hat, her hair had to be washed every day because the sugar dust seemed to seep into everything. Another form of employment was working in a pepper factory—at the time it was mostly white pepper—black peppercorns were unheard of. The one big problem was that Alma seemed to be highly sensitive to the pepper—she was constantly sneezing and her eyes were always streaming. She came to hate the very idea of pepper! Other times she worked in the Peek Freans biscuit factory, helping with the packing.

Members of staff were allocated bags of broken biscuits that they could buy very cheaply.

Having such treats was a rarity in those war-torn times.

Alma could be a bit of a rebel. On one occasion, she wrote a letter to the Prime Minister, Winston Churchill, about her mother's widow's pension and the derisory sum that she got for injuries during the war. She wrote a very strongly-worded letter (sadly, it never came to light) telling Mr Churchill where he could stick his meagre pension, especially when he had rich food and sumptuous dinners while others were almost starving – the letter was replied to by one of Churchill's secretarial staff but sadly, it never came to light, probably because Alma threw it in the bin in utter disgust!

Alma's socialization was going to the local dances. Her brothers played and sang with guitars and Violet could knock out a tune on the piano – she loved nothing more than getting a crowd of people around her and having a good old singsong of wartime melodies. Alma would get invited – she also loved going to a local hop. Glen Miller and other big bands were the order of the day and they had many recordings on an old 78 wind-up gramophone. George would write home every day. Alma kept all his letters, wrapped in a blue ribbon. He had beautiful handwriting – very neat and clear. His letters were extremely touching and completely out of character, in fact, it was hard to believe that *he* wrote them. They were so romantic and loving – he would talk about what it would be like when the war ended and how he would make a home for Alma that would be "like a palace". It all seemed very unbelievable due to his working-class background.

Of course there was no reason why he couldn't have aspirations of grandeur and better things to come but he was in a fantasy world because he was lonely being so far away from home and all that he knew. In 1944, he was given ten-days leave before his next assignment. That was a very precious time for George and Alma as they had had only two days of married life before George was whisked off to Italy back in 1942. So, ten days must have felt so special.

It went all too quickly then George was sent to North Africa. He hated it, especially the heat, the flies, and the mosquitoes. He was in the Transport Corps, driving heavy hot jeeps through the African countryside. The one thing he spoke about with fondness was the beautiful water melons that could be picked at the side of the road or bought from passers-by. Even though the melons were not cold, their sweet liquid juice was like heaven because of the heat of the day. They ate masses of them just so that they could quench their thirst and have something delicious.

Rations were extremely meagre and they would often look for parcels from home or some delivered by the Red Cross Organisation. Home could not come soon enough when Germany surrendered to the Allies on 7th May 1945 in France – it was a time of great rejoicing. George had a reasonably smart de-mob suit and it was time for him to look for work. On his return, he went back to Violet's home where Alma was residing. It wasn't long before she became pregnant.

All the while they struggled to manage on the meagre rations. George demanded bacon or eggs for his breakfast and it annoyed Violet enormously. Alma was quite undernourished and George argued with Violet because she was holding their ration books—eking out extra supplies just for herself. George got extremely angry saying that they wanted to control their own ration books so that Alma was able to have what she was due – such as extra milk and eggs to help keep her strong during her pregnancy.

Violet became so aggressive and angry at George's protestations that she hit him over the head with a full bottle of milk – the contents of which poured down his face. She told him that they could get out of her house and go and find somewhere else to live. By now, Alma was overdue and she had to sit on an armchair on the back of a lorry whilst being driven to London.

Their refuge was in George's grandparents' home. The house was not particularly clean and it backed onto horse stables that were owned by the police. There were rats and mice (and their droppings) in the house and Alma was absolutely terrified. The old grandfather was a very angry, miserable old man and they stayed there for several years. In fact, Alma had two further children whilst residing at the property.

For now though, George and Alma had to concentrate on their first-born – about to be delivered any minute. When she got to see a midwife and local gynaecologist her baby was breached and she was extremely stressed, having very badly-swollen ankles. She was extremely depressed by the whole process. At the time, Alma had a twenty-four-inch waist and very slender hips – it was not going to be easy to be able to deliver a breeched baby. The procedure was absolutely brutal, cutting her open and delivering the child, weighing ten pounds three ounces. It wasn't easy bringing little John Albert home to Poplar, in the East End of London as conditions were very difficult.

If the old boy, George's grandfather, fancied going to the toilet in the back yard he would do so and cared nothing for making sure that it was clean to bring a baby up in. Alma was forever scrubbing the stairs, cleaning and tidying. Each morning she would wash down the back yard and George would set a large copper going to boil the water, and Alma would have to use a wooden mangle to wring the water out of the clothes and then dry them – either in the sunshine or on a clothes-horse in front of the fire.

Alma's only consolation to all this depravation was the love of her son, John Albert. She loved the periods of free time when she could cuddle him and he snuck into her breast for milk. When George returned home from work, John would often cry for attention and Alma, quite naturally, would pick him up to comfort him.

This greatly annoyed George – he was angry that Alma was giving the child too much attention. George would snatch baby John from her arms and say, 'That's quite enough!' and he would place him back screaming into his cot.

Alma was hurt and angry by this wrenching of her child from her arms. She could not understand why George was so cross but she had the foresight to realise that this was due to the emotion of jealousy as George had always been the kind of person who wanted unstinting devotion and attention.

These conditions were not conducive to happiness and although things were tough, it would have been much better if Alma and George could have made peace with Violet but sadly, they only ever experienced a minor truce. Right the way through their marriage there was always tension between them.

Alma could not forgive her mother for sending them packing at such a difficult time and in later years that created a rift that could never be fully repaired.

George found work in a timber yard. He had done courses in carpentry and loved the work. He would often deliver wood by strapping it to his back, when riding a bicycle. On better days, he could have some refuge in driving the lorry. 1947 was a very hard winter and they were absolutely freezing cold. Central heating did not exist. The only heating that they had was a large coal fire and paraffin heaters on the landing that were smelly and smoky.

There was no heating in the bedrooms so Alma would iron the sheets to make them warm to get into, then, she would use hot water bottles, usually of the stone or metal variety. On the bed, Army blankets of either a dark grey or Khaki colour, along with their winter coats, were laid on top of them to keep them warm. It would be impossible to imagine how awful this must have been – it seems that they experienced deprivation at every turn.

Chapter 3

The winter of 1947 was truly terrible—frozen pipes that frequently burst, thick smog—a peasoup thick, yellow fog where you could barely see your hand in front of your face. "Wearing my snow boots and fur-lined coat I was not once warm. All my pipes are frozen, so a bath or a wash is out of the question," grumbled architectural historian James Lees-Milne. The writer, Christopher Isherwood, who was over from America for the first time since before the war, observed that Londoners themselves 'didn't seem depressed or sullen – though their faces were still wartime faces, lined and tired, while many of them stared longingly at my new overcoat.'

A new overcoat was a luxury that many people in the East End of London could not afford. Not only were their faces ravaged by war-torn memories, but they were heartily sick of rationing and bargaining with whatever they could to get some variety into their diet.

Many journalists have written that people were healthier from a frugal diet but people longed for good quality meat and the odd luxury. So often, people would barter using whatever means that they could to get good food on the table. People would often hark back to the days of the VE celebrations where the stress was suddenly lifted from their shoulders.

Many Londoners congregated in central London, particularly around Buckingham Palace, where there was much singing and dancing. They would take hold of someone that they didn't know and start to do "The Conga" and happily dance around or climb the lampposts and railings. Of course there was the happy incident when Princesses Elizabeth and Margaret wore headscarves around their heads to obscure their faces and left the grounds of the palace so that they could join in anonymously with the crowds.

Imagine how everyone must have felt when they were all sharing in the fun of that glorious day when peace would reign. Now, not two years later, people were struggling yet again – jobs were hard to come by, money was even harder to find, especially if you were a working-class citizen. George and Alma were very much part of that era but for now they were caught up in the daily grind of living with George's grandparents and trying desperately to bring up a child under difficult circumstances in such a harsh winter.

In 1948, there was a turn for the better. The National Health Service was founded by Aneurin Bevan who was Minister for Health. At the founding of the National Health Service, Aneurin Bevan made this memorable statement underpinning his principles and all the qualities that the NHS stands for today...'The collective principle asserts that...no society can legitimately call itself civilised if a sick person is denied medical aid because of lack of means.'— *Aneurin Bevan, In Place of Fear, p. 100.*

So, gone was the struggle of finding two shillings-and-sixpence each time that a doctor was called. Now, people would receive hospital treatment at the point of need, including items such as dentures. Many of the cases treated by the NHS in the early days were for illnesses such as Pneumonia, Tuburculinum Bovinum (TB), and infections of various kinds, since the progress made by Alexander Flemming in 1928 with the discovery of Penicillin. The Health Service was going to prove an absolute boon for George and Alma in later life.

John Albert was born in July 1947. Alma only had five months of pregnancy-free life before she became pregnant again. George Philip was born in November 1948. Now, George had his hands full trying to provide for two little children. There wasn't much money around and what there was, had to be stretched somewhat, especially as George loved to bet on the horses – something that he did well into his ninetieth year. There was never any money.

Whenever Alma said that she needed to buy shoes or clothing for the children, George would say, 'Don't go looking at me – I haven't got any money.' But he always had time to go to the bookmaker and put a bet on the horses or dogs, and of course, the Grand National. George was a regular smoker. His pastime was cadging cigarettes off of anyone he could con one from – always with the promise 'I'll give it you back' though sadly, to reciprocate, was not George's forte!

If he could get away without buying a round of drinks in a pub, he was happy. His classic wheeze was to wait until several rounds of drinks had been purchased, then, he would make it abundantly clear that Alma and others close to him, did *not* want a drink and he would always hang back so that the round of drinks required became much smaller as people left the function – something that Alma absolutely detested. She would say before they went out 'Make sure you get off your arse, put your hand in your pocket, and be one of the first at the bar – everyone knows what you're up to and *why* you are doing it and it's fucking embarrassing!'

George always had a reputation for meanness. He was never generous but held on tightly to his wallet. His classic trait was that he never opened his wallet in the same room as other people – he always walked outside, took the money out of his wallet and then came back in and gave it to you so that you couldn't see what he had in his wallet.

Alma would come to detest these kinds of traits. She was a free-hearted, generous person who would give her last penny to anyone that needed it – she was a person that would give the "top brick off the house". She would learn to her cost that George did not reciprocate these feelings of generosity.

Chapter 4

George's mean streak continued and he was the laughing stock of many people because they would tell Alma how he was always making sure that he was well-fed, buying himself bacon sandwiches, rolls, and particularly, fresh cream cakes and so on when he was out and about. Not that Alma ever saw any evidence of such niceties unless she made them herself. George would come in from work and say that he was absolutely starving because he hadn't eaten all day.

Alma would say, 'Don't lie to me; you are not capable of not eating for a whole day!' But he would insist that what he was saying was the truth. However, he was frequently found out as his friends and brothers who visited the house would testify to that fact. That kind of lying put Alma on edge because she felt that she could never trust him. His constant, mean response to everything drove her mad so whilst she struggled to make ends meet, he would carry on regardless. It only served to make for bitter resentment which just got worse as the years progressed because, in the end, he didn't know reality from fiction. He would make up stories to suit himself.

Sadly, he was far from honest. He would do anything to make money but it wasn't to give it to his wife to buy clothing for the children but rather, what *he* wanted to do. There was never any discussion about how money should be saved or spent. Secretly, George was quite clever at saving. It was only after his death that the true extent of his savings and scrimping became known.

People were incredulous at the large amount he had accrued although, that did not take into account the thousands he must have lost on gambling. Alma, found him out all the time – perhaps, secretly, he wanted to be found out. She would search through his pockets before putting the trousers into the wash. There would be betting slips rolled-up in the bottom of his pockets—often, the amounts were incredible—huge by anyone's standard at that time. The more she searched around the house, the more she found evidence.

When Alma confronted him, he would hotly deny it. 'Don't lie to me' was her frequent cry and it would always end up in a row. When she became really frustrated about the lack of money and resources and his gambling, her anger would spill over – she would march down to the local betting shops until she found him. She would drag him outside because she realised that it was an obsession and more importantly, an absolute mug's game. Alma wondered what the future would hold for this little family where money was at a premium and there was no real emotional consolation for all the effort that she was making.

In this very cramped, dirty house, the grandfather would complain that Alma was always scrubbing the stairs. To show his annoyance he would kick a pail of urine down the stairs just after she'd scrubbed them and he would say, 'Now you can do it all over again!'

And of course, she did! She would frequently have to, otherwise the smell was atrocious. It certainly didn't help for good relationships. When George's brother, Alfred, brought his son, Alfred junior round to see the grandparents, Alfred junior, would get on John's tricycle and run it full pelt into the brick wall. He would then constantly crash it into the brickwork until the front spokes of the wheel were damaged and all the paintwork was scratched.

Naturally, it caused John to be heartbroken and although Alma protested about what was being meted-out to her children, George did nothing. So what Alma had to do quite clearly was to 'go it alone.' She was waging a personal war within her heart for the conditions that she found herself living under and the attitude toward her by her parents-in-law. It wasn't many months before Alma found herself pregnant again. It seemed that George only had to look at her, and she would fall!

The third pregnancy did not go well. Alma had deficiencies of iron, folic acid, and was also lacking in general vitamins due to a poor diet. When her baby was twenty-eight-weeks, she went into labour. She experienced bleeding and her water broke. She found herself being sirened by ambulance accompanied by her GP to St Andrew's Hospital, Bow, London E3, causing George to go into panic-mode – he could never really cope with pressure. His way of dealing with pressure was to shout and yell and bang his fist on anything he could find.

As an emergency measure, the boys, John and George, were taken to a local child-minder from early morning until after hospital visiting. George Philip was a very gentle, sensitive little boy who found this whole experience extremely stressful – he hated the fact that the child-minder had a large dog that barked and snarled a lot.

As a result, George Philip went into his shell, and for years, he never really came out of it. It was at that point of the trauma that George Philip started to stammer – he could not complete a sentence without stammering and George, his father, never had any patience. He would say, 'What's the matter with you boy? Why can't you speak properly?' The more his father ranted and raved, the more George Philip (or Georgie, as he was known to the family) clamped up.

For now, everything had to be put aside because at St Andrews Hospital, Bow, baby number three was coming, come what may! Forceps were used and Alma was told that her baby was still-born. She went over to the slab in the delivery room in a total daze. She could not believe that her child, weighing just two-pounds at birth, lay dead on that cold slab. Whilst weeping over the child, she suddenly heard the tiniest of squeaks – rather like the sound of a mouse.

She told the doctor that her baby was crying. He replied 'Don't be silly, mother, your baby is dead.' Alma retorted 'She is *not* – come with me and look!'

The doctor went over to the slab only to realise that Alma was indeed correct – there was total panic in the room. The baby was rushed to an incubator and put into an oxygen tent. The doctor said, 'Although your baby is alive, she is not expected to live, therefore, we should arrange with the hospital chaplain to have her christened immediately.'

No one within the family could be found to fulfil the role of Godparent so, two West Indian nurses took on that role and four hours later, the baby was christened, Linda Jean Berwick.

It was a terrifying time for both parents but particularly for Alma. All George could think about was how he would get the children home from the child-minder and the fact that his dinner was not going to be provided for him!

Chapter 5

The Berwick household was suddenly in total chaos. Alma was devastated and yet totally preoccupied with this tiny baby, weighing just two-pounds at birth. Alma showed people how even dolls' clothes were far too big for her baby and how the child could sit within the length of the doctor's hand. Linda was still in an oxygen tent so it was very difficult for Alma to have any contact within the first few weeks.

Feeding the child was an almost never-ending impossible task – it took two hours to give a normal feed so that by the time that task was completed it had to begin all over again. Alma had to "express" her breast milk by using a pump. This was then fed to Linda using an inner tube of a fountain pen. The milk was squeezed into the baby's mouth – very slowly and carefully.

Alma and George spent three months visiting the hospital with George attending the visiting of the baby at night, and Alma, travelling by bus to deliver the breast milk and see how the child was getting on during the daytime. It was all very traumatic and there was always the thought that Linda might die.

For three months, Linda was still on oxygen which was gradually reduced. Once she had reached the magical five-pounds in weight, she could leave the hospital. Alma had used her skills as a knitter to make all the baby's clothes, blankets, and a shawl to keep her warm. Returning to the home at 13, Alton Street, Poplar, made Alma realise how problematic their lives would be.

George was watchful when he could be there, but he was terrified for the child, and for himself – after all, there had already been disability within his family. His brother, Roy, had severe Cerebral Palsy, rendering him without speech and barely able to stand.

Alma used to get up in the middle of the night to feed Linda. She was horrified at the dirty state of the house and realised that to have to cope with the mice coming out, sitting on the hearth of the fireplace and preening themselves, was not a fit state for a premature baby to be brought up in. All food items had to be covered and put into tins because of the mice droppings leaving Alma absolutely terrified as she waited for the milk to heat up on the stove.

George did not take his turn on the night-shift – that was women's work! He had to get up early in the morning and go to work. There was always tension in the house, never more so as Linda screamed constantly. Visitors did not come to the house very often and when they did, they only stayed for a very short time because of the constant screaming.

It was evident that all was not well – Linda's limbs were in constant spasm, one leg crossing over the other in a kind of scissor-movement – to put a nappy on her was a real feat of endurance for Alma. It was a case of literally prising Linda's limbs apart which was accompanied by high-pitched screaming. Every two-hours or so, this task had to be repeated with the accompanying screams.

One thing that was certain as far as Alma was concerned, was that she could not bring up a child who had obvious disability in this kind of family environment so she set about trying to change things. She was a very astute, determined woman who would not be beaten or fobbed-off with red-tape bureaucracy.

Alma would spend hours massaging Linda's body to try and ease the obvious pain and discomfort. Evacuation of the bowel had to be done manually – no one showed her how she should do it, she just used her own common sense.

Alma spent much of her life observing Linda. She could see the frustration within her child who obviously wanted to move but could not. Her right arm, as well as both legs were in spasm and this was obviously very painful when Linda tried to reach out for things but in vain. The constant supervision continued. Alma was aware that Linda did not reach the same milestones as her other children had done. She would take Linda back and forth to the doctor who would tell her that she was just being an over-anxious mother. 'Your child is three months behind a normal child; therefore you must give her time to catch up.'

Alma was left to go home and ponder all these things and worry herself sick. Each day of survival was a little miracle. Alma started writing letters to the council explaining that she had a three-month premature baby and that the housing situation where she was currently living was not suitable. She constantly wrote these letters and was, of course, continually fobbed-off.

Alma was determined to get answers to her repeated questions. Eventually, the GP agreed that Linda should be seen by a paediatrician at the then, Queen Elizabeth Hospital for Children in Shadwell, E1. Alma was told to take the child's clothes off. The doctor held her by her legs upside down and watched her scream. He said to Alma, 'This child is spastic, take her home, forget about her – she'll never be any good. You're wasting my time, your time, and everybody else's time!' He literally threw the child back into her arms.

Alma was staggered by the brutality of the doctor. She left the hospital in floods of tears. On the bus, going home, Alma was crying and so was Linda. Alma's response was, 'How dare that doctor say, "You're no good." We are going to show them that you are worthy and you are going to make something of your life and prove them all wrong!'

When George returned home, Alma told him what had happened. All he would say was, 'We are not going to put her into a home. We're going to love her and look after her.'

Those sentiments were all very well but of course it wasn't George who was doing the bulk of the caring, but Alma who was dealing with all Linda's physical needs, coping with all the emotions and constant screaming, and still caring for the family. Alma never gave up on trying to reduce the spasms and the tensions within Linda's body – she would massage her back and neck muscles with every spare minute that she had to try to make things better. At least Linda was now in the system for medical care as well as physiotherapy.

There was also a light at the end of the tunnel because, as a result of Linda's special needs, they would now have more points within the system to obtain suitable housing. Eventually, in 1951, Alma was taken to see a property on the new Lansbury Estate in Poplar, East London.

They visited the show house at 14, Grundy Street, Poplar, E14. It was a spacious three bedroom property with a sizeable living room, hallway, and large kitchen. The fact that this property was an end-terrace meant that the living room and kitchen was larger than the other similar houses in the street. There were thirteen steps on the stairs before one reached the landing which had three bedrooms with a small separate toilet and bathroom.

The garden, however, was very small – just thirteen-feet-square, surrounded by a brick wall and a coal shed and barbed-wire fencing, leading to a gated park area which was mostly grass and cement with boulders and a climbing frame for the children to play – in those days there wasn't any protection on the ground to break the falls of the children slipping off the climbing frame or boulders.

Nevertheless, this house was a palace in Alma's eyes. The floors were covered in black, shiny tiles. This was to prove to be a Godsend in later years.

There was an entry in the visitors' book at the Lansbury Estate show house written by His Royal Highness, The Duke of Edinburgh. His comments were, that it was 'A lovely little house but it had been bodged-up.' Some of the doors and windows did not fit properly for example. As Alma left the show house she prayed that she would be allocated it.

Some weeks later she was told to come and view the house that had been allocated to her. She was brought to that same show house that she had visited a few weeks earlier and she was absolutely amazed to be given the key and informed that this was now her home. She was completely overjoyed. Indeed, the whole family could not believe their luck. Were things going to get better at last?

Chapter 6

Linda's medical care was shifted from the Queen Elizabeth Hospital in Shadwell to the Queen Elizabeth Hospital for Children in Hackney Road, E2. She was going to be under the care of the eminent paediatrician, Ursula Shelley and a new physiotherapist, Nancy R. Finnie – later to become an esteemed writer on the treatment of Cerebral Palsy for children. In fact, Linda was Nancy's first patient at this hospital. For something like three months, all that was achieved was gentle massage and heat-treatment, three times a week.

Then, one day, Nancy came in with a determined, angry look upon her face 'Right, young lady' she said, '*I*, am going to sort you out this morning – you can scream and protest all you like, but *I* am going to win!' She started trying to prise the scissored-legs apart and of course, Linda started to scream. Miss Finnie persisted – she was leaving large red hand marks on Linda's skin and Alma, who stood by watching, was becoming more and more distressed. She asked Miss Finnie to stop saying, 'You are hurting my child.'

Miss Finnie said, 'I don't care, I am going to win!' In the end, Linda was beside herself, crying and screaming with pain.

Alma said again, 'Stop! You are hurting my child!'

Miss Finnie replied 'I don't care!'

Alma said, 'You will care!' and promptly punched her in the face.

Miss Finnie was in total shock. It was a great lesson for her to learn that day that you can only push a parent so far. Naturally, Alma apologised profusely.

Miss Finnie's reaction was to say, 'Come and have a cup of tea and a fag to calm down.' This was a surprising reaction because she was a very cultured – one might say, posh lady, who was impeccably coiffured, smelling of My Sin perfume by Lanvin. It was absolutely gorgeous and Alma loved the fragrance too.

Alma pleaded with Miss Finnie never to tell George about the incident because she knew that he would be angry. Alma kicked herself at the loss of self-control but she just saw red – it was all too much and the constant screaming finally got to her. After a short time, Miss Finnie and Alma returned to the couch where Linda was lying.

Miss Finnie said, 'I'm sorry that I hurt you, Linda, but you must understand that we have had to do this today to make you better so that one day you will be able to stand tall.' Linda could never imagine what it would be like to stand tall as she couldn't even move her legs independently but now, thanks to Alma's hard work, she was at least, able to lift her head.

On returning home, Alma continued to watch. She would hold a piece of cotton over Linda's eyes to see if she responded to it. Gradually, with the strengthening of neck muscles, Linda was able to begin to turn her head. That earlier doctor at Shadwell had told Alma that her daughter was not only spastic but totally blind.

Through Alma's persistence she was able to show that although Linda's sight was defective, she could at least see something. She was obviously blind in her left eye, but with her right eye, was able to track the cotton moving and turn her head towards it. Obviously, that right eye was damaged because Linda could only see from the area of around ten o'clock through to four o'clock. Alma had worked this out by acute observation. Then she started to place things within Linda's reach at the position where she would be able to see them.

Alma was absolutely thrilled when Linda turned her head, looking towards the object. All the arguments with doctors who said that Linda was blind and Alma disputing them were proved right. Linda was then taken to see an eye specialist at the Queen Elizabeth Hospital for Children who also worked at Moorfield's Eye Hospital in City Road, London, EC1. He examined Linda in a darkened room with just the ophthalmic torches played into her eyes. He told Alma that her observations were correct – Linda was not totally blind in both eyes, she had a small amount of vision in the right eye which was also affected by the eye-condition known as Retrolental Fibroplasia which was caused by a burning of the back of the eyes due to the use of pure oxygen when she was in the incubator in intensive care as a premature baby.

Alma was overjoyed but very quickly, her joy was shattered because the doctor said, 'I am going to take out her left eye so that what little sight she has in her right eye can be strengthened.'

Alma said, 'You are doing nothing of the sort.'

The doctor was angry and said, 'Let me talk to your husband who will obviously see sense.'

Within days, George and Alma went to the hospital together and George said, 'You leave my daughter's eye where it is because you never know, medical science might improve things later on.' The reality was that this could never happen and in 1976 the left eye was removed, due to intense pain with Glaucoma.

Chapter 7

The physiotherapy continued over the months. Linda was now beginning to cooperate with Miss Finnie much more. Despite the difficult beginnings, Linda almost worshipped Nancy Finnie.

She had got her to be able to sit up albeit with some support, and able to roll onto her tummy. This is where Alma really came into her own. The whole point about Cerebral Palsy as it became known, was that movement had to be continually planted into the brain. It was not a natural, spontaneous process. Alma worked at trying to bend the knees and arms and do whatever she could to plant the idea of movement from wherever it came. One way was that George would tell Linda to hit him and he would encourage her to hit him as hard as she could with her fist. She turned out to be very strong on her left hand but much weaker on her right.

Eventually George would tell her to stop because she was hurting him! George didn't really care as long as Linda was doing something active. When he came home at lunchtime, he would put Linda on his lap and she would take things off his dinner plate and eat them. Alma told George it wasn't a good idea because she had to learn how to manage in the real world but again, George didn't care as long as something was being achieved.

Suddenly, Linda was able to sit up, aged three but still spent much of her time screaming. The only way Alma got any respite from this was to put Linda around her hips so that she could lean on Alma's back and watch what was going on – she watched Alma stirring the pots, cooking the meal, and serving it up for the family, all the while, Linda was quiet until she was put down, hating the restrictions and not being able to see what her mother was doing. Linda could only really see what was directly in front of her face. By the age of four, she was able to speak – *perfectly normally*!

Whilst visiting the Queen Elizabeth Hospital, Alma had the opportunity of speaking with many parents who had children with Cerebral Palsy. It was quite a common circumstance because so many premature babies, or those who had had difficult births for one reason or another, had suffered brain damage.

Alma used the opportunity to talk with parents and discover what they needed. The overriding issue was to get adequate physiotherapy and behavioural therapy for their children. The Spastics Society was formed in 1954 and there were many affiliated groups that stemmed from it, one of them being The East London Spastics Society. The word spastic was much more emotive so it was a way of raising more money for the cause. The Spastics Society which later became known as SCOPE, was instrumental in bringing parents together.

At the first meeting of The Spastics Society George was fired up with enthusiasm to start an affiliated group of his own which became The East London Spastics Society and was intended to initiate change for children and their families in the East End of London. George and Alma had a meeting with parents who felt that the overriding need was for physiotherapy. They had big ideas and very little money but they started fund-raising and became a registered charity. That inaugural meeting was to become the biggest part of George's life – he had found his purpose and used all his available time to raise money. It was done piecemeal in a very small way but, nonetheless, effectively.

Up to now, George had not be seen in a very positive light which was unfortunate because he did have many fine qualities – he would always be willing to help somebody and do whatever he could to enhance the lives of people with disability so long as it didn't personally cost him any money.

He would always freely give of his time but not his cash.

During his forty-five year history with the charity he held the position of transport officer, treasurer, secretary, and chairman. As transport officer he would take groups of children and their families down to the coast for the day and on some big annual trips, a fifty-seater coach was hired to go to the Martello Camp at Clacton-on-Sea. He hated giving speeches in public.

Indeed, he was hopeless at it, but what he lost in intellectual ability he gained in practicality.

He helped to build a new social centre which was opened in 1972 by the boxer Henry Cooper OBE. Sadly, at that point George decided to resign from office and nobody even thanked him for all his hard work. He must have been absolutely devastated. His daughter, Linda, watched all the hard work that George and Alma put in – they literally never had a meal in peace because the telephone was always ringing off the hook concerning the charity work.

When Alma's son John, was almost seven years old, George, his father, treated himself to a new fountain pen. It was Father's Day and John wondered what he could give his father for a gift. He was not given pocket money but relied on contributions that he was given by uncles and other members of the family. For him, he had what he called a "brainwave".

'I'll know what to buy Daddy, I'll give him a jar of Indian ink for his new fountain pen because I think that will please him.' John took the money out of his money box – one-shilling-and-eleven pence-ha'penny. Alma got some appropriate wrapping paper and a card and John wrote his personal message and proudly gave his dad the gift on Father's Day. Rather than George showing pleasure, he went absolutely ballistic. 'What's this?' He cried.

'Are you taking the piss out of me? A bloody bottle of ink? Is that all you could give me?' George started hitting and punching the boy, kicking him up the street. John ran away from him but George continued to follow, catching him up. He grabbed him by his coat, lifted him off his feet and carried on punching. John was absolutely incredulous. He had no idea what he had done. He eventually wriggled away from his father and ran home crying to Alma.

Alma ran after George and they started yet another of their enormous rows which ended in fisticuffs from both sides. Linda sat in the front garden, shaking, wondering what on earth was happening.

What should have been a lovely moment of togetherness turned out to be a total disaster. At that moment, the tide turned with Alma. Her hatred for George really set in. Years later, she spoke of that incident. Their relationship never really recovered from that moment. George's constant bullying, nagging, and lack of appreciation for whatever was done for him, created more and more resentment that became engrained in the fabric of their marriage.

Miss Finnie and Alma continued to plant the idea of movement, moving the hands and arms, trying to develop strength so that Linda could lean on one hand and lift the other. Firstly, she got the idea of moving the arms towards an object and although her legs were still like breaking a plank of wood, eventually the idea of crawling became firmly planted in Linda's mind.

Crawling became Linda's mobility until the age of eleven. George thought it would be helpful to get down by the sea so he bought a caravan on a site at Seasalter, near Whitstable in Kent. His idea was to have green grass and fresh air to strengthen Linda's body. So, the crawling continued on the vast length of grass leading to the public toilet areas and speaking to the other caravan owners on the site.

People would say how awful it was that Linda was disabled but George and Alma just accepted it and still continued to try and make a difference. Life was much easier now that Linda could talk. Fortunately, she had perfect hearing and more importantly, she found her voice and absolutely loved singing. Her education was the next problem to tackle.

Linda was placed into Bromley Hall PH School, Leven Road, Bow, E3, a school for children with special needs so that some education could begin. She was sent, aged five, to see an educational psychologist. The psychologist asked Linda, 'What do I have around my neck and what do I have on my wrist?'

Linda thought that she would not bother to answer because the questions were so stupid. From there, a box was produced with all kinds of different shaped slots in the lid. The idea was to slot the pieces into the appropriate spaces. This was a very difficult task for Linda to execute because she could not see the slots well enough to define how to fit the pieces together.

There were many other tests but the upshot was a diagnosis that Linda was educationally subnormal. It was terrible to put labels upon people that were very difficult to take away. For now, she was stuck with that diagnosis, struggling with poor sight and movement but at least there was some progress.

Due to the fact that Linda crawled everywhere, she was frequently in need of new shoes and trousers so that she didn't hurt her knees. Alma's solution was to buy a pair of jeans that were far too long, cut the bottom off the trousers to make patches for the knees that wore out. Alma would stitch pieces of leather onto the knees of the trousers to give them extra strength and protection.

Alma would frequently say to George, 'Linda needs new shoes,' because now she was wearing the toe-caps out every three weeks.

Typically, George's response was, 'Don't look at me; I haven't got any bleedin' money.' So, with her usual determination, Alma decided to do it herself. She had a small sewing machine and realised that she was highly capable of making things. She would make all of Linda's dresses, making them look really pretty with ribbons and lace and she would plait Linda's hair, tying each plait with a ribbon which had to complement the clothes that she was wearing.

George and his brother Colin began to take an interest in model-making – they would buy highly-complicated kits of model ships and the like, spending hours making them and painting them. Naturally, the boys, John and George, were fascinated by this procedure. Up until now, they had only seen things like this on the television and could only dream of having such a thing.

After George and Colin completed many models, they decided that they would like to build a model racing motor-boat that could be floated on the lake in Victoria Park, Hackney. The boat took months to build – it was powered by a miniature steam engine and it also worked on some level or other, with petrol. When George tried it out in the bath, the smell was horrendous but then came the day when the boat was going to be launched. The boys were extremely excited.

It was a cold winter's morning so they were all wrapped-up warmly ready to go in the car. Suddenly there was a knock at the door and Uncle Colin arrived. When he knew that the boys were coming along too, he was angry. 'Oh, you're not bringing those two along are you?' He said. 'If you are, I'm not coming.'

So, George did no more but told the boys that they couldn't come and he went off with Colin to the lake. The boys were in floods of tears. They said to Alma, 'Daddy promised us that we could go with him, and now, we've been left behind yet again?' And again, they were inconsolable.

On George's return from the lake, he met the full wrath of Alma's anger. She was baking at the time so she tipped a two-pound bag of flour over his head and whacked him with her rolling pin. George was absolutely furious. He said, 'You are a bloody madwoman – just like your mother!'

The language between them was ripe! George showed his fists although he didn't actually strike her. Needless to say, the Sunday morning trips on the lake were no more and it wasn't long before the model-making ended.

Alma went to the area of Stepney, E1, looking for work and found a woman, Mrs Onions, who had a business making children's nightdresses – the job came with its own industrial sewing machine. It was absolute slave-labour, something like, one shilling-and-sixpence for a whole nightdress or pair of pyjamas but nevertheless, it was money coming in – money that would buy shoes and patches for Linda. Alma's sons John and George were very annoyed saying, 'How is it that she always gets things and we don't?'

A perfectly justified comment to make but George, their father would say, 'You can run around and do things – but Linda can't.' That was the start of a build-up of resentment by the boys for how they were excluded. Linda could understand the argument but could do nothing to change it. It did not help for good relationships between the children. The family would go to Seasalter every weekend.

George now had a car. Previously he had a motorbike and sidecar but Alma hated it saying that it was too flimsy and unsafe. Eventually George bought a Triumph Renown car – it was a bit like a luxury limousine with leather seats and a sliding door between the front and back passengers. George absolutely loved it. The boys had the freedom to run around on the campsite and go to the beach. Unfortunately it did not have the luxury of gorgeous sand, it was mostly stones and seashells – cockles, whelks and so on that happened to be thrown up upon the shore.

It was a very difficult terrain for Linda to negotiate as the ground was so hard and the shells so spiky and sharp but it never stopped her from wanting to join in. A great pastime was cockling. Linda and the boys would go out into the mud and Linda would watch for the bubbles that emerged from the mud, then scoop her hand down into the mud and pull out handfuls of cockles.

Naturally, after crawling out into the mud once the tide had gone out, Linda was tired on the return journey and would ask her father to pick her up and carry her home. Returning to the camp site, the spoils of shellfish and dabs of plaice which had been strung-up on a baited-line would be brought back for all to enjoy.

Alma came into her own yet again with the exercising routine. George bought a Triang Mobo Tricycle with the pedals on the front wheels and Linda would sit on the trike with her feet strapped to the pedals whilst Alma turned the wheels by hand. She wheeled the tricycle up and down the hall of the house and through the living room to give as long a space as possible. This went on for six months.

Eventually, one day, Linda suddenly took over and rode the bike herself, unaided. Alma was incredulous. This was to be Linda's means of mobility outside the home until the age of eleven. Alma was terrified to let Linda go off on her own but eventually Linda said, 'Look, you stand there and I'll go to the end of the street, turn around, and come back to you.' This was painstakingly achieved. 'Now' Linda said, 'You have got to let me go out and play with the other kids.'

Alma was reluctant but at least she could keep an eye on her in Rocky Park, as it was known, beyond the garden of their home. It was an incredible achievement of painstaking effort and determination – all achieved by Alma. Nancy Finnie and the other doctors were absolutely thrilled. Linda was going to "motor" now! The Mobo Triang Trike progressed to a fixed-wheel, three-wheeled tricycle with a padded seat and backrest. This was Linda's means of mobility around the classroom where she would ride the bike to her desk, be lifted off by the school attendant, and then put on the chair. When she needed a toilet break, she would get on the trike and ride off.

Nancy Finnie was beginning to make great strides with Linda. She had gone to the Bobath Clinic in Marylebone High Street, later to move to St John's Wood, opposite Lord's Cricket Ground. She had asked Alma whether she could take Linda with her as a sample patient for herself and other new physiotherapists. Roberta Bobath known as Bertie Bobath, was the main senior specialist. Her husband Kenneth, was a neurologist who was a specialist in Cerebral Palsy and brain damage. So they were all working together as a team.

Nancy had got Linda to the stage where she was attempting to stand. But however hard Nancy tried to progress, the contractures of her knees and hips were proving to be more and more problematic, although, because the Bobath Clinic worked to look at the child as a whole and not just at their disability, Linda was progressing in leaps and bounds.

Alma was charged ten-shillings-and-sixpence a session, three times a week – although the overall cost was much higher. It was known that Nancy and her partner, Tommy Barnes, later to be her husband, was the chairman of Sunpat. He was meeting the other part of the costs. He made Linda a promise that if she ever learnt to walk, he would buy her a proper bicycle – that was her goal. She really wanted a beautiful new, shiny bike.

Some of the tasks that Linda was made to perform were, drawing, which was almost impossible, cutting food up and putting it on a spoon or a fork and getting it to the mouth, and eating it. The other task was learning how to wash the face. Typically the head would be brought to the facecloth rather than the other way round. Months of patient training, getting the brain to respond would continue but eventually, Linda succeeded and could take her place at the dinner table along with anyone else.

All these minor victories occurred at an expense to the boys. John was incredibly intelligent and absolutely brilliant at maths, but when it came to tests and examinations he became a total, shivering wreck – he could not revise or concentrate his mind on anything. Whenever he went in for tests he just froze and could not give the answers.

On the day of his Eleven Plus examination he turned the paper over, then his mind went blank. He couldn't even put pen to paper and ran out of the examination hall. Of course, he failed. His father's response was not difficult to imagine. 'You are bloody useless – you're only going to be fit to be a shit-raker or a road sweeper!'

That statement said in an explosive manner, only served to reinforce John's hatred of his father, especially after the "Indian ink" incident a few years earlier. He could not believe that his father would talk like that to him. That started the love-hate relationship that John had with him all his life. John was always trying to please him but sadly, he never got it right. His brother George was always the bright, clever boy who passed his Eleven Plus and it was hoped that he would go to St Paul's Way Grammar School.

However, when it came to discussing George's options, Alma was always taking Linda to hospital and physiotherapy and his father, George, was always "too busy" to attend any school meetings so consequently the number of places at the Grammar School were taken so that George Philip ended up going to Bow Boys' Comprehensive School. He later transferred to the sixth form at Ben Johnson Road School and subsequently, the technical college in Newham, E16, where George passed his Higher National Certificate (HNC) in technical drawing.

From then on, George was known as the "blue-eyed boy" much to John's disgust – John would say to him, 'Of course! You can do no wrong! It's only me who is a shit-raker and a road-sweeper!' That image stayed with John for the rest of his life. He never got over it and he never moved on.

Linda would say to him, 'Forget it – prove him wrong.' But he could never break free from that image. It is well-documented how harsh words can destroy a child's confidence for the rest of their lives.

A further incident showed that George did have some compassion although it was always difficult to find. It was the custom for the children to play in Rocky Park – they'd walk across the road, climb up onto the low wall by the telephone box, and walk the full length on top of the wall. Below the capping of the wall were railings about two or three inches apart.

Alma would watch the boys do this from her front door and tell them not to do it. 'One of you is going to fall and hurt yourself.' Of course, as soon as her back was turned, the boys would jump on the wall, walk the full length, and then jump off it.

John was extremely clumsy. He could trip over a match stick! This particular day he jumped off the wall, catching one of his feet between the railings – he twisted himself awkwardly as he fell. He lay on the ground for some considerable time before getting up and going into the house. He was obviously in pain but said nothing. Later that evening his brother George went upstairs to find John in bed. This was unheard of because you could never get John to go to bed; he was very definitely a night owl.

George found it strange and asked John what was wrong. He said that he'd got a bad pain in his stomach and he was sweating, yet felt cold. All he wanted to do was sleep. George was troubled by this and could not decide what to do. John told him not to tell Mum and Dad because they would go mad. So George left it twenty-minutes or so and then went back to see how John was doing. John looked extremely pale and was obviously in excruciating pain.

George did no more than tell his parents what had happened just over two-hours earlier. The telephone in the house wasn't working at that point so Alma crossed the road and used the public telephone box. She told the doctor that John was far from well so he said he would put a call into the local hospital so she should stay in the phone box and wait for a call back. A doctor at Poplar Hospital, as it then was, called back and asked Alma many questions saying at the end, 'I will come out and examine him myself.'

He duly arrived and on first examination thought that John may have fractured a bone in his back. He said that he would turn him onto his front to make it easier. On doing so, John screamed out in agonising pain.

The doctor said, 'I'm going to revise my first examination and say now that I think that he has an injury to his stomach and he will need to be kept upright when moving him down the stairs.' He was strapped into a Neal Robinson Stretcher, used for confined spaces, and lifted down the narrow staircase to the waiting ambulance. He was blue-lighted to the hospital with his father accompanying him.

The family waiting back home had no idea what was happening. His father George eventually arrived home back from the hospital just after midnight. John had broken some ribs which had punctured his spleen which necessitated its removal. In total, he required eight pints of blood and four bottles of plasma and he was in hospital for almost three weeks. His father George had sat by his side until he came round from the operation.

Naturally, the nausea from the anaesthetic caused him terrible sickness, and the pain of the surgery was terrible. The incision was from the middle of his chest, right down into his stomach. On his return from hospital his father would say, 'What's the matter with you boy – stand up straight!'

John could not do this and walked as if he were an old man for months. Furthermore, sport was out of the question. Sadly, this caused John to have a great many problems. People called him, "sissy" and a "mummy's boy" and generally made his life difficult.

Alma heard all these things being said and it just made her more resentful and angry. She would find herself in a very difficult position trying to juggle with the needs of all the family members as well as to try and do her very best by Linda. It was evident however that not much else could be achieved until surgical intervention could take place. Linda was taken to Mr J C H Hindenache, a German surgeon who had perfected a hamstring transplant. This consisted of moving the hamstrings to the front of the knees, thereby straightening the legs, enabling the child to stand and eventually, walk.

Alma and George were told originally that Linda would have to be taken to Scotland for this operation but eventually it was decided to perform it at the Queen Elizabeth Hospital for Children in Hackney. Whilst George and Alma made the decision the physiotherapy and general training continued at the Bobath Clinic.

Every three months, the clinic had thirteen new physiotherapists to learn the Bobath method. They would come to each of the patients, feel the extent of their disability, and learn how to treat it. Linda was a prize example because she was able to talk to the physiotherapist. It was terrible with everyone sitting in a circle and Linda in the middle with Nancy Finnie. Without fail, every three months Nancy recounted how Alma hit her. This was difficult for Alma and Linda to hear because Alma was so deeply embarrassed although Nancy did say that she absolutely deserved that "treatment" meted-out to her by Alma, saying to the student physiotherapists, 'Never underestimate the power of the mother, because she is your best ally in getting the greatest response out of the child.'

A letter arrived saying that Linda would be admitted to the Goldsmith Ward at the Queen Elizabeth Hospital on the 26th February 1962. That morning the ground was covered with a blanket of snow and it was freezing cold. Linda was kneeling on the sofa looking out of the window at the weather with her two brothers either side of her. All of them were in floods of tears because it was the first time that Linda was going to be separated from her mother and other members of her family.

Little did Linda know that it would not be until May 4th that she would return back home to her family – eleven weeks and four days of an absolutely agonisingly painful experience that would cause her to lose more than two-stone in weight and not know whether her ambition to walk would ever be fulfilled – only time would tell.

Chapter 8

Doctors told Alma and George that this would be a very trying time for the whole family. The surgical intervention of a hamstring transplant on Linda's legs would have been one of the most painful surgical procedures undertaken at that time. The purpose behind the surgery was to enable the knees to be straightened, hopefully enabling Linda to walk. But the hurdles to achieve it were incredibly difficult, not least because Linda had to cope with the trauma of being separated from her mother for the first time in her life.

It was particularly hard as Linda's vision was quite poor and therefore she couldn't always see what was happening. Linda had always experienced loving care from her mother – now she was being handled in a brutally-aggressive way by doctors, surgeons, physiotherapists, and other clinicians. At that time, there was a preparation period of two-weeks before surgery.

Alma started her daily routine of visiting the hospital from 2pm until 6pm every day. Even before the surgery, Linda was traumatised by the whole experience of being in hospital. The food was particularly disgusting and the cries and sickness from the other children on surgical days was traumatic.

There was a small boy in the bed opposite. When Linda was about to be taken off by a hospital porter to the operating theatre, the boy said, 'I'll say goodbye to you now, because we probably won't be seeing you again,' which absolutely terrified Linda. That walk through the corridors and going up in the lift to the operating theatre seemed the longest journey in the world.

Linda had been given a pre-med but she reacted badly to it. Further trauma occurred when the mask was placed over Linda's face and she became distressed as the anaesthetic took effect with the stench of ether along with that woozy 'sinking feeling.' Because she was distressed, and fighting her situation, it took longer for her to 'go under,' so she was informing the doctors that she would be having a visit from the actress and comedienne, Hattie Jacques, president of the

East London Spastics Society (TELSS), as it would be her twelfth birthday on Sunday.

Hattie had been president of TELSS for several years – she was a frequent visitor to Alma and George's home. The very first time she called at the house Alma was airing washing in front of the coal fire. Alma went into a panic and said, 'If I'd known that you were coming, I would not have had the airing in front of the fire.' Hattie's response was, 'If you came to my home, I wouldn't move the clothes horse for you so don't worry about doing it for me!'

Just over a year later, this story was recounted by Alma on "Hattie Jacques: This is Your Life" on BBC 1 Television with Eamonn Andrews. This came about as a result of Alma receiving a telephone call from a BBC researcher. She told Alma that Hattie was going to be the surprise subject for "This is Your Life" and they wanted a "mother to mother" approach concerning Hattie's connection with her work for The East London Spastics Society.

Alma's immediate response was to refuse, but the researcher, picking up on Alma's nervousness, asked if she could at least come and talk to her. When she did so, Alma made it abundantly clear that she still did not want to know anything about it. At the end of the conversation, it was agreed that the researcher would talk to other members of The Spastics Society to see if one of them would appear on the show instead.

The next thing that Alma heard about it was from receiving a telegram thanking her for agreeing to appear on the programme, saying that she was to meet someone at a railway station in order to be given over a script. This was collected by George. Alma's immediate response was to run to the toilet and be sick. She just couldn't bear the thought of it. On receiving the script, Linda read the part of Eamonn whilst Alma learned her lines.

She purchased a beautiful pale lemon grosgrain silk dress. Her hair was done by the make-up artist at the BBC. George went to the studios to watch the show and attend the party afterwards. Some of the people who appeared on the show with her were Hattie's Husband, John Le Mesurier, Eric Sykes, Shirley Eaton, Bernard Miles, Lesley Philips, and Max Bygraves to name but a few. It was a lovely occasion for Alma and George and the whole family watched with eager anticipation and excitement as it went out.

Unlike the later programmes of "This is Your Life", the BBC programmes were live, produced at the Lime Grove Studios. Little did Alma and Linda know that the tables would be turned on Linda some years later in 1977, when she herself became the subject of "This is Your Life", when Alma and George, and their two sons, John Albert and George Philip, would also be present on the programme.

Hattie was a very warm, friendly person. She arrived with her bottle of ice-cold milk, a box of a hundred John Player Cigarettes, and a bottle of brandy. Brandy and milk, was her regular tipple, and she was a chain-smoker. There were two comfortable armchairs, but Hattie was a rather large lady with flowing velvet dresses which took up quite a lot of room in the chair.

Rather than relaxing into the chair, she had to sort of "perch" on the edge of it. The family were somewhat overawed by her presence but they need not have worried. She visited on many occasions over the years, so for Linda to be talking about a visit from Hattie Jacques for her birthday was not unusual and was nothing to do with the anaesthetic! The doctors and nurses realised that Linda was actually telling the truth when they saw Hattie come into the ward, carrying a box for Linda with a silver charm bracelet for her birthday.

It was quite a remarkable feat for Linda to be sitting in a wheelchair that day – she was doped-up to the eyeballs but managed to make sense. Once Hattie left the building, Linda was absolutely exhausted and in intense pain.

One leg was operated on and Linda awoke to the most agonising pain – she just screamed and cried in agony, not knowing what was happening or what to do apart from the constant sickness. The only salvation was that Linda was aware that her father was by her side. He had waited for Linda to come out of the operating theatre doors and came back with her onto the ward. The situation was really bad. Linda could not sit up or move due to the heavy weight of the plaster-cast that went from her toes to her bottom on her leg.

One week later she would have to endure it all over again as the second leg was operated on. Now, the pain was doubly difficult. The hips were abducted and a piece of wood, rather like a broomstick handle, was placed between both knees. The only way that Linda could try and eat was to lie on her tummy but it was not successful. She also had to pass "water" and "motion" on her tummy – with everything being "captured" on a rubber sheet.

Linda had never endured anything so horrible. She hated being dirty. To aid a bowel-movement she was given liquid paraffin which made her violently sick. Everything was traumatic and the pain was intense. It was at that time that Linda learned the art of coping with life at just five-minutes at a time, then waiting for the next five-minutes to occur, and so on.

There was to be yet another trip to the operating theatre because both knees had to be manipulated under anaesthetic. It would have been far too horrific to manipulate the legs in full consciousness. There was an infection of dysentery on the ward and most of the children, including Linda, went down with it. Alma arrived at Linda's bedside only to find her covered in excrement, crying because she hated the smell, and being dirty. Alma went straight to the Sister on the ward and asked, 'Why is my child dirty?'

'It's because she is heavy and it takes three nurses to move her,' came the reply of the Sister on the ward.

Alma was furious. She said, 'Get your nurses together and come to Linda's bedside and I will show you how it should be done – without any nursing training!'

Alma handled Linda with tender loving care and she naturally responded. Alma cleaned her up, washed the plaster, and put clean, fresh night clothes on her. The nursing-staff were absolutely amazed just how well Alma handled her daughter. Alma's response was, 'There you are – I told you that it could be done quite easily. If I ever see Linda in that kind of disgusting state again, your feet won't touch the ground until you reach the Matron's office!'

'Oh my God! Don't report us to the Matron!' The nurses said. Alma said that it was not her intention to do so but if there was any further such "treatment" meted-out to her daughter then she would have no hesitation.

Any movement with Linda had to be done manually, as there weren't any overhead electric hoists at that establishment in 1962. Pain-injections also had to be administered before she could be moved. On one occasion, Linda was picked up by a very strong German nurse by the name of Mary Ann Eham. At that point, because Linda's legs were bent and were dangling, the pain was so excruciating that Linda fainted.

Further pethidine injections were administered to "knock her out" and the lovely German nurse, who had the best of intentions to help, but nevertheless, it should not have been allowed to happen, was removed from the ward. Linda was heartbroken because Mary Ann was the only person on that ward that was kind, but on Linda's case notes it was stated that she was not allowed to be moved without pain-relieving medication because the surgery was so serious.

All this served to make Linda even more distraught. The nerve pain in her legs was terrible and she desperately wanted to be with her mother. Other visitors came to the hospital to give Alma a few hours rest, but Linda could not be pacified. She was terribly unhappy. The paediatric consultant, Ursula Shelley, visited one day and expressed concern at Linda's mental state. The pain had just been too much to bear.

Years later it was found that the circulation in both of Linda's legs had been accidentally, partially restricted by the surgeon, hence the terrific pain. It was excruciatingly painful even if someone were to simply walk across the floor in front of her—that action also caused her pain—such was her sensitivity due to the restriction of the circulation. This error was not found until further surgery in 1978 – some fifteen years later!

Winter had suddenly turned into spring but Linda still spent much of her time on her stomach looking at a green-tiled wall. Doctor Shelley was becoming increasingly alarmed. It was suggested that Alma could take Linda into the hospital garden when she visited and Dr Shelley asked Alma to encourage Linda to eat whatever she could bring to tempt her. Alma took salmon and cucumber sandwiches, cake, fruit, and ice-cold drinks.

It was vital to get Linda's fluid levels up and to try to put a little weight on. Linda was becoming more emaciated by the day. Those couple of hours in the hospital garden were a Godsend and Linda was beginning to respond to eating some food. The hospital food continued to be absolutely disgusting. On one occasion, the ward Sister offered Linda a meat sandwich. When it was brought the bread was green and the meat was minced-beef that had been the meal three-days earlier. The sandwich was full of greasy fat and was completely inedible hence, her absolute misery.

It was now April and Ursula Shelley was becoming even more concerned at the weight-loss situation. Linda had now lost two-stone in weight since her admission on the 26th February. It was Ursula Shelley's opinion that if Linda did not get home as quickly as possible, she would have a nervous breakdown.

The East London Spastics Society minibus was used to transport Linda home. It should have been done by ambulance because the pain in the legs as they went over the various pot holes in the road sent Linda absolutely mad with pain. On reaching home, Alma said to Linda, 'I know what will make you better.' She chose a piece of smoked haddock with butter and pepper, and an egg and milk custard with nutmeg on the top.

Naturally, Linda refused, so Alma just had to coerce her to try and eat a little. Not much food was taken and sickness regularly occurred. Linda was in a totally agitated state and Dr Shelley prescribed phenobarbitone, to tranquilise and painkillers to help with the pain.

For weeks, the family went on struggling like this. Alma took Linda back to the hospital at weekly intervals. All this stress made the relationship between Alma and George even more difficult than it already was. Linda's bed was placed in Alma and George's bedroom so that they could turn Linda at night and deal with whatever had to be done. Due to Linda's many difficulties, this arrangement remained in place for three-years until Linda was fifteen – which did nothing for the sexual health and general well-being of Alma and George.

The bar between the knees was still in place but it was removed around July. The legs still had to be splinted – this was done by wrapping bandages around the back splint to hold the leg tight then physiotherapy could begin. The physiotherapy wasn't with Nancy Finnie but with a physiotherapist by the name of Miss Greenhill from The Queen Elizabeth Hospital for Children. One day she announced, 'We're going to take the bandages off and try to bend Linda's legs.'

A rubber ring was placed in Linda's mouth so that she could bite on it to ease the pain – it was torture. Linda suddenly lashed out, screaming in agony, and hit Miss Greenhill. Alma rebuked Linda for lashing out but was told by Miss Greenhill that they expected that to happen because the pain would be so intense. Gradually, as the weeks went on, Linda was able to manage without the wooden bar between her legs and later on, attempted to stand.

The plaster-cast came off completely, one year from the start of the surgery. The progress was marked. Linda now had straight knees but the spasm had gone into her back, causing her to have a bent back with a protruding bottom. However, at least her knees were straight and her feet were flat on the floor. In that one year, Linda had taken her first steps, just four of them, at the age of thirteen. What a victory! The whole family were overjoyed. They just stood in a heap, hugging each other, crying. The victory was hard-fought and hard-won but now things would begin to happen.

Chapter 9

Alma's eldest brother, William, known as Bill, and his wife, Kit, announced the wedding of their only son, Alan, to Iris, in June 1963. Initially, George's comment to Alma was, 'You can't go.'

Linda said, 'Of course she can, *you* can look after me, Dad.'

George was horrified. All Alma said was, 'I haven't got anything new to wear, and I can't afford to buy anything.'

George gave his usual response, 'Don't look at me – I haven't got any bleedin' money!' He never had any money so there was nothing expected of him anyhow. Linda had been given money by friends and relatives for coping with her ordeal at the hospital. She said to her mother, on the quiet, 'Don't worry Mum, I'll help you. Go out and see what you can find.'

Linda sent her mother off with some money in her pocket which was a very rare occurrence for Alma at that time. She came back from one of the local shops, having purchased a lovely suit and a beige, pure silk blouse. Foolishly, she was so excited that she couldn't wait to show George. He got her to put it on and then he went absolutely berserk. He was so angry because her bra could be seen through the silk blouse. He started screaming and yelling at her, then, he hit her and she protested, crying and screaming. He ripped the jacket off her back, grabbed hold of the blouse, tearing it into little shreds, wrenching it from her body.

Alma was upset and incredulous because she had never done anything disrespectful in her life. She just could not believe his outburst. He was enraged with jealousy saying, 'Just because you want to go and see your family!' He struck her extremely hard.

Later, when he had gone back to work, Alma came down the stairs, sobbing. She showed Linda her bruises. George was clever because he only hit her where the injuries couldn't be seen. He punched her in the chest and on her back. She said to Linda, 'How can I go now – I have nothing to wear?' Linda's response was, 'You *can* go – even if you have to wear something that you have worn before. All the family will love you whatever you wear just for the fact that you have made it to the wedding.'

Linda knew how tough things were within the marriage, and felt guilty because of the pressure that her surgery had put on her parents. George's outpouring of rage was caused by the stress he had gone through in those last few months, but it was irrational. However much it may have been understandable, it was, nevertheless, unforgiveable. He should never have struck her and been that abusive.

It just hardened Alma's heart all the more, causing yet more bitter resentment. Linda was Alma's confidante. They talked about, and shared everything. George was incredulous when a few weeks later, Alma suddenly announced that she was going to the wedding, and he wasn't going to stop her.

Linda waited for the explosion to occur yet again but amazingly, nothing happened – probably because George was feeling quite ashamed of his past behaviour.

Linda was not looking forward to being left in George's care. Alma assured her that she would not be away from the home for too long. She would just go to the church service and then come back. But Linda told her, 'After all the problems you have been through, just go and enjoy yourself for a few hours.'

George could have taken Alma by car but he offered no help which both surprised her, and made her feel angry. Linda said, 'He must not win. It's about time you stood up to him.' Everyone was sick of his aggression. No one could ever do anything right.

Linda was now left to George's devices. The first comment he made was, 'You are not having any drink until *she* gets back.' Linda knew that her mother would be away for several hours and her main concern was what she would do if she needed the toilet. Alma had looked after Linda since she returned from hospital, as well as assisting with the care needs whilst recovering from surgery. All of which was done without complaint.

Now that George was being asked to do something, it was a different story. It was not too long before Linda required the toilet. Her father was furious. He would now have to manage her on his own and he didn't want to. George carried her upstairs putting her legs up on the chair to make her feel more comfortable but his handling was far from gentle, indeed, it was anything but. Having come back down into the living room, Linda decided that she would like something to eat.

This was another barrier between them but they got through it, and Linda thought that it was a salutary lesson because he'd not done any food preparation since her return from hospital.

Nothing was done with good grace – whatever the request.

On Alma's return, George showed no early interest in what had gone on at the wedding. Alma had just stayed for a cup of tea and a few items of the buffet but George was not satisfied with this. He then wanted to know the "ins" and "outs" of everything with aggressive questioning then refused to talk to her for three days when he wasn't satisfied by the answers. His mood-swings were very common but this was one area where Alma would not tolerate his behaviour. Linda's answer was that she shouldn't give in to him. In a way, he was like a naughty schoolboy.

Chapter 10

Nancy Finnie's next priority with Linda was to instil the movement of putting one leg in front of the other and to assist her to climb short stairs. Normal stairs, at that time, were far too high for Linda to manage. Nancy asked Alma whether George could make some miniature staircases for Linda and the other children to practise on. In order to do this, George came to the Bobath Clinic to watch what went on and how the physiotherapists were helping the children.

George was impressed by how they were managing the treatment and he also watched how Miss Finnie carefully managed Linda. His response was, of course, that he would help and he would make four miniature staircases at no charge to the clinic. When they offered to pay, he refused it, saying, 'If you can get my daughter to walk up a flight of stairs, I'll do anything to help.' George willingly gave of his time and energy to this project, making four sets of stairs which were used within the centre for many years.

On the day when Linda attempted to climb her first four steps, she used vacuum cleaner pipes to help her stand. Every step was agonising torture, but those four magical steps happened and then she could move on to greater things. It was a case of getting the brain to respond differently to movement as was the case when Linda was seven, riding her bike. Months of Alma's dedication eventually paid off and now it was Nancy Finnie's turn to do the same with the stairs.

At first, bending Linda's knee and pushing up on the step seemed totally, physically impossible but, as in all things, her brain suddenly grasped the idea. No physical movement comes naturally to someone with Cerebral Palsy – it has to be "planted" again and again so that the brain receives the messages enabling the person to take over. Climbing the stairs was just like that – planting the idea of movement again and again to the point that Linda was utterly fed up, even though she had come so far.

But now was not the time to give in. Eventually, using the staircase that her father had built paid off. She was able to achieve it but had to always have her hand on both banister rails. Then, each step was made a little higher, then a little higher and so on until Linda could lift over a normal-sized step.

Nancy arranged for some tripod sticks to be made that were height-adjustable, at a surgical instrument maker in Hackney Road. These were the best kind of tripod sticks that Linda had attempted to use because the base of the sticks were narrower than the average tripod, although they could still be placed upon a normal step. Linda had these sticks from the age of thirteen through to the age of twenty-five, when a new pair was made for her.

At their home in Grundy Street, there was only one banister rail, so George set about making a rail, attached to the wall, that went from the top to the bottom of the stairs allowing for the dog-leg turning half-way down the stairs. That was a scary thing to do because it meant that Linda had to lean further forward and grab hold of the banisters on the right hand side.

Linda had a pair of quadripod sticks at the top of the stairs and the use of her tripods and the handles of the wheelchair that sat at the bottom of the stairs. It was quite a good place for answering the telephone or piling up items of washing and so on that had to be taken upstairs to the other bedrooms. George also made a set of parallel bars with a seat at either end to encourage walking, standing, and sitting, without the use of sticks.

Naturally, the parallel bars gave all the support that Linda needed when she was practising walking. This was done religiously, every night, and Linda hated it. She just wanted to go out and play with the other children and do normal things, but that wasn't to be. The physiotherapy had to come first.

By now, Linda had achieved her goal—walking around the house and getting around the school—not on a tricycle, but now using a walking frame to go to the classroom and sit at her desk. All this strengthened her arms and legs. The children loved to ridicule and bully Linda. They would gang-up on her during the school lunch break and whatever she tried to talk about she was shouted down and laughed at.

Linda became very frustrated. Her school friends would call her, "posh" because Alma had made sure that she spoke very well to adults, doctors, physiotherapists and the like. In fact, when school inspectors came to the classroom the headmistress would say to them, 'Here is a child that speaks two languages.'

'Oh really?' They would say, 'What are they?'

The headmistress would answer, 'English and Cockney.' This caused much laughter at Linda's expense.

Out in the playground Linda was a real "Cor Blimey" East ender but when it was necessary, she could speak perfect Queen's English. Linda was not afraid to speak in public, probably because she had been involved in the meetings held at The Spastics Society so she knew how things should be conducted.

Alma decided that she was not making enough money sewing children's night clothes so she looked for further work. It was found by home-working for the Sabina Shirt Company. The firm made cheap men's shirts in different kinds of fabric but mostly nylon which created its own irritating dust that got into the eyes and up the nose.

Alma would do a series of jobs for Sabina in the eight years that she worked for the company. She would either label and stitch the body of the shirt, or, put the collars and cuffs on the shirts. Making the collars was a much more difficult task. But what was good was that once Alma got on a roll, she could make two-dozen bodies of the shirts and the collars and/or cuffs, so that her money increased, not by a huge amount, but at least it was more than she had been earning. She would pull twenty-four shirts through her machine, and then Linda would cut off the ends of the cotton, making the finish of the shirts very neat.

The only way that Linda could achieve this was to hold the material very close to her nose and then use a pair of small scissors to cut the cottons, either on the labels that had been attached to the inside of the shirts, or to cut the cottons from the collar and the cuffs.

Naturally, there would be many pieces of cotton on the floor and this would have to be swept up. Linda would sit on the floor and gather up the cotton from the carpet and dispose of it all in the bin, then fold up the shirt and place it into a bundle of a dozen which Alma would then tie up and place in the sack which would be collected every other day.

Alma would work for much of the morning, then, when Linda returned home on the bus at 3.30pm, they would have a cup of tea. Then, Linda would be helped by Alma to do her physiotherapy. Afterwards, Alma would prepare an evening meal and after the meal was finished, more physiotherapy would take place. Then it was time for bed. The only break in the routine occurred if Linda was ill.

There wasn't much time for enjoyment other than the visits to Seasalter where now, since Linda's surgery, she could not crawl on the grass, so felt very frustrated. However, the quadripod sticks came into their own because the ground was quite uneven. Either Alma or George would encourage Linda to walk with her quadripod sticks for exercise. This was extremely exhausting.

Alma and George's main socialisation was to visit one of the many public houses in various parts of Kent. There were some wonderfully eccentric characters, in a particular pub at Chilham, and of course, the most frequently used was the Pearson's Arms at Whitstable – home of the oysters. Many of the caravan fraternity would also attend, and the family had happy evenings singing, eating, and laughing with the owners in the pub "after hours". Sadly, they have long since passed away but their characters live on.

Chapter 11

Gone were the days of Linda crawling on her hands and knees, but she still had to find ways of fulfilling the household chores that she had done in the past by crawling and kneeling. Now she could clean bathroom sinks and toilets standing on her feet, but to fulfil the role of polishing the floors, she would sit on her bottom and slide herself along the floor so that she could roll over onto her side to put the polish on the cloth, and then polish the floor. Needless to say, the home was, "spic and span". One day, however, Linda went into the toilet and was horrified to find blood in her underclothing. She went to her mother. Alma's reaction was, 'Oh my God, you're normal!'

'Of course I'm bloody normal!' Linda cried.

'Oh no, I didn't mean it like that,' said Alma, 'You are having what's known as a period and it is perfectly normal for a woman of your age. There is nothing to be frightened of. I didn't tell you about it before because doctors told your dad and me that you would never be able to have them because you probably wouldn't live that long. But there you are, you've proved them all wrong, and it's absolutely wonderful. I have worried ever since you were born that your insides might not function because that is what we were told by the doctors, and here you are performing well, and now, that part of things and the worry about it, is over.'

Linda did not think that it was so wonderful. She had stomach cramps, her legs were in spasm, and extremely painful. This was going to be her lot every month from now on. The stomach cramps and coping with the menstrual bleeding, was not going to be easy to manage. Sanitary protection was very basic and it could easily move when the person had to "drag" their body around or struggle to get on and off chairs and so on.

But for now, Linda and Alma could forget all those difficult ramifications and just rejoice in the normality. It was never easy, having to cope when Linda's vision was poor, and she did not always realise when the menstrual bleeding had occurred. Linda did all that she could to keep clean and clear up if there was any blood on the toilet seat and the like. But if her father walked into the toilet and found any traces of blood anywhere, he would go absolutely ballistic and say to Alma, 'Stop whatever you are doing and come and clear this up now because I'm not bloody doing it.'

So, menstrual cycles were always a little problematic. It made Linda all the more grateful for the fact that she was not crawling anymore and would not have to cope with the indignity of having sanitary protection visible under her clothing. Thank God she had struggled to succeed to get on her feet and that she could hold her head up and know that she was as good as anyone else. Alma and George were always saying, 'Don't worry, no one is going to be looking at *you*.' This did nothing for Linda's self-esteem.

As a result of the surgery, Linda had lost so much school time – more than eighteen months which is a long time in educational terms. Linda was still in a great deal of pain, even though she was beginning to succeed. She was weak and fatigued from the whole experience of what she had just gone through. Her nerves were still shattered and she suffered from extreme anxiety. It was decided that Linda should have some home-tutoring from a Miss Glazebrook.

Miss Glazebrook soon realised that apart from supporting Linda, her two brothers needed help too. She tried to discover what interested the brothers. Once she had got their confidence, John became her favourite. She encouraged him with his maths and although he was brilliant at mathematics, he could never fulfil the promise of passing examinations, as has previously been mentioned. One of John's loves was watching and listening to horse racing. He used to borrow Miss Glazebrook's newspaper and study the form. Little did anybody know that this was to be one of John's greatest downfalls in his future life – more of that, later.

Now it was time for Linda to go back to Bromley Hall School. She received even more bullying from the group of boys and girls than she had in previous years. It is hard to imagine how cruel disabled people can be to one another. It would seem that they should have some sort of "fellow-feeling" because of all their shared experience, but sadly, in many instances, it was a case of "dog-eat-dog" and there was no room for such sentiments as compassion.

Many of the children in Linda's class suffered from Duchenne Muscular Dystrophy. This was a genetic disorder, passed on from the mother, predominantly to boys, but not in every case. It was tragic to see their struggle from walking as toddlers, to dying at around thirteen to fifteen years of age. They became philosophical about their situation, but some were also extremely angry. As they got weaker, their anger grew stronger, and if someone got in their way – God help them! The boys would take bets on themselves as to who would die next.

Linda found it upsetting when one of these lads passed away because they had been in her class and she had made friends with them. Death was not uncommon so the whole grief process was always present. Linda would contemplate how the doctors kept repeating that she would not live long so she would wonder how long it would be before it was her turn—a fear that she continued to live with until she had reached the point of amazing the doctors who firstly said that she would not live beyond her teens—then it was her twenties, then thirties, then forties, and then, the doctors gave up. Their final prediction was that at the very least, she would not live beyond the age of sixty-nine.

Chapter 12

Now that Linda was back at school full time, Alma could concentrate on her machining for the Sabina Shirt Company as well as doing household chores and looking after her family.

She also continued to provide daily support for Linda's physiotherapy. The boys had sports days and parents' evenings but George never attended and Alma was too occupied with Linda nothing must spoil the evening routine. Linda had been successfully assessed for Keeler Aid glasses which meant that she could read the blackboard as well as reading close print. The glasses were very expensive – something like £1500 for a pair in 1963.

They were on loan from the London County Council Education Department, and so the effect was that they had to be treated like gold dust. They came in a wooden box, with a lock, which was padded in velvet and silk. The left side was totally blackened out because Linda had no vision in that eye, and the right, had two lenses. One, which was for close work, looked rather like a pudding-basin turned on its side, and then protruding from the centre, was a short, tube-like structure to enable her to read longer distances, say on a blackboard, or watching a television.

They were quite ugly-looking things with very thick frames to carry the weight of the two lenses. The bullying by the other children still continued, especially when they saw Linda's new glasses. They said that she looked like something from outer-space. Linda was more and more terrified and stressed-out, but the more that she squirmed, the more the children loved her discomfort and the more they bullied her, especially at playtime and lunch break.

Linda had now reached the age of fourteen. Things were just going on in the usual way and it seemed that not much progress was being made. Then, one day, in April 1965, Linda awoke and looked out of the window. As she did so, she noticed that the sky was bright yellow and every time that she looked down at the pavements, they were dark green – she screamed out and both parents came running.

Alma advised Linda to rest because it was probably a migraine. It was, for Linda, as though a penny was being held in the bottom right hand corner of her eye – all very frightening for everyone. The next day, the dark shape wasn't there so there was a big sigh of relief and, after one week, Linda went back to school. As she looked down at her notebook, it was as though a large black "rim" had encircled the page and the lines "bulged" outwards. Linda was terrified and tried to cover up her fears.

Something was obviously not right but she felt, if she voiced it, the world would come crashing down upon her head. Miss Chapman, the form teacher at Bromley Hall, could see Linda's sense of panic and kept asking if everything was alright,

'How's your mother's back, because your writing is going all over the place,' she said, thinking that Linda's issues were to do with home and her mother having a bad back due to her, "machining" and the lifting of Linda. Linda assured her that there was nothing wrong – yet inside she was still totally terrified.

A few weeks later, there was an LCC Medical which all children had to have when they were fifteen. Linda knew that her problem would be "found out", so she refused to have the eye test and a letter was sent home to her mother as a result. Alma picked up the letter and read it. She gave it to Linda and asked her to read it.

Linda pushed it to one side, 'You don't want to take any notice of those people, they are stupid,' said Linda.

Alma took a hold of the letter and cried, 'Do as you're told – and *read* it!' What Linda didn't know was that Alma had given her the letter, upside-down, deliberately. Then, Alma realised the horrifying truth, that her daughter couldn't see the print. Alma was crying and very frightened but picked up the telephone and rang Moorfields Eye Hospital, where Linda was taken a few days later.

Alma was very pale and tense as the doctor looked into Linda's eyes, 'Your little girl is very brave,' he said.

Alma's response was, 'Yes, she's a fighter.'

The doctor said, 'Yes, and she's going to need a whole lot more of it too. We will have to have her in.'

Linda thought that her worst nightmare had just come home to roost. Examination under anaesthetic proved that Linda had a detached retina in the one eye that she could see out of, and it had so severely detached, that it had broken-up into little fragments so that nothing could be done. Doctors broke the news to Alma and George. The story was recounted by George many years later. His response was that Alma ran around the room, screaming, 'Don't tell me, don't tell me – I *don't* want to know. I can't cope and neither will Linda.'

She would realise just how resilient her daughter would be in later life. Whilst Alma and George were having this life-changing conversation, another doctor was sitting by Linda's bed. On Linda's waking, he said, 'Well, you'll be blind within three months, so you might as well get used to it.'

Linda replied, 'Ok, when can I go home?' That evening she got her father to take her to the Wingfield Music Club for the disabled, where she was learning to play the flute. The tutors and staff, who looked after the children at the club, asked Linda how she got on at the hospital. She told them what the doctor had said and then turned away to carry on teaching a small child to play the flute.

Apparently, the other teachers said that there was nothing wrong with Linda and that she was just attention-seeking. If only they'd known the truth! When the staff and tutors at the Wingfield Music Club were later told by George that Linda would in fact be blind within three-months and it had now actually happened, everyone was totally shocked. They realised that, rather than Linda being attention-seeking, she was firstly, in a state of shock, and secondly, was brave, in continuing to live her life. But in reality, of course, she didn't have a choice.

It was approximately, five-months before Linda became totally blind. She had some terrifying experiences when walking into a room, such as a bathroom or a kitchen, to find that all the white objects appeared to be in a great "fog". Any light from the window would mean that Linda saw colours of yellow and green, and dark black "rims" as a result of the retina detaching. Linda was now suffering from a condition known as "Charles Bonnet Syndrome".

This is when the brain is geared for "seeing", rather like having an electrical appliance of some kind which is geared to work but the plug has been taken off the end. This is a terrifying experience because of the shapes and colours that she was experiencing. It is because the eyes cannot receive the signals from the brain. This gives a person a feeling of nausea and great fear.

Linda would often sit in the kitchen with her back to the window, shaking, because of what she was seeing. Alma was completely at a loss as to what she should do. Although Alma and George had been told that Linda would lose her sight by her teenage years, they never actually thought that it would happen because she had made such good progress with the Keeler Aid glasses. Suddenly becoming totally blind, seemed impossible to get their heads around.

School was not a good place for Linda. The bullies were still in evidence. Boys would go down to the football pitch, get a handful of mud, come back to the classroom, and rub it into Linda's face, jeering, 'Can you see that, Berwick?' To the great hilarity of the other children.

Linda just felt like screaming, 'Get me out of here!'

Each and every day was a nightmare, not helped by the situation at home. George was so terrified that he just went quiet and said nothing. Linda could often hear Alma crying and saying that she could not cope. One day, George got very angry with her. She tore down the stairs and ran out of the house.

Alma took herself off to the family doctor – a very lovely, understanding man. Alma naturally expressed her fear. He told her that the best thing that she could do was to get involved and fight Linda's corner at every turn. One sunny afternoon, as Linda got off of the school bus, she walked forward, and instead of finding the gate of her home, she slammed her face on the brick wall beside. There was a young boy on the school bus called Christopher Benson, he wasn't a nice little kid, in fact, he would spend more time jeering at others and generally being horrible. He thought that this situation was uproariously funny. Alma saw red.

Within seconds, she was on that bus, picking up this boy by the collar of his jacket, lifting him off the seat and shaking him. She told him, 'Don't you ever laugh at my daughter like *that* ever again you little *shit*, otherwise, I will not be responsible for my actions – you little *sod*!' She shook him again as she landed him back onto the seat and then she got off of the bus.

The attendant driver and care assistant were very sympathetic to Alma. They had been told what had happened to Linda and they were deeply shocked and very understanding. They put their arm around Alma and gave her a hug as she sobbed. She said, 'I know that it was wrong but I just couldn't stop myself.'

Their response was, 'Yes, it was wrong, but understandable – something *like that* should have been done to that boy a long time ago.' The boy was totally shocked and it got around the school like wildfire that you better not mess with Mrs Berwick! In fact, some twenty-years later, Christopher Benson met with Linda and humbly apologised for his actions.

The headmistress told the children about Linda's diagnosis of going blind and that she would be struggling, needing some help and they would have to do whatever they could to help her. All they ever did was to put things in her path so that she would fall over them and tell Linda that the glass doors were open when they were in fact shut, so that she would crash into them yet again. It was all extremely upsetting.

Now that Linda had been registered blind, although she could see some variation in light and dark, it wasn't of any real, practical use. Linda's form teacher said, 'What are you going to do now that you are blind?'

Quite frankly, Linda did not know. What she did know was that, if she was going to get out of this situation, she had to learn Braille and find out how to respond as a blind person. Social Services provided a tutor for two-hours a week to teach Linda Braille – it was very difficult to learn and extremely frustrating. The first Braille book that Linda ever tried to read was a book on the life of Kathleen Ferrier, the famous English contralto singer.

The dots of the Braille felt to Linda as though they had been sat on by a very heavy person because they were so squashed that they had almost gone to powder, nevertheless, she ploughed on. Alma was given the Braille lessons in both Braille and printed form by the social worker each week to help Linda learn the Braille system.

As Linda began to differentiate the Braille characters under her finger, Alma would write Linda's answers by hand and then read the passage back at the end of the lesson. Linda thought that she would *never* succeed, but, as with the learning to ride the tricycle, Alma was determined that Linda would make it.

Chapter 13

Suzanne Peel came to Bromley Hall as a home-teacher for the blind. She was also partially sighted and used Keeler Aid glasses. She spent several days really getting to know Linda. Her aim was to help Linda integrate more as a blind person and talk to her about how she was feeling. Linda was both terrified and exhilarated at the same time by all the changes. Linda had already purchased a Braille watch, a Stainsby Braille Writer, and some Braille paper. She was now able to communicate on paper for the first time since she went blind.

Suzanne Peel's other remit was to help train finger-dexterity and recognition of objects. There were many tests. She and Linda had some fun times recognising objects by touch, along with identifying smells and textures, especially of food, some of which, Linda hated.

Linda was very good at these tasks but she found recognition with her right hand hard to manage as Cerebral Palsy made the definition of touch much harder to define. Suzanne introduced basket-making to help with the dexterity. Linda used to like making the plaited tea-trays – Alma and Linda made many in Linda's training sessions at home. The children at the school showed their annoyance at Linda, asking Mrs Peel, 'Why is it that *she* can do basket work, and *we* can't?'

'That's because the school budget doesn't run to it, and Linda's needs are greater as a newly blind person. She has to learn new skills that you can barely imagine,' replied Mrs Peel to the children.

Linda thought, '*You lot have no idea how tough all of this is.*' Alma quite enjoyed doing the basket work with Linda. They made all shapes and sizes as well as using thick raffia twine to make stall seats and shopping baskets. Linda got quite good at it and it really helped to develop the use of her hands. Alma really enjoyed these times at the kitchen table, although George was always complaining about the "bits" on the floor and the "drips" of water over the table.

Alma showed George her annoyance, 'It doesn't fucking matter so long as Linda is progressing!' But it obviously mattered to George and he resented the time that it all took. All George could think about was what was the next meal going to be, and when was it due!

It was Linda's fifteenth birthday and Suzanne Peel gave her a gift of a recording of Beethoven's Symphony Number 6, "The Pastoral". Linda absolutely loved it and realised that she wanted to hear more. So, George actually bought one of those cheap classical recordings that you used to find in newsagents. He had no idea what he was buying but he knew that Linda liked Beethoven and Mozart. He bought a copy of Beethoven's Spring Sonata, played by Fritz Kreisler. Later on, George went to a record store and asked the owner which pieces of music might be good to buy for a newcomer to classical music. He ended up buying a Piano Trio with Daniel Barenboim, Pinchas Zukerman and Jacqueline du Pré.

Alma also purchased a recording for Linda of Grieg's Piano Concerto in A minor, which both she and Linda came to love. Linda's two brothers, John and George, asked, 'How is it, *she* gets records and *we* don't?'

So Linda was getting a barrage of comments through no fault of her own. Alma could understand the boys' feelings but she told them that Linda just needed help to find something to interest her, and help her to relax, because of recently losing her sight.

Suzanne Peel also tried to introduce Linda to many more pieces of classical music. Linda herself purchased the Elgar Cello Concerto, played by Jacqueline du Pré, which probably remains one of the most iconic classical recordings to this day. Linda loved all of them and that started her quest for classical music – she went on to collect hundreds of recordings and they became a most welcome and pleasurable pastime throughout her life. Linda more importantly, wanted to have the experience of live music.

The first ever live concert that she attended was Daniel Barenboim and Jacqueline du Pré, which was absolutely fantastic and fuelled the fire for more live performances. Naturally, Linda's brothers were not very enamoured with the idea for they loved "pop" music. Her brother John would say, 'What do you want to listen to *that* stuff for, you posh *cow*? Are we not good enough for you? Your working-class background not posh *enough* for you?'

John was absolutely right. Linda *wanted* to progress, something that none of her family could really understand. Linda had spent so much of her life being labelled "Educationally Subnormal". This was a label that she wanted to forget and, instead, she wanted the opportunity to listen to good music, read good books, and engage in intellectual conversation and the like.

The reading of good books was difficult due to the sight-loss but the RNIB Talking Books Service rescued the day. Linda read many books; one of her favourites was Emily Brontë's *Wuthering Heights,* read by Alvar Lidell. Alma and Linda spent many happy hours listening to Talking Books together.

The headmistress, at Bromley Hall, Margueritte Turnbull, told Linda's parents that she knew of a lady who was a teacher for the blind and she would talk to her about trying to get Linda into Linden Lodge, which was a school, run by the Royal National Institute for the Blind. Linda and her parents were full of hope because Linda realised that she had to get properly educated as a blind person.

In September, Linda was waiting for the school bus, and Alma was surprised to see it go past the front door without stopping. Alma telephoned the school to speak to the headmistress who replied, 'Oh, didn't you realise, *mother*,' she said sarcastically, 'that your daughter left school in July?'

Alma was absolutely furious, saying, 'Why didn't you tell me? And what happened about the school for the blind in London?'

The headmistress replied, 'Oh, they wouldn't take her because of her disability, so, that's *it*, I'm afraid.'

Alma said, 'You will be, because I am afraid that no one is going to write my daughter off. You cannot behave as though she doesn't exist. I will leave no stone unturned to get this put right. You-mark-my-words!'

Alma just couldn't believe that there was no consultation as to the difficulties, and that decisions were made by the head of Linden Lodge to decline Linda's admittance to the school without even meeting her. Alma's first port of call was to contact the Labour Member of Parliament, Ian Mcadoo, who then wrote to the Minister for Education. He had also got a contact with a school called Dorton House School for the Blind in Sevenoaks, Kent. Robert Bolton, the headmaster, agreed to interview Linda. It was a vast place with difficult steps at the front and a big, sweeping staircase, rather like you might see on a film set.

The first person that George, Alma, and Linda met was Joan Brown, the deputy head. She was very warm and friendly and knew that the whole family was nervous. Eventually, the door opened and Robert Bolton, the head, came in. He had a strong Birmingham accent. The first thing that he did was to say, 'Linda, follow the sound of my voice.'

Alma instinctively got up and proceeded to help Linda out of the chair, grab hold of her skirt, and walk her towards him. 'Mrs Berwick, stop what you are doing,' said Mr Bolton, 'Leave her alone. Now, Linda, follow the sound of my voice.'

He walked Linda around the room, past the desk and chairs, and told her to turn around and back-into a chair, and sit down. She was now on the opposite side of the room. Linda had followed his voice, perfectly. She had not walked into a single object. What a revelation! Linda always hated the way that she was, "grabbed hold-of" and almost pulled off of her feet by other people.

Mr Bolton chatted to Linda for some time. His main question was, 'Why do you want to come here?' Linda's response was that she wanted good education as a blind person so that she could make her way in the world. After a while, Joan Brown and Robert Bolton went outside for a chat, leaving George, Alma, and Linda in the room.

The three of them couldn't believe how well Linda had avoided the obstacles and was able to walk around without any problems. It showed them in that one simple lesson, what could be achieved with training.

On the headmaster and deputy head's return to the room, Joan Brown said, 'We are very impressed with you Linda because you have learnt Braille perfectly and even though it is a difficult thing to learn, you have applied yourself to it very well.'

Mr Bolton said, 'I also like the way you are saying that you want to be educated and do well, so we have decided to give you a six-week trial-period at the school. This will show us how you fit in and what your aptitude is for learning and how we will cope with the logistical problems of having a multiply-disabled person in a school for the blind. All of the children are either blind or partially sighted but we have never had anyone who uses a wheelchair to transport themselves around the school. Your dormitory will be on the top floor so it might be helpful if we see how you negotiate the stairs without using your wheelchair.'

It was forty steps, up to Dormitory 10 and then of course, Linda had to come down again! By the time she had struggled to get up the forty steps, she was exhausted. She had to use even more concentration when walking back down the stairs because the tripod had to be placed one step lower so that she could place her feet in the right position beside the tripod when coming off each step. The other hazard was that the blind children were just coming out of their classes.

Some of them ran up the stairs, hopping onto the bannister and riding down on it to the bottom, jumping off, then going on their way!

Alma and George were incredulous and wondered just how Linda would cope. After all, she'd been wrapped in cotton-wool from the moment that she became blind and now she was going out into the big wide world. Linda couldn't wait but all Alma could think was how lonely she was going to be without Linda. It was a six-week trial that would be a make-or-break situation, but Linda was absolutely determined that she would do her best to try and be successful.

Chapter 14

When Linda was in Moorfields Eye Hospital, and she had to stay in a side-ward all by herself, she realised that she could manage without her parents in close proximity. Later, when she realised that she'd be leaving home and going to a residential school, it was imperative that she developed her new-found independence. George had made a tall bookcase with lights and a glass sliding door for Linda to be able to put her bed underneath, Linda could sense when the light had been left on by the heat coming from it.

The light would also help someone else coming into the room. It was good to be back in her own room and no longer have to listen to her parents' nocturnal "happenings" and conversations. She had always felt very awkward about the way her presence in their bedroom impacted on her parents' sex life. The only unfortunate part was that her room contained the sewing machine and bundles of shirts, placed in sacks, which all exuded dust and fumes. All in all, it wasn't the greatest experience for anyone to have to cope with, let alone someone with Linda's limitations.

Getting out from underneath the tall book case necessitated half-rolling out of the bed and grabbing hold of the sewing machine table to pull herself up. In those days, there was no such thing as a variable-height bed. It would have been useless anyway as the bed was placed under the bookcase.

Linda and her parents had received a letter from the secretary at Dorton House School asking Linda to start the six-week trial period from the 2nd of October. On that weekend, the family had been at the caravan in Seasalter and everyone had had a pleasant weekend. Now, it was a case of making the forty-mile journey from Seasalter, near Whitstable, to Seal near Sevenoaks in Kent. It was quite a long journey which took around an hour. Linda was on edge.

Music was played in the car so that they would all sing along to take their minds off what was about to happen. At least, this parting would not be as difficult as the stays in hospital. To Linda, everything felt so vast and confusing.

When they arrived at Dorton House, they were all met by Miss Brown, the deputy, and shown into tea. Sunday teatime, at Dorton House, was probably the best meal of the week, but even that wasn't saying much! One of the items on the menu was cold beef-dripping on toast, which Linda detested. The noise, as Linda entered the dining room, housing two hundred-and-fifty children, most of whom were totally blind, was deafening.

Someone dropped a plate of food on the floor and everyone in close proximity, cheered uproariously, banging their knives and forks on the tables, and stamping their feet on the floor. It felt to Linda, like a "mad-house". Alma and George were asked not to go into the dining room, but to leave her to "get on with it".

'What have I done?' Linda thought – but there was no going back. Then, Miss Brown took Linda with Alma and George, to the Dormitory.

Linda was totally shattered by the time that she got into the room. What greeted her was the sound of girls singing and playing their guitars. One of them, Jean, who had just received two new, artificial eyes, was introduced to Alma. Jean said to Alma, 'What do you think of my new eyes, Mrs Berwick? Do you like the colour?'

Alma was already in a heightened state, and this finished her off completely. She ran out of the room in floods of tears. It made Linda feel angry – she suddenly felt really protective towards her mother. There was no need for this girl to be so pointed in her comments. That put up a barrier between Linda and Jean, right from the start, which remained throughout their school lives, and was never repaired.

The staff guided Linda down the corridor from her Dormitory into the large, communal bathroom; three baths, four sinks, and toilets behind doors in cubicles. Linda was afraid to move but was assured that there were no steps – a welcome realisation. Miss Brown, was the teacher on duty that evening – obviously planned to coincide with Linda's visit so that she could make her observations and report back.

One of the girls in Dormitory 10 called out, saying, 'If you're in the bathroom, will you pick up the box on the hand basin that contains my eyes and bring it with you?' These boxes had Braille and printed labels on them with the names of people.

Linda's response was, 'Oh, blimey, I'm not doing that – you come and get it yourself.'

The thought of having artificial eyes filled Linda with absolute dread. She couldn't begin to imagine what it would feel like and, for now, she already had, more than she could handle. Linda could only deal with one thing at a time as it was all too overwhelming with all the noise and so on.

Linda had a restless night's sleep, not only because she was worrying about what the next day would bring, but all the noise from the other nine residents in the room that was Dormitory 10. They were carrying on their lives as normal, especially when the "tuck" boxes with various goodies of food etc. came out after lights out.

It seemed very strange to Linda, orientating her way in the blind world. She had never been in this sort of situation before. Even at this early stage, she realised that there would be a certain level of freedom as her mother, Alma, would not be watching over her every second of every day. Although Alma's help had been wonderful, it was also suffocating. Of course, Linda was grateful for all that her parents had done but she had already had to cope with the feeling of constant "gratitude" which was incredibly difficult to handle.

The windows in the dormitory were always open, however cold it might get. Later, the experience of snow on the inside of the window sills with its freezing temperatures did nothing for making her feel cosy and warm. Linda was to experience a rude-awakening by the House Mother at five-fifteen in the morning. She guided Linda around and stood there talking to her while she was washing, in order to check on her that she was doing it properly.

By the time she got back into the dormitory, Linda was freezing cold and other members of the Dorm-Share were starting to complain about the help that she was being given and how long it was taking. They had plenty of experience when it came to coping with blindness but not understanding all the ramifications of physical disability, wheelchairs, tripods and the like.

Breakfast was another noisy affair – tinned tomatoes on toast and fish-fingers. What Linda couldn't understand was that the food quality was so bad; everything seemed to smell the same. She was parked unceremoniously next to a radiator. The warmest that she had felt for twenty-four hours. Then it was time to go into the main hall for morning assembly.

Everyone was given a Braille hymnbook and the church organ was played by Michael T Campbell, the organist and flute teacher who was himself totally blind. In fact, the first meeting between Linda and Michael T Campbell had him accidentally catching his shins on her wheelchair and yelping in pain so much that he almost fell into Linda's lap!

It was a very pleasurable meeting and he seemed a really nice man. His voice was very gentle and caring – just what she needed at that moment. She struggled to read the Braille and to find the appropriate hymn in the book. One of the teachers offered her a guiding hand, putting her fingers on the appropriate line of Braille. It was obvious that Linda was way behind most of the other children.

In the form-room, Linda was tested as to her Braille-reading speed. It was sixteen words a minute. Other pupils read between eighty and one hundred-and-thirty words a minute. Linda realised just how inadequate she was and felt very despondent. Teachers tried to assure her that she had done really well to learn the Braille system. Mathematics was a complete anathema to Linda, especially when she had to use the Taylor-Type mathematical symbols.

These were eight; eight-sided shapes that depicted, in Braille, dots or shapes, either numbers or mathematical signs on the top and the bottom of each piece. By the time, she had found the position and how to turn them, and slot them into the board, the other members of the class had already completed several sums. Linda thought, '*How on earth am I going to master all this?*'

At the end of the lunch break, Miss Brown came to Linda and told her that she had a visitor. The person said hello and Linda responded with a warm greeting. It was her father, George, who said, 'What's the matter with you? You've only been away for twenty-four hours and you don't even recognise your own father!'

Of course, Linda profusely apologised. She said, 'Everything here is so big and strange and echoey. I'm feeling terribly confused.'

George said that he had brought some spare shoes and a dressing-gown. Linda realised that it was just an excuse – he wanted to know that she was alright.

The English lesson was reading Richard The Third by William Shakespeare. She was never going to get this at sixteen words-a-minute because by the time she'd worked out the Braille and got to the bottom of the page, she'd forgotten what it said at the top. Later that day, a tape recorder was brought in so that she could listen to the sections and make comments. Linda had never read Shakespeare – it was all very strange. Her aspiration, to meet people and read things of culture, seemed very far off.

The last session of the day was choir practice. Jill Smith was the choir mistress. Linda was brought into the hall and told to listen and to "join in" where she could. The choir was learning parts of Handel's Messiah. This sounded incredible, particularly when Michael T Campbell played on the organ. Hitherto, Linda had not heard The Messiah so this opened up yet another world of sound.

At the end of the session, Jill Smith came over to Linda and said, 'Let's take you to the piano so you can show me what you can do.' She played some scales and asked Linda to sing the sounds that she'd heard, then she asked if Linda could sing a third, fifth, and seventh of a chord. It was discovered that Linda had perfect pitch. Jill Smith was very pleased. Then Linda was asked to sing *O Waley Waley* – this had been played in her other school so she knew the words well. Some of the children stopped their chattering and said, 'Who's that singing?'

'Oh, it's the new girl in the wheelchair,' someone answered.

Linda had a beautifully-clear soprano voice and she absolutely loved "shining" in this way. This had certainly been the best part of Linda's first day at Dorton House. It made her feel glad that she was there and she decided that she wanted to remain. But only time would tell.

Chapter 15

Linda had been at Dorton House School for two-and-a-half weeks when she heard about the terribly tragic disaster at Aberfan in Wales on the 21st of October 1966. One-hundred-and-forty-thousand cubic yards of black slurry cascaded down the hill above the village, destroying everything in its path and killing one-hundred-and forty-four people, most of them children, sitting in their classrooms.

Naturally, the reporting of it on the radio was extremely graphic and the anguish felt by the people who were there was very well documented. Linda was a compassionate, impressionable soul. She felt that she wanted to do something. She spoke to Miss Brown. Miss Brown, in turn, had a discussion with the head, Robert Bolton. Linda asked whether a collection could be made on behalf of the pupils at Dorton House, to be given to the victims of Aberfan to help with the rebuilding of their lives.

It's not known exactly how much was raised, but this one action put Linda in the spotlight in the school. There will always be the cynics who said that she was only doing it for attention – nothing could have been further from the truth and Linda thought, '*Here we go again.*' She tried to do something to help, but others put her down just as they did when she became blind after going into Moorfields Hospital. She was misunderstood then, and was further misunderstood now, as to her motives. But Linda carried on regardless, and earned the respect of all the members of staff.

Linda suddenly realised that it was her parents' Silver Wedding Anniversary on the 21st of November but what could she do to make it a special occasion for them? She spoke to a staff member who offered to put up the funds temporarily, for two tickets to see the musical *Oliver!* Along with a meal for two in a local restaurant.

Linda was very excited about being able to give her parents a present and each week her pocket money was used to pay back the cost of the event. It was, "all-systems-go" and Linda was to put the tickets and letter, together with a twenty-fifth Wedding Anniversary card so that her parents would receive it in good time. However, tragedy struck. George's mother, Alice, was rushed into hospital after Alma found a lump in Alice's breast that was the size of a golf ball. Sadly, nothing could be done as she had had this lump for years and not spoken about it.

It had suddenly started to increase in size, causing deterioration in her general health and she died in early November, three days after being admitted to hospital. Her funeral was some four days before George and Alma's Anniversary.

So, Linda thought, '*What to do now?*' She thought the only way was to come clean and tell them of the surprise. They decided to go to the theatre but naturally, they had no appetite for it, particularly as the opening scenes were set in a funeral parlour, which was a disaster, given the situation. What should have happened was that Alma and George should have had a happy time, and been grateful for Linda's thoughtful gesture.

But George didn't see it that way. Linda was prepared to cancel it all but Alma's response was, 'There's no point in cancelling it, we just have to press on regardless.' Linda felt entirely flat and the next day, when she called her parents, she had a totally unenthusiastic response which was not unlike the rest of her life. Any occasion usually resulted in negativity. George always refused everything unless it was something that he himself had arranged, which was virtually never.

George never saw the point of trying to make something nice for someone else. Linda had flowers delivered to her parents on the day, to make it feel like a special occasion. But nothing would shift the doom and gloom.

Back at school, life went on at a pace. There was one student, Kelvin Williams, who had offered to give up his prep-time to read for Linda – he was a brilliant Braille reader and would obviously go far. He had a beautiful speaking voice and he knew how hard it was to cope, and that Linda was struggling. They got close over the months although no sexual contact could occur between them, according to the rules of the school.

Kelvin decided that he wanted to become a boarder. His reason for doing so was that he would be able to see Linda for social time between eight and eight-thirty in the evenings. The only thing they were allowed to do was to sit together, chat, and hold hands. It was very awkward because the staff would walk through and separate anyone who started getting "familiar".

Kelvin was lucky because his home with his parents was in Seal Drive at the bottom of the lane from the school so it was easy for him to go home and visit his parents. But it was not so easy for Linda and the only way that she could meet with Kelvin was during the school holidays.

Kelvin was a very good pianist and he and Linda loved playing music together. Every morning as Linda came down the stairs in her home back in Poplar, Kelvin would wait until he heard her footstep on the first group of stairs, then he would play the first movement of Beethoven's "Moonlight Sonata". It was a piece that Linda loved from then on.

Linda and Kelvin were together romantically for five-and-a-half-years but it was not without its problems, one being Alma. Kelvin could never do anything right. Alma hated his long hair, long beard, and the fact that he smoked a pipe – a present that Linda gave him on his birthday with some Dutch Clan Tobacco. It was quite a sweet-smelling tobacco which filled the room and Linda loved it. What she didn't like however, was the ash that went over his clothes which occasionally set fire to things in his pocket – also all very problematic to Alma who wanted to keep a pristine home. Alma would say, 'I don't know why you two have to sit so close to one another, and cuddle one another?' It drove Kelvin and Linda mad because they could never do the "right thing".

After the school holidays, it was back to work with a vengeance. Now Linda had started to study "O" Levels in English Language, English Literature, and Religious Knowledge – later known as RE, Religious Education. To have reached this stage was truly amazing for Linda.

For someone who was labelled "Educationally Subnormal" to have got to the stage of taking "O" Levels was incredible. In June 1968, the exams dawned. Linda would be writing her answers on a new type of Braille writer – a "Perkins Brailler". The keys were quite spacious but a significant amount of pressure had to be applied in order to operate them. Miss Brown knew that Linda would find the experience of examinations stressful and debilitating and would be exhausted by the end, not least because of the sheer physical effort required to write fourteen pages of Braille.

As a result of the intense effort required for blind students to take exams, an extra hour was allocated to each paper. At the end of it, Linda was so exhausted, using her Brailler "like the clappers", going as fast as she could, so that she could get everything down, that Miss Brown had to arrange for her to be carried up the stairs to her dormitory to rest. Kelvin had taken even more examinations and got selected to go to Worcester College for the Blind and then on to Swansea University to complete his BSc in Social Work.

Linda's parents were very proud of her achievement – three subjects and three passes. Linda never thought that she would do it. Sadly, Kelvin never had any acknowledgement of his achievement from Linda's parents, which was a great pity.

Chapter 16

Linda's father had fulfilled the role of transporting her to and from Dorton House for two-and-a-half years, collecting her from Dorton House on a Friday afternoon, then returning her on a Sunday evening with Alma accompanying them so that she could be a companion to George for the return journey home. That also meant that they had five days of uninterrupted time together which should have worked really well, but they were always arguing, partly because Alma did not know what to do with her so-called "free-time".

On her return home on a Friday, Linda would get chapter-and-verse from her mother as to how horrible it had been concerning her father. It didn't matter how much Linda said that she should try and make the most of this time and to do things together like going for a drink or a meal, and learning to relax in each other's company, the truth of the matter was that Alma felt lost.

She had relinquished her daily role of caring for Linda and now she had nothing to replace it, because they had both lost the art of working at their marriage. Almost every week when Linda returned home, they started to argue with one another. Anything small would spark them off and then it would escalate within minutes.

Alma had a temper that mirrored her own mother Violet's. Violet would swear profusely and run to the knife drawer, take out a sharp knife and flail it around, shouting to her husband, 'I'll kill you, you bastard!'

So, Alma had learned this kind of behaviour. All her anger and pent-up emotions were meted out to George. She would say and do exactly the same things to George as her mother had said and done when she'd argued. Linda would sit in the kitchen, shaking and thinking, 'Oh my God, here they go again,' anticipating the inevitable slanging-match, or much worse, which would surely follow.

One day, it got so bad that Linda went to the cutlery drawer and started emptying the contents of the knife section because she was so fearful that they would clash with one another, escalating the fight to something more dangerously physical on Alma's part. Alma came running into the kitchen shouting, 'I'll kill you, you bastard,' just like her mother, Violet, and opened the drawer only to find that the knives had been removed. She asked Linda, 'Where have the fucking knives gone?'

Linda told her that she had taken them away, out of her reach for her own safety because she could not be trusted, and the arguments were getting out of hand. 'Quite frankly,' Linda said, 'I can't wait to go back to school. It's all just too much.'

When Alma and George started bickering, they would use Linda as the go-between, 'Tell *her* there's a cup of tea, if she wants it,' George would say, and, 'Tell *him* his dinner's on the table,' Alma would say.

Linda was sick of hearing this toing and froing, with her parents trying to point-score with one another. One day, she sat them both down and said that she was not going to be a go-between for either of them and that this had to stop. Sadly, it made no difference and the arguing continued. The knife drawer was constantly being emptied by Linda. She was obviously taking a risk when she removed the knives because she could have easily fallen and cut herself in the process of handling them, especially due to her heightened state of anxiety and of course, the fact that she was totally blind. So this kind of behaviour was highly dangerous and of course, counter-productive.

George was always "spoiling for a fight", and Alma readily "took up the bait". Linda unwittingly got sucked in and was able to see the injustices meted out towards her mother. She knew that her mother was working all the hours that God sent and that she worked unceasingly for the family, whereas George did whatever *he* wanted, regardless of the consequences for others. If Linda defended her mother, George would say, 'Oh, *she* can do no wrong!' and Linda's response was always, 'No, *she* can't, in my eyes, because I think *she* has been bloody marvellous.'

George would then go off in a huff, sulking – not speaking for some three days, other than in monosyllabic "grunts". Although there was always an uneasy truce between them, the consequence was that there was always an "atmosphere" around the home that could be physically felt. Linda never knew when it would lift. Linda used to pray to God, asking him to help her find a way out of all this – she was trying hard to cope with everything, and make her way in the world. All they wanted to do was to fight, not acknowledging all the effort that Linda was making. It was soul-destroying – for all three of them.

Chapter 17

September 1969, found Linda leaving the safety of Dorton House and heading for Heathersett, the RNIB Vocational Training Centre for the Blind, in Surrey. It was a three-month training course which turned out to be a complete disaster. The speedy, erratic movements of visually-impaired people chasing up and down the stairs, which were not wide and spacious like those at Dorton House, meant that people met each other face to face, one coming up the stairs, the other coming down, with nowhere to go. They would frequently have to squeeze themselves against the bannister so that the other person could pass.

This training course was to teach independence. The first hurdle was breakfast. Trying to lift a jug with four pints of milk in it was almost impossible for Linda and she had the same difficulty with large jugs of coffee and hot water. Linda was really nervous because she knew that she was being watched and any spillages or difficulty would be "marked down".

Linda decided, after trying to lift the milk jug that she wouldn't bother – a member of staff came over and said to her, 'I see you drink black coffee?'

Linda smiled pleasantly and said, 'Yes, it's quite nice, isn't it?' Linda had never drunk black coffee before but after a couple of days, she got quite used to it and indeed, found that she preferred it. Also, the same principle occurred regarding sugar. Linda did not want to spoon sugar from a large bowl so, for a similar reason; she didn't struggle with it for fear of making a mess – much better for her waistline too!

The morning found tests in typing, dexterity, and touch tests for switchboard work. There were various box-structures with lights in to ascertain as to whether Linda had any light recognition – this failed miserably, unfortunately she had none. So a series of very small light bulbs were switched on to ascertain whether she could tell whether or not they were on just by touch from the heat that they gave off. This was fine, providing there were only two or three close together. But if there were twenty or so, by the time Linda reached the end of the row, it was impossible to know whether the earlier lights were still warm because the time from when they were switched off caused the heat to have dissipated.

It was decided, based on these simple tests that Linda would be able to manage a "PABX1 Switchboard" that worked on the basis of twenty outside lines and one-hundred extensions. The new technology for the blind on this board was a system whereby the lights were replaced with electrosolenoids with an indicator that made a "clicking" sound, similar to that of an indicator on a car, where a pin popped in and out, pulsing under the finger to inform a person when, what would have been a light, was flashing – simple, but effective.

Touch-typing was another no-go area. Linda could only manage two fingers and a thumb on her left hand, and one finger and a thumb on her right hand, although she knew the layout of the keyboard very well.

The tutor's attitude was, 'Don't worry about the "Pitman Method" of touch-typing; I will accept whatever you can do so long as it is accurate.' It was painfully slow, but Linda managed to type a letter with which the staffs of the vocational training team were pleased. At least, it would mean that if Linda had to write a message in print, it could now be done.

At the end of the first week, Linda would have to learn household skills such as washing, ironing, and some cooking. This was done in the domestic science room which was at the bottom of a narrow staircase down in the basement. One of the tutors said, 'Bloody hell, I'm not helping you down that staircase because I have a bad back!' From then on, all thoughts of domesticity went out of the window for Linda.

After two weeks, she was sent home and asked not to bother to return. It was terrible for Linda that she had failed, for all intents and purposes, through no fault of her own. She felt that the rigidity of the RNIB Training Centre was unfortunate at best, and, darn right ignorant at worst. Where to now?

It was decided that Linda should go to Pembridge Place, Notting Hill Gate in London. This was the RNIB Commercial Training College for the Blind. In this building there were many obstacles, not least, the stairs, having reversible swing-doors at the very edge of the stairs which made things very difficult, especially when pushed open by students from the other side when Linda wasn't expecting it. The female training administrator for telephony said, 'I am here to teach the blind, not spastics!'

An approach was made to St Dunstan's, for the war-blinded veterans, but because Linda was not war-blinded, even though she had great difficulties with her hands, St Dunstan's constitution meant that they could not go beyond their remit. This was a great pity because organisations for the blind or disabled should have worked in collaboration with one another. But for Linda, no help was given, and she was left just sitting around for a whole year doing virtually nothing.

When the tutor had said, 'I am here to teach the blind, not spastics,' the pressure that had been put upon the RNIB and Pembridge Place in particular, meant that she was forced to resign. Linda had felt that it was terrible that one person could hold her life to ransom in such a way that she couldn't progress.

She had something to occupy her mind in the meantime because she was asked to set up a charity providing social activities for spastics over the age of sixteen. The East London Spastics Society wanted someone with a bit of spirit to provide activities for younger people and Linda was chosen to do that work. Her remit was that the social club should include people of all disabilities and visual-impairment, together with able-bodied people, to encourage greater integration between the two groups. This concept was not greeted with much enthusiasm by The East London Spastics Society but Linda was adamant that this should happen and the people with disabilities themselves were very enthusiastic about this new concept – someone was taking their needs seriously.

Linda started to raise funds. A grant of £50 from TELSS, The East London Spastic Society was given, but most expected it to fail. Linda was determined that it would not, and that it would only happen if they did their own fund-raising. Whatever they did, the problem of transport dogged them – anything with four wheels and an engine, was commandeered to pick people up and take them to the centre!

In the first instance, musical entertainment was arranged. Thank God that they had got away from wartime melodies and singing with a piano. Now there was folk music, pop music, some classical, and of course, singers of various kinds. As funds slowly trickled in, Linda's group became more adventurous. The members wanted to go out to the local pub for a drink, to the local restaurant for a meal, or to take in the latest movies at the cinema. "James Bond" movies were particular favourites of the group although Linda hated them because for her, her blindness meant that they were too visual. However, groups were organised to go out. Transport and volunteer helpers were sought at every turn and the club progressed.

Pembridge Place was still negotiating as to whether Linda could attend. A trial period was arranged. She had two volunteers from the British Red Cross

Society – they had little or no experience in dealing with a blind person. After three days, it was decided to abandon the help of these particular volunteers and Alma, "stepped-in" to fulfil this role. The only difference was that the able-bodied-blind had up to a maximum of one year to complete their training, but in Linda's case, being also physically disabled as well as blind, only three months were allocated.

Linda felt this to be distinctly unfair but she pressed on regardless, trying to prove a point. Between training sessions, lunch and tea breaks, Alma would occupy herself by knitting. If she was to keep this role on, she would be doing a great deal of knitting during that three-month period. Every evening when Alma returned home, George would ask whether it had gone well, not that he ever offered to take any time off work, or do a shift at Pembridge Place.

It was always left to Alma, despite her being with Linda from eight-thirty in the morning until five-thirty in the evening; George did nothing in the house but still expected his meals put on the table. There was never any sense of concession on his part. He might accept the occasional take-away, but that would be a very rare occurrence.

Back at Pembridge, Linda was continually tested on Braille-writing speed, Braille-reading speed, and the making of a directory of useful numbers and places. Alma watched with great interest, marvelling at the way Linda had mastered the PABX1 Switchboard. She frequently said that she could never have coped with the strain of learning and coping with so much.

One test that Linda had to do was to memorise five-hundred STD national dialling codes. Linda was given these weekly, and by the end of the three-months-training she had to recite them in random order, being given the place names by the tutor. A further task was to place Linda in a telephone booth whilst wearing headphones. The tutor would then give Linda six London telephone numbers, and would then ask, 'What was the third number I gave you?' then, 'What was the fifth? The first? The Sixth? The second? And the fourth?'

To hold six new London telephone numbers in her head and then to recite them in random order was incredibly difficult. She was allowed to fail for the first three times, then, if she persisted in forgetting one, she would be failed on the whole course. Linda did not fail but excelled at the course.

The outcome was that a person who was trained by the RNIB Commercial Training College was better than the GPO-trained telephone operators. Blind people had to prove that they were better than their sighted, able-bodied counterparts, and this certainly stood them in a good position for outside employment. They were so amazed by Linda's remarkable memory that she was awarded "Student of the Year" by the RNIB and was awarded a Braille watch by the American Embassy in Grosvenor Square as it then was. The "Tutor of the Year" was Geoffrey Jackson – also one of Linda's tutors who was himself, blind. He too, was given a Braille watch by the American Embassy at the same time. Linda was absolutely thrilled by this recognition and the beautiful meal that was provided on the occasion, especially the "American Martinis"! Linda was accompanied by her father on that day which she felt was a little out of order because it was in fact, Alma that had done all the hard work and sacrificed so much to get her through. Every evening after getting home from Pembridge, Alma had to cook the meal and then do several hours machining until bedtime – she was completely shattered. Neither Alma, nor Linda, could wait for the weekend when they could have a rest, and not have to dash to the centre of London, to complete a week of study.

Chapter 18

Now Pembridge Place was over, and the harsh reality of work would begin. There were only one-in-twenty people with disability who manage to get a full-time job with normal prospects and salaries. The RNIB Disabled Resettlement Officer was meant to help Linda look for a job, but he wasn't very effective because he spent most of his time getting her to write job applications for switchboards that she couldn't even operate. There was only one thing for it, Alma would have to spend time looking at the job advertisements in the local and national newspapers and give Linda the telephone numbers to call for application forms.

Alma and Linda looked through many newspapers until they found some that had a PABX1 Switchboard. There were many false starts but eventually Linda, accompanied by her mother, was invited for an interview at The Commonwealth Trading Bank of Australia – later to become The Commonwealth Bank of Australia. It was right in the heart of the city at Old Jewry, London, EC2. Linda was asked to bring any equipment that she might need. So Alma, and Linda struggling with her tripod sticks in the pouring rain, were armed with a Braille Short-Hand Machine and some files, as they struggled with the revolving door at the bank's entrance.

They asked to speak to Mr Chandler, the accountant. His first reaction was, 'I didn't realise that you would be *this* disabled, but you might as well sit down anyway.' He proceeded to ask Alma every single question about Linda's training and Alma was becoming more and more unsure and exasperated as the interview progressed. In the end, she said, '*I* have not trained as a switchboard operator. Why don't you ask my daughter?'

Turning to Linda his response was, 'I thought, being spastic, you would have had a speech impediment.'

As the questioning was going on, Linda was going red in the face with anger and Alma was kicking her under the table, in an effort to keep her quiet. But

Linda replied, 'Well sir, I'd hardly be applying for the post of senior telephonist if I couldn't speak.'

Mr Chandler said, 'Oh Blimey!' As he placed his hands on his head, 'I've really blown it now, haven't I? Let's begin the interview all over again, shall we?' To his enormous credit, that is what he did.

The interview went well but then he took Alma for a walk around the bank so that she could see some of the obstacles. Linda was left with the telephonist in the switchboard room. She was invited to answer some calls and although she couldn't see the switchboard lights because it wasn't an adapted board for a blind person yet, the senior operator told her which lines were flashing. Mr Chandler and Alma slipped quietly back into the switchboard room, unnoticed by Linda who was busy concentrating on the calls.

After a while, Mr Chandler said that it was the best telephone technique that he'd ever heard. So Alma and Linda went back into his office. Linda thought that he had decided not to take her on but there was only one chance, so she may as well go for it. Linda said, 'Look, if you'll give me a chance, I will work for you for one month without salary and at the end of it, if you like what you see, give me a job, and if not, I will walk away having had the work experience.'

They said their goodbyes and Linda thought that she'd blown it. It was a difficult and emotional time for both Linda and Alma.

The next morning, the telephone rang and it was Mr Chandler. He said to Alma, 'I'm going to give that daughter of yours a chance – she's got guts.'

Alma passed the telephone onto Linda – they were laughing and smiling. Linda just hugged her mother with delight before asking Mr Chandler how many people worked at the bank. He told her it was two-hundred and-fifty and there were some hundred departments or so.

Linda asked him to put a list of names into the post so that she and Alma could work on Brailling the list and committing it to memory. Alma would throw a name or department at Linda and she would recall the full name and the departments, their numbers and extensions.

There were some four weeks before she started work at a salary of the princely sum of sixteen-pounds-a-week. The transport for ferrying her into and out of work was supplied by Access to Work – that government office was to support Linda all through her working life and she could only give them credit for everything that they had been doing. But, sadly, the taxi was frequently late in getting to Linda's home to pick her up.

On her first day, the switchboard had still not been adapted which should have been done in the previous four weeks. Once that was done, Linda readily committed everything to memory and handled the switchboard beautifully. Mr Chandler kept popping in and out to see how she was doing. After just three days, Mr Chandler told her that she had gotten the job – a permanent position with a pension. Linda was ecstatic. However, after two weeks, Linda was called in to Mr Chandler's office and he said, 'I know that your transport has let you down badly, but I have to say, that if this problem cannot be resolved, you will have to give up your job.' He then went on to say, 'Do you know anyone who would like a job in the post department here?'

'Yes,' replied Linda, 'My mother.'

'Well give her a call and see what she says,' replied Mr Chandler.

Linda would have done anything to get her mother away from the lonely isolation of working on a sewing machine and of course, having a regular wage with a pension would be fantastic.

Linda called her mother and she was incredulous saying, 'Well, it would really help *you* if I were there wouldn't it? I could help you during lunch time, tea break, and be there to guide you around the bank, up in the lifts to the toilets, and so on.'

The next hurdle would be to tell George. As predicted, he went ballistic, 'What about my meal at lunchtime and what about the dog?' Nicky, the poodle had been the family's companion since 1962, when Linda needed a pet to help her recover from her nervous breakdown.

Alma's response was, 'You'll just have to eat at night. I will try to prepare something for you at lunchtime while you spend some time with Nicky.'

George was not happy but Alma's mind was made up. Linda was to tell Mr Chandler that Alma would be delighted to accept the position. The Sabina Shirt Company was not too happy but Linda was absolutely thrilled that her mother would have some easement of pain from her back, and that she herself would now have a properly-decorated bedroom with no machine or sacks of work in it. It was decided that Linda would have a lovely new bedroom suite of furniture and a new carpet. So, for the first time in her life, at the age of twenty, Linda felt "normal" and realised that she was not devalued with the "anything-will-do" mentality so as long as it earned money.

George continued to protest relentlessly. He wanted a hot meal provided at midday so the fact that Alma would not be there, to dance attendance on his every "need", made him extremely angry. He protested without ceasing. Linda thought that it could never be overcome.

It was great to know that Linda had the security of having Alma with her at the bank and it did not take long for Alma to become a very popular member of staff. However, there was a downside. People had given Linda assistance around the bank for the first three weeks and it was good that she could get to know people without Alma's controlling influence. Alma would tell Linda when she could speak and even what she could have at the canteen – control, at every turn. This was the price that Linda had to pay for helping Alma to get a new job.

The way that the transport problem was resolved was that George got the sack from his employer so he then decided to look for a job in a bank as a messenger so that he could drive himself, Alma, and Linda, into work each day. Once Linda knew that she was going to keep the job at the bank, she then had to gain a certificate from the City of London to obtain a disability parking permit.

Unlike the normal disability badges, the City of London, Westminster, Camden Borough, and the Royal Borough of Kensington and Chelsea, did not recognise the regular disability badge scheme, as is still the case to this day. Having obtained her permit, she could then get down to the business of being fully employed and achieving her goal.

Now that George was part of the equation, the question of who paid for the petrol reared its head. George would put the petrol in the car each week and he would claim the cost back from Alma and Linda. Linda protested, 'Why can't we split the cost.'

George's response was, 'Not bloody likely, I'm *driving* the bleedin' car – and what's more, *you two* are going to have to pay my car tax.' The exemption on the car tax could only be achieved if the vehicle was for Linda's sole purpose which seems unfair when her parents were enabling her to get to work. Alma had never learnt to drive so, yet again, George had total control over *his* car.

In 1972, Alma's mother, Violet, died. Linda was told that she'd better go to work because she would only "get in the way". Linda was heartily sick of the fact that it was always thought that she would not wish to attend a funeral, or indeed, any family gathering – it was as though George didn't want the embarrassment of a disabled daughter on display for all to see – everything had to be kept "under wraps".

Violet had said to Alma that what little money she had would be for Linda's future, but the reality was that she did not make a will. Therefore, others got it, and Linda had nothing.

George and Alma received a letter from Tower Hamlets Council saying that, because they had lived in Grundy Street for thirty years, they would have an opportunity to purchase the property at a great discount. George's immediate response was, 'You can forget that. Where do you think I'm going to find a thousand pounds for a deposit on a bleedin' mortgage?'

Alma said that she would like to do it as a means of providing Linda with an investment for her future. Both the boys, George Philip and John Albert, were now married and both had children so they had their futures well-established. Alma turned the screw on George a little tighter. Eventually, he agreed to seek out a mortgage with The Clydesdale Bank. It was a relatively meagre sum of nine-pounds-fifty-a-week.

Linda went to see Mr Chandler and asked whether she could be considered for a bank loan to assist her parents. Mr Chandler said that he would ask senior management. However, because of her disability, it was refused (something that would become illegal in time in terms of it being discriminatory). Mr Chandler was incensed by the management's attitude so he wrote out a personal private document offering Linda a bank loan of £500 to be paid back in two years out of his own personal bank account.

Linda saved hard and paid it back in less than fourteen months. She went home and gave Alma and George the remaining money for the mortgage on Grundy Street, as a gift. Alma was delighted but George showed no feelings of gratitude. Indeed, because he had to find nine-pounds-fifty-a-week for the mortgage, he docked Alma's forty pounds-a-week housekeeping money by five-pounds-a-week. His meanness was incredible.

Chapter 19

It was 1975 and Linda was just twenty-five-years old. Alma, George, and Linda, drove to the bank as usual. Everything seemed normal. On their return, they noticed that the front door of their house in Grundy Street was open – both Alma and George accused each other of leaving the door open. Linda said, 'Don't worry about all that now, don't you think you ought to see what might have happened?' On entering the house, George quickly found out.

The house had been broken in to. It was a two or three-person job, with a small child being put through the kitchen window, landing on the draining-board. The child then let in his "friends". They had had a field-day! They had sprayed Coca-Cola all over the walls of the sitting room, the hallway, and in to the bedroom. They had obviously got over-excited and excrement was found on the carpet.

Every cupboard and drawer was emptied of its contents onto the floor and the burglars went rummaging. What they couldn't take, they smashed – Braille machines, Braille books, and Braille watches were all either torn or smashed. The record collection was taken, but leaving some classical music discs behind. Jewellery was also taken – several pieces of Linda's and some of Alma's. The dog, Nicky, was knocked unconscious having been hit over the head and then placed under the sofa – from then on, Nicky's hearing was severely impaired.

There was a huge carving knife placed on the sofa. It was all very distressing and Alma could not stop crying. Linda did not want to express her feelings because Alma was doing enough for everyone. Linda just sat quietly. Alma said, 'I don't know how you can be so calm?'

'Well it's like this Mum,' said Linda, 'Did *Dad* get hurt? Were *you* hurt? Or, did *I* get hurt?'

Alma's answer to all three questions was, 'No.'

Linda said, 'So why are you worried? All that has been taken are just material things – either insured, or they can be replaced.'

Alma replied, 'But look at the state of the place!'

Linda responded, 'But all these things can be replaced or renewed.'

'I can't make you out, you're so bloody calm,' replied Alma.

When Alma entered her bedroom she broke down in tears. The first thing that she saw was her mother's death certificate, lying on her bed. She was absolutely distraught. Linda said, 'It's only a piece of paper, Mum.'

Crying, Alma said, 'No, it's an invasion of my private space and my home and all the things that I hold dear.'

Alma was sobbing and Linda tried to comfort her but there was no consoling her, and George was not very sympathetic – after all, he would have the job of redecorating and it would probably be better to have a new carpet. The police gave the story of the robbery to the East London Advertiser and they ran it the following week. The good old "East enders" put their hands in their pockets to try and help. Money came in via the newspaper office and people put money in envelopes through the family's front door. The insurance company started to deal with the claim of replacing the jewellery.

The newspaper article was quite graphic. Linda had already decided that she would only replenish or replace the items rather than buy extra from the money that accrued from the proceeds of the article. This local news item captured the interest of the local television news which also held people's interest. A further programme was planned for the afternoon slot in which Linda also appeared live on air.

As a result, Linda had a letter from some of the inmates at Wormwood Scrubs Prison. Some of them wrote to her to say how sorry they were that this had happened to her. If you are a hardened criminal, there's more of an honour among thieves when they can see that the person has special needs, and they wrote, 'We don't normally go around smashing up people's possessions in the way that happened to you.' They sent twenty-six pounds of their collective pocket money to say sorry. Linda was very touched by this. As a result of the various broadcasts, Colonel Alexander from International Artists Representation asked his secretary to contact Linda for her address so that he could send her seventy-five pounds of record-tokens to help replenish her collection.

Linda was very grateful but she did not want to make money out of other people's wrongdoings. It was decided that Alma, George, and Linda would have a few days rest at Cromer by the sea, in Norfolk, to recover from the ordeal. One week in a very mediocre hotel for a largely, freezing cold, windswept time for the most part. It did not make them feel better but Linda's main goal was to use the spare cash that she had acquired to give a holiday to two disabled people. They were absolutely incredulous that Linda should do this and were delighted by the holiday.

All in all, something good came out of a difficult situation, perhaps the nicest part of all, was a friendship that Linda made with Colonel Alexander's secretary, Mary Spain – a friendship that continued throughout the rest of Linda's life to this very day.

Chapter 20

Now that the Berwick family was becoming more affluent, George decided that he would like to own a speedboat. It was a very fast boat, powered by Volvo engines and it was the type of boat that was used for water skiing, so it could cut through the water with incredible speed. Linda was quite happy chugging around in the Daily Mirror dingy with a single engine. She had been especially happy because she had helped with the building of it some eight years earlier.

Linda's job was to sandpaper all that she could reach. George liked her work because she felt the wood, carefully, and sanded it in the natural direction of the grain. It was perfect. Once this little boat that was built in 1965, in the back yard of the house in Grundy Street, was lifted over the wall onto a trailer and taken to Seasalter, much fun was to be had.

But now, George had this forty-foot beast that roared more like a lion. George took Linda and a friend out in the boat and opened it up – it was freezing cold and the water surged over the side, soaking the occupants. Linda asked her father to go slower because the water was so cold that she could not cope.

George couldn't really hear her above the noise of the engine and he ignored her hand signals to go slower. He thought that he would do her a favour and make it go even faster. Linda felt as though she could not breathe and went into a panic. Even when the boat came to a stop, Linda couldn't cope with the wind in her face. This fear of wind and water persisted for many years. It was only when a psychotherapeutic counsellor told Linda that her phobia was an outward manifestation of inner tension, and that once that tension had gone she would be able to cope much better. This made a great deal of sense to Linda.

The situation hovered between work and the East London Spastics Society, where the centre was now officially opened by the boxer, Henry Cooper OBE. Alma was regularly serving disabled people and their families from behind the bar at the monthly socials and generally being a great assistant to so many as well as a wonderful support to George. So things were on a fairly even keel.

Linda was developing work with the East London Spastic and Handicapped Club, raising money for its first tailgate-vehicle. This was achieved by staff at the Commonwealth Bank of Australia having a regular weekly prize draw. Sidney Crook, who worked at the bank, was the transport officer for the club. Linda involved the Rotary Club, and Sidney Crook approached The Worshipful Company of Cutlers and The Worshipful Company of Drapers for fundraising. Linda was also giving media interviews, both newspaper and radio, in particular, with Joan Shenton and Tommy Vance at Capital Radio.

The East London Advertiser took up her calls and this is where Joan Shenton and Tommy Vance got involved. So fund-raising was launched on Capital Radio on a very regular basis. Alma and George felt that this was ridiculous, thinking that no one was going to find this interesting. But the public did due to Linda's unique situation as a multiple disabled person along with her enthusiasm for the project. A vast amount of money was raised to purchase the club's first vehicle.

Everything seemed to be going really swimmingly until one day, Alma and Linda went to the canteen for coffee at the bank. As they waited at the lift for the doors to open, someone came out, carrying a cup of tea, splashes of which fell to the floor. Alma walked forward to press the lift buttons and as the doors opened, Linda walked forward on her sticks. Suddenly, Linda's tripods went from under her as the rubbers connected with the "spilt tea" and she fell, hitting her head on the marble floor. Alma was powerless to do anything about it as she had already stepped into the lift. Naturally, a crowd of people gathered to see what had happened.

Linda said, 'Don't move me yet, I've got a terrible pain going through my eye.' Eventually, Linda was able to sit up and was helped to her feet but she felt very strange and knew that the pain in her head was different to what she usually experienced. Linda said to her mother, 'I think that we are going to have to go to Moorfields, because there is something very strange going on.' Alma called George and he was not happy because it would mean that he would have to have permission to take time off work.

On reaching Moorfields Eye Hospital, they were seen by a consultant who, after x-raying, said that the left eye had burst and there was no hope of saving it because it had haemorrhaged and it would have to come out. It seemed ironic that George was the one who doggedly confronted the doctors all those years previously, telling them that he would not give permission for Linda's eye to be removed, but now, when Linda was able to make her own decisions, she knew from the pain that she was suffering, that there was no choice.

The pain was absolutely intolerable. Linda was taken into hospital – obviously very stressed because it had all happened so very quickly. The person who spilt the tea on the floor was absolutely beside himself when he heard what had happened.

It is quite a traumatic experience to have an eye totally removed. During the evening before the surgery, Linda was wide awake, thinking about it all. She tried to sleep when everyone was quiet, but it was impossible. The Staff Nurse on duty said, 'Let's give you something to help you sleep.' However, at four in the morning, Linda was still wide awake, even though she had been given 5 milligrams of Valium. She had only asked for two, because she had experienced previously that when the milligram dosage was increased, it made her more excitable and agitated.

But to her dismay, five milligrams were administered which meant that she was awake for the whole night. The hospital staff was very kind but her agitation persisted. However, Linda used this time for prayer. Naturally, she prayed fervently that all would be well. Then suddenly, the words, 'Take this cup away from me,' came into her mind. At that moment, she would have given anything in the world to have had "that cup" taken away.

Later on in the night, the words, 'Not my will, but Thine be done,' came clearly into Linda's thoughts. She was suddenly filled with a peace and serenity that she had not experienced the whole night. She knew that whatever happened in that operating theatre, she would be able to cope. It was as though she had been given a great sense of security and that she was being held by God. Throughout her life the church had been very important.

Alma and Linda regularly went to church together and had daily bible readings and prayer together. One year earlier, Linda was confirmed by Bishop Trevor Huddleston, which had meant so much to her. Bishop Huddleston was a deeply spiritual man and he was very encouraging to Linda when she wanted to "walk forward" to receive the laying-on of hands at the communion rail. His comment was, 'This is something worth standing for, isn't it?' So, her faith meant a great deal and at that moment, was very real. Linda's mind was taken back to the time when she was seven years old.

Alma had taken her to a healer by the name of Harry Edwards. People were encouraged to join a prayer group and pray for each other each day at eight in the evening. Linda was taken up to her bedroom and whilst sitting on her bed, she saw a cross, illuminated with a blue light, surrounded by a circle of white light.

Naturally, she was anxious. She called her mother from downstairs and told her what she was seeing. Linda said, 'I expect you think that I'm mad?'

Alma's response was, 'I don't, because I can see the same cross on the wall at the foot of your bed.' Alma contacted the healing centre and spoke to Harry Edwards. He told her that her daughter had been given a very special sign that God had something important for her to do in life. So both Alma and Linda trusted in the fact that God was guiding them through all the circumstances that were to come.

Back at Moorfields while Linda was awaiting her operation, she was asked whether she would like to see the hospital chaplain. They obviously did not inform him as to why she was going down to the operating theatre because his prayer was that Linda would get her sight back and all would be well, which of course, was impossible. This made Linda feel angry because he simply hadn't understood what she was going through and how frightened that she was feeling at that moment.

After the operation on waking from the anaesthetic, Linda complained of pains in her chest and was told that it was because of the way the optic nerve had to be removed. The nurse said, 'They had to hold your shoulders down by kneeling on your chest, whilst pulling out the eye and optic nerve.' Linda was never sure if that explanation was correct, but what she did know for certain, was that her chest felt bruised, and her head ached terribly.

Because of the anxiety that Linda felt after the operation, it was as though she was going to throw up at any moment, not helped by all the pain that she was suffering, which by now was extremely intense. Various medications were given and on the first night after the surgery George was there doing his usual bedside vigil. He never failed to amaze Linda, because as soon as he got her home from hospital, he would relinquish all responsibility and pile everything upon Alma.

One touching moment was whilst in recovery, a Chinese nurse brought a gift from the Reverend Douglas Wallend, curator of the John Wesley Museum at Wesley's Chapel in City Road, EC1. It was a plaque of a picture of John the Baptist being baptised by Jesus in the River Jordan. It was something that Linda always treasured. The nurse's comment was, 'Jesus loves you, Lin,' as she injected her to help her sleep after the surgery.

The next day Alma visited, and Linda was distinctly unwell. She kept complaining about feeling nauseous and needing more medication. Tablets and an injection were administered.

Then, within an hour, Linda's throat and tongue enlarged to the extent that she could hardly speak. Everyone was wondering what was happening. Fortunately, a Chinese nurse who was on duty, said to one of the doctors, 'I've seen this before. It is because two drugs have been administered together.'

The drugs that were used were Fentazin and Stemetil and they should not be used together. The Chinese nurse told the doctor to be quick and go to the library and check. Minutes later, he came rushing back into the ward. Linda was by now, foaming at the mouth and making very frightening noises. An injection of Valium 10 was given along with an antidote for the Fentazin which tranquilised Linda very quickly.

The next day, Alma came into the ward to speak to the nurses. She and Linda were obviously traumatised by the previous night's events. She asked the nurses whether there was anything else that could go wrong. They assured her that Linda would now be fine.

'Well,' Alma said, 'I want to bring her home. I know it's only been two days since the surgery but I think it would be the best thing.' They showed Alma what she had to do to clean the eyes and put a prosthetic inspection-cover into the eye socket. Linda was aware that, when they were showing her mother what to do, Alma suddenly dashed off to the toilet and was promptly sick.

That didn't make Linda feel great and she wondered, *'Was her situation that bad, and, did she look that horrible?'*

During the surgery, Linda's head was heavily bandaged to keep the bruising inside the eye-socket space. Then, a shield was put over the eye and then the head was further bandaged. Linda would need to return within a couple of days to have the clear inspection-cover, with its tiny hole, inserted to release the fluid which acted as a natural cleaning agent. The body is wonderful in how it provides just what is needed to heal.

George was utterly disgusted. He would shout at Linda, 'Can't you stop making that "clicking" noise,' that was caused by the liquids "squirting" out of the little hole inside the prosthetic inspection-cover. George was absolutely revolted and was shouting at Linda to stop what she was doing but Linda had absolutely no control over this – it was just nature doing its thing, cleaning naturally.

Alma had to remove the dressing which covered up the eye-space and keep it clean – not a good procedure for anyone to have to do. George was terrified. He would not come anywhere near Linda, and would not touch her, or speak kindly in any way. When Alma asked him whether he would help, his response was, 'Not bloody likely, you're on your own.'

Linda was terrified when it came to washing her hair because the headache from having an eye removed was terrific and she asked her mother to be as gentle as she possibly could. Alma was absolutely brilliant and they had a tearful, yet reassuring hug together. George just could not comprehend it, and throughout her life it was always to be the same because George could not accept her blindness whereas Alma just had to get on with it.

The people at the bank were totally shocked. One of the bank managers came to see Linda, bringing flowers, chocolates, and fruit from all the staff at the bank that had kindly contributed. There was a very funny moment when Linda went to meet the prosthetic engineer, or rather, "artist", Mr Wilson. There was a man sitting in the room with his guide dog. He had recently had an eye removed so a discussion took place as to what colour he would like for his new eye. He said, 'Well I understand that my guide dog has beautiful brown eyes so could I have the same as him?'

Mr Wilson turned to Linda and asked what colour she wanted.

She said, 'Well, I'll have a different colour for every day, depending on my outfit and a bloodshot pair for when I have too much to drink!' Much laughter ensued and he told her to 'clear-off!' Linda found him to be a fantastic person, giving her loads of confidence.

Within the space of four weeks, the measurement for the new artificial eye had been taken and a coloured, temporary shell was put in. Linda went back to work within a month. Everyone was amazed to see her so quickly. Alma and Linda were laughing and smiling together. They were just relieved that they had got over this hurdle. People at the bank commented, 'We don't know how you can be so bloody cheerful!'

Linda said, 'You would know, if you had been experiencing the kind of pain that I was in when I left here that day. It was something I hope that I will never have to experience ever again.'

Chapter 21

The telephone rang one evening. George picked it up and it was Joan Shenton, the radio and television presenter, who was becoming quite a good friend to the family. George asked if she wanted to speak to Linda. Joan replied, 'No, that's just what I don't want! I want you to go to the telephone box across the street from your house, and call me.'

George was confused. He went into the kitchen where Alma was doing some baking – she had her hands covered in flour.

Alma said, 'I know what it is. They want Linda for "This is Your Life" and if it *is* that, the answer is no!'

George said, 'Don't be so stupid. I'll go and see what she wants,' He left the house and went to the telephone box.

Alma told Linda much later, that when George returned, he was as 'white as a sheet,' saying to her, 'You're right. How did you guess?'

Alma said, 'I hope you told them the answer is no?'

George said, 'Of course I didn't, if the nation wants to give Linda a tribute, then who are we to deny it?'

There then followed many weeks of the researchers on "This is Your Life" visiting Alma and George when Linda was at Radio Moorfields, broadcasting her weekly programme to the patients. The researchers would arrive and sit in their cars across the road and wait for Linda to go out in a taxi. Naturally, all of this preparation was done secretly and with total confidentiality – any "slip", however small, would have meant that the project was cancelled.

Linda had been broadcasting on hospital radio at Moorfields Eye Hospital for the last year or so, since her first eye was removed. She had initially been a guest on the show, appearing on a two-hour programme, choosing her favourite music and talking about her life to one of the Moorfield Hospital Radio's presenters.

After this, the presenters on the programme were so impressed with Linda's technique and broadcasting style that they offered her a two-hour, weekly programme of her own together with a producer-type assistant, where she interviewed many famous celebrities over a period of some five years or so.

Linda continued to battle with all the pain and side-effects of taking some fourteen lots of medication to try and save her right eye. There was one particularly nasty drug called Daranide, which had horrendous side-effects. For Linda, within half an hour of taking it, her hands and the back of her neck went ice-cold. This drug had the effect of lowering potassium levels, and lowering glaucoma pressure in the eyes. It made her feel particularly unwell.

Every day was a tremendous effort, simply to cope, especially when Slow-k (potassium) was taken with the instruction that five pieces of fruit or vegetables had to be eaten every day, and bananas were essential and could not be excluded because of their potassium-loaded property. The pain in the remaining eye was terrible, like having a migraine every single day for five-and-a-half years.

One day, David Wood, the bank manager and accountant for the Commonwealth Bank of Australia, went in to speak to Linda, 'What are you doing on Wednesday afternoon, Berwick,' he said, 'I never know whether you're "in" or "out" these days.'

The bank was very proud of Linda's efforts with the club that she formed to help people with their disabilities, so much so, that she was featured in the Commonwealth Bank of Australia's magazine "Bank Notes". To have been featured three times was relatively unheard of. Some people had worked there more than thirty years and they had never got any recognition other than competitions or obituaries. Linda told David Wood, that as far as she knew, she would be available.

'Good,' he said, 'Because you're coming on a "gin-sling" with me.'

Linda's response was, 'Stop mucking about, and tell me what all this is about.'

'Well, you know the bank's policy is to tell the staff as little as possible? Well, that's it!'

He was walking round and round the switchboard room, nervously rattling the keys in his pocket, 'No, what it actually is,' he said, 'Is that we are doing a PR exercise which is going to be filmed at a Christmas party. We want to film you at the switchboard, wishing employees at the banks in Australia, a Happy Christmas!'

Linda said, 'I've heard it all now. What a bloody waste of money!' But naturally, she agreed to help.

On the day of the filming, Alma woke Linda at five-fifteen in the morning. Being on the drugs made the start of the day terrible, feeling freezing cold on the hands and neck, having to plunge her hands in warm water to ease the pain, and always, with a really bad headache.

Alma said, 'Come on, get going. I've got to wash your hair.'

Linda's response was, 'Oh, go away, I just can't cope with it today.'

Alma said, 'Ok, get back into bed and I'll tell Mr Wood that you can't help him.'

Linda then dragged herself out of bed and into the bathroom, leaving the house at seven-thirty. Alma was, "supposedly" going on a Christmas shopping trip. Linda rang the house in a panic because one of her tripod sticks suddenly broke in two. So, another pair was brought to the bank. There was a buzz about the people at the bank that day, watching and wondering what was going to happen. Later that morning, a large vehicle turned up at the entrance of Old Jewry with the words "Australian Newsreel" painted over what was actually, a Thames Television outside broadcast unit.

Nobody knew the reality except, Mr Wood, the accountant along with the chief manager of the bank, and Alma. Then, Christmas decorations and a Christmas tree, food and drink, were taken into the main entrance hall of the bank. Once the doors were shut to the public at three o'clock, the transformation of the entrance hall into a party scene began in earnest.

Linda was taken to the toilet by one of the senior secretaries because Alma wasn't there. Linda thought that it was rather strange as the secretary had never accompanied her anywhere before, let alone engaging in conversation. Later, Mr Wood came into the switchboard room and asked Linda to put the switchboard over to "night-time use", and to come and join the party. She was offered a drink but declined it due to her medication.

'Well just hold it,' said Mr Wood, 'For the sake of the film.'

Everyone around seemed quite excited. Suddenly, the door opened, and a voice that Linda knew very well said, 'Hello, assistant manager David Wood.'

To which David Wood replied in his usual Australian greeting, 'G'day.'

Then, Eamonn Andrews said, 'It's my pleasure because I can say to a very remarkable lady – Lin Berwick, Tonight, This is Your Life.'

Linda was totally shocked and so were all the onlookers. All that she could say was, 'Oh no, oh crikey!'

People were laughing and applauding. Linda tried to stand up but couldn't, so her father George, who had been hovering unseen, behind the Christmas tree, suddenly appeared, picking her up and carrying her out to the waiting Daimler limousine. Many people had gathered outside the bank, probably expecting to see someone famous walking out with Eamonn Andrews. Instead, they got Linda or Lin as she preferred to be known. The PR film was a front for the surprise television programme "This is Your Life".

Eamonn Andrews told the people assembled, 'You're all invited back to the studios to watch Lin's programme and there is a coach waiting outside to take you there.' People were absolutely agog. By now, Linda was sitting in the limousine, feeling thoroughly bewildered. Jack Crawshaw, the producer, was also there with Linda's good friend, Joan Shenton, the Capital Radio presenter, who also happened to be Jack's wife. When Eamonn and Jack got into the limousine with Linda, Eamonn asked her how she was feeling. Linda's response was, 'I feel sick and need some fresh air.'

The window was wound down immediately and the car sped off to Thames Television Studios where Linda was taken to the green room. She was told that she would not be able to see anyone who would be appearing on the programme.

'If I can't see my mother, I'm not going on,' said Linda.

Alma was brought immediately. They wanted nothing to spoil this great occasion. Linda and Alma laughed and cried together as Linda said, 'So this is what was going on when you went to Dad's Christmas party last night, and Christmas shopping today, was it?'

Marylin Gaunt, one of the researchers who had visited Linda's home when Linda was at Moorfields Hospital doing her radio programme, saw the clothing that Alma was about to put on Linda and said, 'What did I say to you Alma about Linda not wearing red? I told you that it would not work for the cameras and lighting. I think that you have done this deliberately to stop the programme because you didn't want it to go ahead? Do you realise that you would have jeopardized thousands of pounds because you wanted to take control?'

Linda's original outfit for the "PR" "exercise" was a black skirt with a red blouse, and a grey velvet jacket with a black and silver waistcoat. Marilyn went away and on her return, said that the programme would not be stopped because little of the red blouse would be seen, and the grey velvet would take off the emphasis. So, disappointingly, Linda would not be able to wear the special red velvet jacket that Alma had chosen for the show, unbeknownst to Linda.

Linda was then seen by the sound engineers who put a belt around her waist and a battery pack inside her coat. A microphone was attached to the lapel of her jacket. Eamonn then came in and practised walking and guiding Linda. There was a very high step up onto the stage so George was assigned to lift Linda onto the edge of the stage before the doors swung open.

Eamonn said, 'Right, Lin. Three steps forward, then turn right,' At which point was heard the familiar theme music of "This is Your Life", The programme may have only been twenty-eight minutes and thirty-five seconds long, but it was recorded as one continuous film from the start to the finish.

Just before Linda went on air with Eamonn, he said, 'Don't worry, it won't be seen by too many people,' But when the filming was over, he told her that the programme would be seen by thirty-million people! This seemed incredible to Linda.

It was a wonderful occasion. Family members were brought in to give their tributes. A priest spoke from Pakistan. Others represented Linda's various charity works, and Hattie Jacques spoke of her time visiting Linda when she was in hospital having the operation on her legs. Linda's good friend, the actor, Andrew Cruickshank, better known as Dr Cameron of the television series "Dr Finlay's Casebook", spoke of his admiration for her, and the programme also flew in a good friend from Canada who formerly worked at the bank along with two people from Australia, one of whom Linda had never met.

After the programme had ended, Linda and her family were first given a private reception of champagne where Linda was also given a beautiful bouquet of flowers before they were led out to meet all the two-hundred-and-fifty participants at the party, who were then invited back into the studio to watch the programme again because they always knew that the subject of "This is Your Life" was usually so stunned by it all, that they couldn't take it all in the first time around.

Not all of those who would have liked to appear on the programme, who were interviewed, could be chosen, due to the constraints of time. The fifty-three people who were hand-picked by Alma to appear on the Christmas party PR film for the bank were also at the party, having a whale of a time.

The "This is Your Life" programme went out on the 21st December 1977. The following day, Linda and Alma, were given a day off work to recover from the shock. The officials at the bank were highly delighted with the response – it was all very good publicity. On reaching the bank, forty-eight hours later, as Linda got out of the car, people in the street came up to her and said, 'I have just got to shake you by the hand. Congratulations and very well done!'

It was lovely that people responded in that way but Linda found it rather precarious when people wanted to express their feelings, just as she was going up or down the steps to the bank, as when people enthusiastically grabbed her hands they took them away from her sticks.

The wonderful outreach of television meant that Linda received more than a hundred letters from viewers of the programme. Of course, all this was done before the advent of the internet so it was a much slower process.

The researchers on the programme, and Eamonn himself, kept in touch with Linda, right up until the week of his death, some ten-years later. On a seemingly regular basis, Linda would receive a telephone call from one of the researchers from the programme, who would say, 'We can't tell you who's going to be on "This is Your Life" tonight but would you like us to send a car for you so that you can come to the programme and the party afterwards? We will arrange for a car to pick you up and take you back home.'

Naturally, Linda was up for this, loving every minute of it.

Linda was quite unsettled about what had happened on "This is Your Life" regarding the mystery of the red jacket. She asked her mother why she had chosen for her to originally wear a red, velvet jacket for the occasion, knowing that red was the one colour that was not permitted, due to the problems with the cameras.

Alma's response was, 'Well I didn't want it to happen, did I?'

Linda said, 'How could you do such a thing when so much effort had been made for a lovely programme. You could have ruined it for me – which would have been incredibly unfair and unkind. You knew that, on the day that we went shopping, that my first choice of velvet was the green that you chose for yourself, simply because you wanted to scupper the event, especially when you chose a red blouse to go with the grey velvet that you purchased for me?'

Linda found this action incredible because Alma had been waiting, and almost got, total control, and it would have been terrible if the whole programme had been scuppered by her mother's actions. Alma had made it abundantly clear, right from the start, that she didn't want anything to do with it, and would have been happy had it been cancelled. Yet, she loved the comments that were made by so many people about how gorgeous she looked on the programme. Indeed, Linda felt disgusted because her mother's green suit was the topic of conversation, and Linda hardly had a look-in. The famous "This is Your Life" red book, together with photographs and text in Braille, was delivered by a chauffeur-driven car some weeks later.

Chapter 22

It was a bit of a heavy fall-to-earth after "This is Your Life", but life had to go on. Linda was still in deep trouble regarding her eyes. She had started her training as a counsellor, doing psychotherapeutic counselling with the Westminster Pastoral Foundation in London. She had successfully completed her first course and then wanted to go further. This would necessitate a morning a week in Chelsea, with the Reverend Dr Denis Duncan and the Reverend William (known as "Bill") Kyle.

She learnt about the writings of Carl Jung, Carl Rogers, Sigmund Freud, Alfred Adler, and many more in the field of psychotherapy. It was compulsory for all students to have personal therapy for themselves at least one hour per week, possibly more. Linda had to travel to a church in Chelsea and negotiate difficult stairs, but at least all of the staff did their level-best to help. Linda was making great strides, both on a personal level, and on an academic level.

Alma and George could not understand this work at all. Indeed, it was totally beyond them.

Alma deeply resented the fact that Linda was having personal therapy. It didn't matter how much Linda said that it was compulsory – all Alma could see was that Linda was being "disloyal" to her family. Every time that she arrived back home, she was quizzed over just what she had been telling the therapist. When Linda said that she was not permitted to disclose things about the session, Alma called her disloyal, stupid, and secretive.

'I suppose you told them about the row we had last week,' said Alma.

When Linda ignored those comments, Alma became angry and would occasionally try to gain the information that she wanted by giving Linda a "thump". This gave Linda an even stronger resolve, not to disclose things about the session.

Linda had become very interested in the whole issue of counselling. She used to listen to a Radio 4 programme called "If you think You've got Problems" with

Dr Wendy Greengross and Dr James Hemmings. It was a wonderful programme which expressed a great deal of compassion and sensitivity to the problems that people presented.

As Linda listened to them, she realised that here was a subject that she could get her teeth into, and wanted to learn more about it. She contacted the BBC but was told that telephone numbers of presenters could not be given out to listeners. So, Linda knew that Dr Greengross was a practising GP in London. She called the number and found to her utter amazement that Wendy picked up the telephone herself because the line had been transferred to her home that day. They had a very interesting conversation.

Wendy wanted to know how Linda was coping and feeling about the issues relating to her eyes. Linda explained that things were going really badly and the pain was almost intolerable and she did not know how she would be able to cope. Wendy said, 'You need to talk much more about how you feel, concerning the loss of your eyes.' She asked whether she had ever been able to discuss it with her parents.

Linda told her that her mother's response had always been, 'I'll cope, as long as you don't tell me that you want to "see" and that it's not fair.'

Wendy's response was, 'You have been put under an intolerable burden. You should have been allowed to express your feelings, even if it was painful to you, or your mother.' Wendy wanted to talk to Linda more about it in view of the pain that she was having with her right eye.

'Things are not good,' said Linda, 'And I don't know how much longer I can cope.'

The answer came within a matter of weeks. Thanks to the Daranide and other medications, Linda was losing weight and beginning to get quite thin. One morning she was suddenly very sick, losing blood, and having terrible aches in her head, hardly being able to hold her head up. All her father would say was, 'What's the matter with you girl? You've got your head permanently on your chest and all you seem to do is act like you have a permanent cold, constantly blowing your nose?'

In the end, Linda asked her mother to take her back up to Moorfields. The doctor's response, after looking into Linda's eye, was that they would have to stop all the medication because it now wasn't helping and that there was a haemorrhage at the back of the eye. Linda told the doctor that she now felt that she was at the end of her rope and could not stand the pain any more, and that she wanted the eye removed.

The doctor's response was, 'I'm so pleased that you've said that because there is no hope for the eye – it is in such a mess.'

Linda said, 'Well if it was that bad, why the hell didn't you tell me?'

The doctor said, 'You had to be the one to tell us because once we remove it, we cannot give it to you back.'

'All I want you to do now,' Linda said, 'Is to get rid of it as quickly as possible.'

Linda went back to The Westminster Pastoral Foundation and met with her personal therapist.

'You look absolutely terrible. What's wrong?' She said to Linda. 'Come in and sit down, before you fall down.'

'I just need a hand to hold,' said Linda.

But that hand was not forthcoming. The therapist questioned Linda until she broke down in floods of tears. Later, the therapist said, 'I think that we'd better get you a taxi and get you home.'

When Linda arrived home, her father was there. She told him about the conversation she'd had at Moorfields. He said, 'I suppose you're *happy* now?'

Linda was incredulous, 'How can you say that I am happy when I've had to make this decision today?'

'Well, you don't want *anything* to interfere with your studies, do you? It's all a bloody load of nonsense anyway!'

Even at a time like this, George and Alma couldn't resist having a "poke".

Alma said to Linda, '*You* and your *big* ideas, you're all full of piss and importance.'

'Thank you for that vote of confidence,' replied Linda.

George said, 'I want you to tell those doctors that your father is not happy unless you have exhaustive medical tests to see whether or not the eye could be saved.'

Linda felt too exhausted to care but arranged another appointment to see the specialist. Her father bludgeoned his way through with the doctors, banging his fists on the table to make his points which Linda found extremely embarrassing. The doctors told him that even if she lived for another twenty-five years, there would still be no hope – but George was his insistent self. At the end of the consultation, Linda was taken to have some underwater infrared photography on the back of the eye.

This was a horrible procedure, especially as Linda had a phobia of water going over her face. A framework was put around her head and a four-pound bag of water was tipped in to a receptacle. Infrared pictures were taken with the eye immersed under water so that the back of the eye could be clearly seen. One week later, Linda went with her mother to see the consultant.

'I don't know how you have coped with this terrible pain,' he said. 'You must have been in agony? The Glaucoma has caused your eye to burst and the pictures of the back of your eye look like a "cake-mix". The only part left intact, is the front, and it's got to come out as quickly as possible.'

Alma said to Linda, 'Whatever decision you make, I will support you, but this is something that you will have to decide for yourself.'

The night before Linda was due to go into Moorfields, she lay in bed, crying. Suddenly, the bedroom door opened and Alma said, 'You can cut that out, you've made the decision and you'll just have to get on with it.'

Linda could not believe it. She thought that her mother was heartless. There was no comforting hand or even a cuddle, probably because Alma was hurting too much herself.

Linda had remembered all too clearly her last experience and told the doctors that she would not be able to take Stemetil but needed a better anti-sickness pill. The operation went without a hitch. The doctors were aware of what happened to Linda the last time and none of the awful drugs were administered this time. Within three days, Linda was able to go home. As before, within a month, she was back at work.

This time, Linda would have totally normal looking eyes. Previously the prosthetic artist had to make the eyes look blurry with cataracts and so on, so that the eyes were not strikingly different but now, having had both removed; she could have two new prosthetic eyes that looked "normal" and beautiful. They were lovely, smiley eyes. The prosthetic engineer interviewed Linda to ascertain her character.

Because she was a happy individual, ready to laugh, it made the task easier, 'We are going to give you two lovely, smiley eyes that will look gorgeous,' he said.

Family and friends could not believe the transformation. Alma and George seemed more content now that Linda looked normal. Everything had to "look right" as far as her father was concerned. Alma took on the role of cleaning the eyes and managed it beautifully. The only problem was that Alma preferred to take both eyes out at the same time. Linda hated it because it highlighted just how awful the reality was, although at the same time, at least there was no further, "pretence".

After Alma had cleaned the eyes and put them back in, Linda would often feel very emotional. She would go into the toilet, bolt the door, and sit on the loo and sob quietly. Eventually, she would exit the toilet, only to find her mother, standing outside who would say, 'Are you alright now, you stupid cow?' Which Linda always ignored. At least though, Linda had some kind of "serenity of self" because that momentous decision had now been made.

When Linda was in the hospital, the doctors asked her what she was going to do now after her operation.

'When I leave this place, I am going to a company called "T J Howarth" and I am going to buy myself a solid-silver flute,' said Linda. Playing the flute had been banned for the last few years because of the Glaucoma but now, she could do what she liked. Alma took Linda by taxi to look at the flutes. There was a beautiful, second-hand, solid-silver Rudall Carte that had a lovely filigree design all over it. It had once been owned by a flautist from The London Symphony Orchestra. However, the cost was seven-hundred-and-fifty-pounds.

Alma said, 'Don't be so stupid, you can't buy that and I won't let you.'

Seven-hundred-and-fifty pounds in 1978, was a lot of money. However, Linda could well afford it. So with great disappointment, Linda was instead, "allowed" to purchase a solid silver Yamaha flute, costing five-hundred pounds. George felt that Linda was absolutely crazy, but Linda was overjoyed with her purchase. The people at the bank could not believe how well Linda's artificial eyes looked. Neither could they believe just what she had gone through to get this far. On reflection, neither could she.

Chapter 23

Linda had been attending St Anne's Anglican Church in Limehouse, Poplar. The celebrant was The Reverend Christopher Idle. He became a very famous hymn-writer. John, one of the trainee students at the church, became very friendly with Linda. "This is Your Life" was a great draw to him. He loved the fame, recognition, and popularity that Linda was getting. Over the months they got quite close. He would visit her home and they would play music together – Linda had a very good cassette player and turntable. They would also read scripture and theological books.

John had been a student at Oxford, reading Theology. Unfortunately, John was the type of person who thought that offering ladies "tea and sympathy" was all that was required of a minister. He loved nothing more than to be "invited" for a meal or afternoon tea, and he had a hearty appetite. Alma was not happy, 'He slummocks around, and all he wants to do is *eat*! I don't know what you see in him?' She said.

'What I see is his intellectual mind and his prayerfulness,' said Linda.

But Alma would say, 'He is just taking you for a ride and loves to come along by taxi to the concerts, soaking them up at your expense.'

Linda said, 'Why do you always have to be so critical – and only think the worst of everyone?'

'I'm just looking after your interests,' Alma replied. 'He's never going to be bothered to look after you as I've done.'

'You don't know that,' said Linda. 'You're only assuming.'

'I know that I'm right. His sort will never look after you as I've done,' said Alma.

And of course, Linda could not argue with the level of devotion that she had received from her mother. But it was always incredibly difficult to show the sense of gratitude that she had always felt when her mother spoke like this.

Linda and John got closer as the months went on, but he was always forced to leave by nine-thirty in the evening so that George and Alma could go to bed. Naturally, Alma's mind was working overtime. If Linda closed the door of her study, then suddenly it would reopen, and Alma would burst in with some excuse or other. John was becoming more and more exasperated. He spoke of Alma's "suffocating" control.

Linda said, 'Oh Blimey! You've learnt *that* pretty quick! I'm afraid that she does this to every person that I make friends with because she is terrified of my leaving home and leading an independent life.'

John was saying that he wanted the two of them to be more than just friends, but Linda queried why she had never met any of John's friends or family. John decided that he would try and rectify this. His mother came down to London from Yorkshire to meet Linda. Naturally, Linda was extremely nervous. John and his mother, Linda and Alma, sat together at the kitchen table for breakfast.

Linda was chatting away with a piece of toast in one hand, and a cup of coffee in the other. Suddenly, there was a "ping-like" sound as one of her artificial eyes catapulted-out; landing eye-side up in the cup of coffee that Linda was holding. If ever Linda wanted the ground to open up and swallow her, this was the moment!

Fortunately, Alma was sitting opposite Linda. Linda looked at her imploringly, thinking, '*Oh God, what do I do now.*'

Alma was trying to suppress her own laughter because she knew that Linda wanted to make a good impression – she certainly did that! Alma went to the cutlery draw and took out a teaspoon which she used to fish out the artificial eye, saying to Linda, 'I don't suppose that you want to drink this now?'

Linda's face was getting redder by the minute. John and his mother quietly rose from the table and left without so much as another word. Alma and Linda fell about in peals of laughter–after all, there was nothing more to do than laugh because the situation couldn't be changed.

Whenever John wanted to socialise with his friends, Linda was not included. She felt it to be a little strange, to say the least. John talked about his aspiration to be a Church of England Clergyman and to have his own church. There are many difficult procedures that candidating ministers and their potential or actual partners have to go through. Linda would have to take part in various interviews and have letters of recommendation for her to be considered as a suitable partner for a potential new minister.

Linda passed these question and answer sessions with flying colours. They were mostly conducted over the telephone. Linda explained her personal difficulties to the people concerned and they were not put off by the problems, rather, they could see the potential for the work within ministry. Linda had some wonderful references of recommendation. So for now, they would just have to wait and see.

It was now autumn heading into winter. When Linda's legs got extremely cold, she would have ulcerating blisters at the back of her legs and just above the ankles. They were always exceptionally cold, even on warmer days. Linda was having severe pains in her legs – quite agonising pain, so she realised that something was wrong. She told Dr Greengross about it.

Her response was, 'I will get my husband, Alex, to see you.' Alex Kates was an eminent orthopaedic surgeon. He was extremely kind but very concerned. He examined Linda very thoroughly and found to his dismay that the pulse on both her legs, had been partially severed by the surgeon JCR Hindenach, when he performed Linda's hamstring transplant operations previously, on both of her legs in 1962. Mr Kates said, 'I am so concerned that I want you to be seen by a colleague of mine, Howard Jayne, who is an orthopaedic surgeon at St Steven's Hospital in Fulham. He is an extremely eminent surgeon, dealing with the problems of circulation.'

Linda and her mother went to see him a few days later. His diagnosis was that Linda's situation was extremely serious. The blood was just not pumping correctly into her legs and he needed to find out why. Various tests were carried out and x-rays taken. Linda was admitted to St Steven's Hospital in Fulham on the fifth of December 1978 for an operation the next day.

The idea was, to keep Linda at home for as long as possible until the date of the surgery. She had to be kept as warm as possible so that her legs didn't burst open and ulcerate further. It was decided that Linda would have a bi-lateral lumber sympathectomy on both legs. Wendy Greengross called Alma early on the morning of the operation to explain that this would be a very, very serious operation, necessitating hours of surgery and it could all go wrong.

'We will just have to pray that it doesn't,' said Dr Greengross.

This was probably the worst operation that Linda had endured up to now.

John had visited Linda the night before the operation and they had spent time in prayer asking God to help. During the surgery, Linda had an amazing experience – it was indeed, a near-death experience. She had the sensation of now being sighted, and then being lifted off the bed, heading towards the wall of the room. The wall suddenly opened up, and a long corridor was revealed with bright, shiny lights at the end of it. As she moved through the corridor, the lights got brighter and closer. Suddenly, she heard a group of female voices in unison saying, 'You are coming to us.'

Then, a voice that was very deep and echoey, said, 'Yes, you are coming, but not yet. I have special work for you to do.'

Linda was in no doubt that it was God speaking to her. At the point of the words 'I have special work for you to do,' Linda had a sense of being dragged backwards into the room. It was the side ward that she had been admitted to. She was aware of floating up towards the ceiling and looking down at her body on the bed. All that she could think was, 'I don't want to go back into my body. I am quite happy to be free for the first time in my life.'

Linda could see that there were others in the room, as she looked down, including George and Alma, doctors and nurses. She heard her mother crying, saying, 'She's dead, isn't she?' George told Linda later that her heart had stopped at that point and the "crash-team" had to be summoned. Eventually, after several attempts, Linda regained consciousness by being violently sick with all the drainage tubes coming out of her mouth – she just screamed in the utmost agony. That would be her experience for more than two-weeks.

Due to the cutting of the pulse in 1962, there was so much damage where the blood could not pump properly that a new pathway had to be created. The tissue matter that had died in the intervening sixteen years had to be cut away. Then the lower bowel and all Linda's intestines were placed on a rack in front of her so that the surgeon could cut and re-join part of the sympathetic nerve chain to increase the blood-flow to the legs. Once the nerve was reconnected, the lower bowel and the intestines were put back into Linda's body. This was a very lengthy procedure – some three-and-a-half hours in surgery. When Linda was being violently sick, nurses said, 'We are just going to put the tubes back down your throat.'

'No you're not,' Linda said.

'Oh yes, we have to do that, otherwise you'll be very ill later,' said the nurses.

Linda refused to cooperate, making the team's task even more difficult. Linda was in total agony and could only function with the aid of Morphine and heroin-based drugs. The family joke became, if the surgeon had sneezed, Linda would have been cut in half! Her body looked like she'd had a game of "noughts and crosses" played on it due to the excessive scarring.

Alex Kates and Wendy Greengross visited Linda the next day. Things were still very bad but at least she was still alive. More importantly, her legs were now warm for the first time since 1962. The operation was deemed to have been a great success. Alex said to Linda, 'I'm so pleased that I did not have to operate on one of my friends and I am so sorry that you are having such a terrible time but it will get better.' Wendy advised, 'If you can't eat, don't worry as long as you have four squares of dark chocolate a day, you will survive.' Fortunately, Linda loved dark chocolate.

The following day, Linda's friend John, went to see her parents, Alma and George. He told them that he did not want to be friends with Linda any more. Alma said, 'We fully understand that you don't want the burden of caring for someone like Linda. She is a fulltime job for anyone. But please, she is so ill just now, still on the critical list, so we don't want to do anything that might push her over the edge. Please wait until she is well before telling her that you want to break it off with her.'

Two days later, on the Sunday morning before visiting hours, John went into Linda's ward. He said to her, 'When I saw you on Thursday, when you returned from theatre, with tubes coming out of every orifice and blood plasma and saline, being dispensed into your veins, and I could see how much pain that you were in, I realised that you would take up too much of my "drinking time" with my mates. Therefore, I'm breaking it off with you.'

Linda was in a daze, 'Well,' she said, 'If a pint of beer means more to you than I do, then all I can say is that I feel sorry for you and that I have had a narrow escape.'

The nurses came into the ward and were party to all of this aforementioned conversation.

When John departed, they sat on Linda's bed, many of them in floods of tears and they summoned the Registrar, Dr Dixey, to the surgical team. Dr Dixey was a lovely man – very kind and gentle. He was told by the nurses what had happened and they were worried because of Linda's fragile state. He sat beside Linda, holding her hand, 'What do you want to do now?' he said.

'I just want my mum,' replied Linda.

Linda's mother and father would be visiting that afternoon. Dr Dixey said, 'When I see how you have coped with the pain of this operation, holding onto the bars of the headboard to stop yourself from screaming, all I can say is, *you* have not lost, *he* has. He doesn't know how lucky he is to have you. You have been superb, and I don't know how you have done it.'

Linda said, 'I have coped, five-minutes at a time, counting down the seconds until the next five-minutes. Eventually, I know that I will win through.'

When Linda was into her eighth day after the surgery, she had to go into one of the rooms to have her dressings changed. Suddenly, she started heaving and was violently sick. The nurses rushed to get one of the medical team. He looked at the situation – Linda was covered in blood. His comment was, 'My goodness, you've done well there! This is because you wouldn't let us put the tubes back down, but I can assure you that you will start to feel better now.'

It was very scary when Linda had to have her stitches and the clips that were holding things together, removed a few days later. This was done in the side-ward with Alma, George, and one of the nurses in attendance. It was the first time that George had seen the state of Linda's back since the surgery. It was black and blue from her neck, right down to her bottom.

George said, 'My God! Just look at you – I've never seen anything like it! I never realised that you suffered so much.'

Linda couldn't believe that he wasn't aware, or perhaps, he just couldn't face it. All he would say was, 'No wonder, you get fed up with your brother, John Albert?' John had married in 1968 and he had left his wife, Jenny, when their two children were six-years old. He had found someone new and by now, she was also pregnant. This was to be how John worked out his relationships with people.

Linda thought that he was always looking for a "mother-figure", trying to find perfection but sadly, it could not be obtained. Right from the age of seven, with the incident of the ink, and the incident where his father referred to him as nothing better than a road-sweeper and a shit-raker, he had lost all confidence and was forever searching. He substituted excellence for new relationships, gambling, smoking and drinking. He never got over the success of his brother George Philip, or indeed, for that matter, Linda's. He was deeply jealous of them both and he never got over it.

Alma and George came into the ward and saw the state of Linda. They were absolutely furious with her friend John because they had specifically asked him not to break it off while Linda was on the critical list. Immediately after leaving the hospital, they went to see The Reverend Christopher Idle. He was also incredulous that John could be so insensitive. He waited outside John's flat until eleven o'clock that evening but John didn't show up.

The following day, Christopher Idle contacted the Church of England Candidating Board. Their verdict on the situation was that for now at least, John would not be allowed to go forward for ministry for reasons that his actions did not smack of pastoral care. In fact, he never did. He seemed to spend much of his time on a building site and getting drunk.

When Linda returned home from hospital on 23 December, she rang John and told him his fortune, saying, 'Being a minster of the church is not all about "tea and sympathy". It is about taking the rough with the smooth and being there in times of great trouble and seeing the person through it. Sadly, you did not do that for me but I wish you no ill. I hope that your problems can be resolved and that you will eventually make the grade as a minister. Sadly, that was not to be.'

Chapter 24

The Reverend Douglass Wallend was the minister at Poplar Methodist Church which was a stone's throw from the Berwick family home in Grundy Street. He had pastoral duty to the people in the immediate neighbourhood and as such, he used to visit Linda. He was also a great friend of The Reverend Christopher Idle. Linda told him what had happened with her friend John, whilst she was in the hospital. She said, 'I can't go back to my old church now because John will be there and I don't particularly want to bump into him.'

'Well come to my church,' said The Reverend Douglass Wallend. 'It's wheelchair-friendly and it will be a lot easier than St Anne's at Limehouse because of all the steps.'

Linda visited the church and instantly felt at home. Reverend Wallend was a great preacher as well as the curator of the aforementioned Wesley Museum in City Road. But he only had just over a year until the end of his ministry which was then taken by The Reverend Brian Rippen. Brian was also a superb preacher, speaking as though he had a bible in one hand, and a Guardian newspaper in the other. He preached with a fantastic social conscience and he really made his listeners want to listen.

In the intervening years, Linda listened intently and wanted to influence others by the teachings of John Wesley. One Sunday evening when Brian Rippen was preaching, Linda felt that God was calling her to the work of ministry. As she waited at the end of the service for someone to take her home, she felt a hand on her left shoulder. She turned and asked, 'Who's there and who wants to talk to me?'

A voice that was very deep and echoey said, 'You've got to get off that pew, go to the front of the church and witness for *Me*.'

Linda was incredulous but knew that it was God speaking to her.

Linda replied, 'Who, *me*? Lord? Who's going to want to listen to me? I'll never cope. How will I manage the study and preaching?'

Linda felt quite unsteady as somebody helped her out of the building. She was utterly amazed by what had just happened. She didn't say anything to her parents because she knew that she would be laughed at and it would be ridiculed. She decided to keep this experience in her heart and share it with no one until she had internalised it and come to terms with it. After all, she had been a committed Christian all her life and had often told Bible stories to the young children in the playground when they asked about what she had learnt at church.

Linda kept all these feelings secret, praying about the situation and asking for God's help. She kept asking herself, 'Why me? Surely it would be better for an able-bodied person to do this work.'

But then came the realisation, 'Why *not* me?' She thought that perhaps the church would be open-minded enough to realise her potential. Three weeks on from that evening church service, Linda had a conversation with Brian Rippen, telling him what had happened to her. His response was, 'But Lin, Aren't you already doing God's work with your counselling, and the work that you do for people with disabilities at the social club that you founded? I want you to go away for one month, and think about all of this and what it would mean, and then, come back and speak to me again.'

Linda did exactly that but the issues about preaching, rather than filling her with dread, made her feel that she was compelled to preach and wanted to become a Methodist local preacher.

One month on, Linda returned for another meeting with Brian Rippen. He said, 'You do realise what hard work it will be? You will have many obstacles put in your way?'

Linda said, 'I know, but I feel compelled to witness for God.'

'In that case,' said Brian Rippen, 'I had better give you a note to preach which is the first step on the road to becoming a fully-accredited Methodist local preacher.'

There was much opposition, not least from the secretary of the local preachers' meeting. His first comment was, 'I don't know how you will cope with the public speaking.'

Linda responded with, 'As I have done more than three hundred radio broadcasts and several television appearances, I don't think that will be a problem.'

He then said, 'I don't know how you'll cope with the academic study.'

Linda said, 'I have "O" Levels and the equivalent of a degree in counselling.' However, her passes with the Westminster Pastoral Foundation at that time were not recognised by the British Association for Counselling and Psychotherapy. Now, things are much more rigorous and one has to pass a degree. Things were very different in 1979.

The secretary's response was, 'Oh, you can *learn* then?'

If Linda hadn't been a Christian, she would probably have thumped him! She couldn't understand how people could be so insensitive. She wondered why they couldn't look at someone's potential rather than seeing everything that they did as a problem.

He then went on to say, 'I don't know how you will cope with the logistics of movement around the church buildings.'

Linda said, 'Ah, now there, I am inclined to agree with you, but obstacles are meant to be overcome.'

His prejudice that no one in Linda's position could possibly do this, had to be seen to be believed. Linda was beginning to wonder whether she had bitten off more than she could chew, but she went on regardless. She got one text book in Braille, and readers to read the other books onto tape for her. She also got a Braille bible from the Wesley Memorial Church Congregation in Oxford, where Linda had stayed at Mary Marlborough Lodge – a rehabilitation unit for people with disability which was part of the John Radcliffe Hospital.

Linda had visited them because of gynaecological issues and whilst there she was asked to attend a conference on sexuality and disability. It was a three-day workshop. Linda would be woken up at eight in the morning, and driven to the John Radcliffe Hospital Conference Hall where many eminent doctors and therapists attended the workshop. Linda lectured on the issue of sexuality and disability – at that time, there was very little done by the medical profession to acknowledge that there was a real problem in this area. The issue was hardly even recognised.

Linda felt that it was her duty to understand the needs and try to convince others that people with disability were just as entitled to a normal relationship as anyone else. Of course, one would have to convince parents, therapists, and other clinicians of that right and need, but it could be done if people had the will to create change.

On Linda's return to Mary Marlborough Lodge in the evening, other residents in the unit asked her about the conference. There seemed to be quite a bit of opposition and aggression on the part of people with disability. One of the residents said, 'Why is it that you get let out of here every morning and we are stuck here?'

Linda said that she didn't know the answer to that, but that everyone is working to create change. Linda formed friendships with one of the doctors, Pat Fletcher, and an occupational therapist, Catherine Le Tissier. These friendships lasted for many years. Catherine's new partner, later to be a Church of England clergyman, did a great deal of work in Africa. Catherine went with him so that she could work with people with disabilities. Linda would frequently receive letters from Africa telling her how their lives were progressing.

This was all part of Linda's spiritual development, helping her to realise that God moves in mysterious ways – His wonders to perform.

If anyone thinks that keeping a close religious observance is easy in a predominantly secular world, then they should think again. Linda's parents, Alma and George, could not understand the obsession to go to church on a daily basis during Holy Week. Linda had to organise transport to get her to and from the meetings as her father said, 'Don't expect *me* to help you every day for a whole week. We can't see why you have to go?'

'Because it's Holy Week?' said Linda.

'Well, we can't understand what all the fuss is about. We just want to sit down and watch the television, but *you,* have to be *out*!'

Linda felt incredibly frustrated. She couldn't even deal with her own religious observances without comment from her parents. She wondered why they couldn't just leave her alone.

The whole week was, "got through" until Good Friday morning. Alma got Linda up early so she could attend the church. Linda expected yet another outburst but instead, Alma apologised for not understanding her need.

'That's alright,' said Linda, 'The most misunderstood person was Christ.'

Alma said, 'Don't be so bloody cheeky!'

Linda wasn't being cheeky. She was just stating a fact, and feeling ever more frustrated. Her parents did not understand how important all this was to her – it was certainly a test of her commitment and endurance.

Chapter 25

The East London Spastics Society Committee could see that there was great progress being made in the socialisation of their people with disabilities. Linda decided that if they were going to do God's work, then the organisation needed to grow further. There was only one way – to get a second vehicle. Fund-raising continued in earnest with Linda doing many talks in church meetings about the need for equality and opportunity.

Then The East London Spastics Society saw Linda's success and wanted a piece of the cake. They decided to make an approach to the Variety Club of Great Britain to ascertain if they could be allocated a "Sunshine Coach", a large Ford Transit vehicle equipped for wheelchairs and passengers. Linda then got more charities involved in raising money for their second vehicle which was also a Ford Transit. So now, the club and the society were really in business.

The members expressed a desire to go on holiday. Linda made an approach to Doug Muncey, of the Ilford Rotary Club, to see what could be achieved. The outcome was a holiday costing just £100 per person for transport, food, and entertainment. They stayed in a local holiday camp near Bideford in Devon. Alma and George were commandeered into helping. George had never dealt with the personal care of disabled people.

Some of them had great issues of incontinence, yet the parents did not adequately prepare Alma and George for just how difficult it would be. The three vehicles were now put into service to drive people from the East End of London to Bideford, with a stop on the way at Yeovil Rotary Club in Somerset, for afternoon tea twenty-seven passengers in all. They also had two cars with first-aiders so it was quite a convoy setting off, with a car leading the three tailgate vehicles and another car at the rear following behind. All in all, everyone had a wonderful time and it showed just what could be achieved with cooperation.

There were other, more pressing considerations for Alma, George, and Linda. It was becoming increasingly more difficult for Linda to drag herself up the stairs (fourteen of them) without a great deal of pain. The worst of it was that George did nothing but complain about how Linda's walking and subsequent "dragging" was putting holes in the stair carpet about which he was not happy.

However, he still expected Linda to persevere, even though she was virtually on her knees trying to achieve it. The doctors at the hospital said that they did not know how Linda had managed to struggle up the stairs regularly since 1978 when she had her back operation. Their advice was that the family should look for a bungalow.

Alma had always wanted to leave the East End so that she could be nearer to members of her family but George's attitude was that he wanted to be in Poplar until the day that he would be "carried out" in his coffin. One weekend, when Linda was on a counselling course, Alma had George looking at Bungalows.

When Linda arrived home around lunchtime, Alma and George said, 'We're taking you to Hornchurch so that you can give us your thoughts on a property that we have found there.' It needed work doing to it but it had potential. What pleased Alma and George even more was that it had a large garden with a fish pond and a fountain in the middle. On visiting it, they all liked the house but Linda said, 'I think that you ought to keep looking.'

Further properties were rejected but in the end, they decided on a bungalow in Ardleigh Green Road in Hornchurch.

When the property in Poplar was sold, they could not believe how much they got for it but the question now was what was going to happen about a mortgage? The bank allowed Linda to take out a mortgage over twenty-five years which cost two-thousand pounds more than the house in Poplar. Alma was in heaven but Linda did not like the property because it was on a very busy main road with cars and lorries going up and down all night long and her bedroom overlooked the street, whereas her parents' room had a beautiful view of the garden.

Linda's needs and how she would cope with her own personal socialisation was never taken into account except for the fact that there would be no stairs. But it wasn't just about stairs for Linda. She realised that the first thing that would go as a result of the move was her work at Moorfields Eye Hospital Radio Station – Radio Moorfields.

She was deeply saddened by this as she'd had so much fun interviewing famous people and making programmes with their favourite music, sometimes putting it together with Hugh Vale, the producer or Linda doing face-to-face interviews with the guests. No more, the weekly challenges, and the work to get the programme out by the end of each week. Radio broadcasting was something that Linda had always wanted to do but now, all her mother would say was, 'Well you won't be able to go to that radio station every week,' Alma had no idea just what it meant to Linda to give pleasure to others who were otherwise confined to bed on the hospital wards. If Linda had had the funds, she would have happily paid the cost of a taxi from Hornchurch to City Road herself. But now it was impossible.

Alma was now in receipt of the Constant Attendance Allowance. It wasn't financially lucrative but at least it gave some recognition of the hours that she and George gave to looking after Linda. The idea was that Linda would pay the mortgage, gas, electricity bills and the bills for the two telephone lines – one was Linda's private line and the other was for her parents. Every time Linda picked up the phone to make a call out, she was shouted at about the cost of the calls.

'But you're not paying it,' Linda said, 'I am?'

George now complained that it would now take longer to drive from Hornchurch to the City each day so he would be wanting extra money for the petrol. This had already been an issue when Linda first got the job at the bank but there was no way that George was going to be out of pocket. The idea was that Alma would put the Constant Attendance Allowance money into a bank account and Linda was asked to be a joint signatory of the account.

Alma's view was that she would only take money from it if Linda was ill and she needed time off work to look after her. Any surplus would be left in the account and given to Linda for her future needs if anything should happen to Alma. For a number of years, all was peaceful.

In 1981, just after the family had moved from Poplar to Hornchurch, they enjoyed looking at the Royal Wedding of Prince Charles and Diana just a couple of days later. The club that Linda founded was going down a storm – almost every week there were events to go to or places for people to visit. A new member arrived at the club and his father offered to drive one of the new vehicles, but this was a very ad hoc arrangement and they needed to get more permanent help.

This came, in the form of Hornchurch and Essex Policemen who drove the vehicle and helped with first aid and physical care for some of the members. The man who volunteered his services was a scrap metal dealer. When Linda wasn't on one of the vehicles, he would talk to the other people on the vehicle about Linda, saying, 'Let's get rid of her, she's been doing this work for far too long.

You vote for me at the AGM and then we can push her out so that I can show you what a good time we can have.'

Linda had no idea what was happening as it had all been very "cloak and dagger". As the officers of the committee were voted on, Linda's role as Chair was also voted on. Alma and George were incredulous to see so many hands go up in favour of the scrap metal dealer as he took over Linda's role. Suddenly, Linda was being asked to take on the role of chief fundraiser which she refused. So many of the people at the meeting that day did not have the mental capacity to know exactly what they were doing. Indeed, the scrap metal dealer had deliberately targeted those who were not intelligent enough to realise what had happened.

Linda was absolutely heartbroken because she knew that the scrap metal dealer didn't care about improving people's lives. He would often drive the vehicle around for personal or business reasons, as he was also one of the drivers. The members could not understand why Linda just left the building.

Some months later, Linda was getting phone calls from the seventy members asking for her to come back because they didn't like what the scrap metal dealer was doing. They said that they didn't understand.

Linda's response was, 'Well, you're going to find out, aren't you?'

It wasn't that she wanted to be top dog; she just wanted people to have a happy time. Linda had started this club with a donation of £50 from the East London Spastics Society and she had left the charity with two hydraulic tailgate vehicles, and £700 in the bank. The charity had also had many hundreds of outings under its belt during her tenure.

Within six months of Linda leaving the club, the members were calling her asking why they never went out any more. They told her that "he" (the scrap metal dealer) had made so many promises to them but had kept none. He ran the two vehicles into the ground by putting his scrap metal goods into them by taking out some of the seats. Linda's attitude was, 'better the devil that you know than the one you don't!'

One mother of a club member asked whether Linda could start again and do it as they did before, but Linda was too hurt. It may have seemed childish but it was the way in which he had contrived and controlled the meeting with false promises behind her back. There was nothing wrong with healthy competition, but this was a man who used the weakest people for his own ends, and Linda couldn't tolerate that.

Chapter 26

For the next two years, life was fairly stable for Alma, George, and Linda. With no major health issues – all was peaceful, until one fateful day. Linda was called into the office at the bank. Mr Brian Sullman, an assistant securities officer, suddenly said to Linda, 'Is it correct that your mother is due to retire on the 3rd of August?'

Linda had a sense of foreboding due to the atmosphere in the room. Alma had also come into the room and sat down.

'Well, when your mother leaves in August, you are going as well,' said Mr Sullman. Linda's response was one of incredulity as he continued speaking to her, 'You will be given a pension, which is calculated for the rest of your life and, you won't have to do anything for it.'

'But I don't want to retire at thirty-three,' protested Linda, 'And I'm not going to sign any of your paperwork. I haven't done anything wrong and I'm still doing my job as a telephonist perfectly well.'

Mr Sullman said, '*That* was never in question.'

'So why, has this happened?' Linda asked.

'Your mother came to us suggesting that it would be better if you retired at the same time as her so that the bank wouldn't have to take any responsibility for your toilet breaks, coffee breaks, and meal times,' replied Mr Sullman.

Linda turned to her mother and said, 'I don't like the way you have been scheming behind my back.'

Alma said, 'Don't be stupid, I'm doing it for you.'

'But I don't want you to do it for me and I am not going to accept this. I will take it to the senior management – and beyond, if I have to,' replied Linda.

Alma said, 'Now you are being really stupid.'

Linda replied, 'It's got nothing to do with stupidity, this is against human rights and I'm definitely not signing the papers.'

Mr Sullman said to Linda, 'You don't have to, because it has already been signed and sealed by your mother.'

Linda's incredulity held no bounds. She was so angry that she didn't care if she ever spoke to her mother again. This was Alma being a control-freak and manipulating Linda's life.

Linda said, 'There is no reason why this has to happen. I could ask for personal assistance from Access to Work and I feel convinced that it would be granted.'

Access to Work had seen Linda through all of her training as a telephonist and her subsequent thirteen-and-a-half years working at the bank. Mr Sullman was adamant that because Alma had signed the papers, nothing could be done. He walked out of the room, leaving Alma and Linda to it.

Linda said to her mother, '*You,* of all people, should know how hard I worked to get this job and that I am bloody good at it. It's ok for you because you're retiring, but I'm just being put on the scrap heap at thirty-three just because I cause a little inconvenience. I cannot believe your devious mind – what you've done is disgusting. If it was left to me, I would never speak to you again, but as always, I don't have a choice – you take control! I have to swallow my feelings and my pride because *you've* decided what's best for *my* life! I know that a life-long pension is a wonderful help from the bank, but I can't believe that you would do this, and what's more, I hate you for it.'

Alma's response was, 'You are just being stupid, *you* ought to be grateful to *me!*'

Linda said, 'I've spent the whole of my life being grateful to you and it will never stop, but you cannot control somebody's life like this when they are totally capable of making their own decisions.'

The next thing that Linda had to endure was a leaving party and presentation to both her and Alma. Alma said to Linda, 'You can make the speech and vote of thanks because I'm no good at that sort of thing.'

Staff members had a substantial collection. Linda's present was some tapes of Beethoven Piano Sonatas played by Alfred Brendel but her heart wasn't in it because every time that she played the music, all she could think of was the horrible way it was all done at the bank. The situation at home was very difficult with Linda only speaking when she had to, and Alma being annoyed and aggressive most of the time.

Linda had a phone call from Dr Wendy Greengross in which she told Wendy what had recently happened at the bank. Wendy said, 'Well, in one way, I'm glad because I realise I have been extremely short-sighted. Here you are, a fully-trained counsellor, and I am going to need one to set up a project that I am involved with.'

She explained her idea to Linda, 'CareMatch, the residential care consortium, has been given funding by the Greater London Council. We have the office, staff, and a large computer, but what we don't have, is a counsellor who will help people with disabilities and their families to find a suitable residential care home, and deal with their obvious grief when the suitable home cannot be immediately found. I would like you, Lin, to be that counsellor, helping people to fill in the forms, and give the reports to me. Would you like this job?'

'You bet your sweet life I would,' replied Linda enthusiastically.

Having taken the job, occasionally Linda would have to travel by taxi to the office for group meetings and general progress reports – this expense was met by CareMatch. The wage was actually more than what she earned at the bank – over three-hundred pounds a week at that time.

Alma and George should have been delighted but they were not. They didn't want their home cluttered-up with boxes of paper and they refused Linda's request to put shelving up to make life easier. In the end, it was decided that Linda should take over the main sitting room where she had a desk, a Chesterfield sofa, and two individual winged-back leather chairs in the area where she did her counselling work.

George said, 'You're bloody earning more money than I am! That's not fair and you can pay even more of the bills now.'

Linda said, 'I thought that I was already doing that and you are both in a comfortable position?'

It was evident that Linda was going to need help to read the reports and paperwork so she asked her mother whether she wanted to earn some extra money. Alma said that she did not. So, Linda contacted the volunteer Bureau in Romford. They found her a lovely person to help do this work. She did not receive any payment, but Betty, just wanted to be occupied as her husband had died and she was living with an elderly mother in her nineties. So it was important for her to have good conversation. Betty had a small Escort car and she asked Linda whether she'd like to go out to lunch with her. They struggled to get Linda into the car because there wasn't much legroom, even though the front seat was pushed well back.

It was, however, just wonderful for Linda to be out, free, and to smile for a while. The following week, Betty turned up with a very nice Volvo Convertible with plenty of space and lots of legroom. The only problem was that because the car was so close to the ground, it was hard for Linda to get out of but despite this, she was determined to have a good time.

There were aggressive comments from George and Alma thrown at Linda when she got back home from these outings with Betty. This went on for several months. These comments soured the outings somewhat. Then, one day, Linda said to Betty, 'My mother would love a trip out like this because Dad never takes her anywhere.'

So, Betty invited Alma to come along. This weekly event kept Linda going, and all was well for more than four years.

Chapter 27

Linda was developing her counselling skills, more and more. She had been asked to be a counsellor for the leading disability newspaper, Disability Now. She was paid for eight hours a week – four hours on a Thursday afternoon, and four hours on a Monday evening. Issues were many and varied. Linda used to get many calls from parents of people with disability as well as the people with the disabilities themselves. At the same time, Linda was increasing her workload in general counselling practice. Alma wasn't sure about this. She hated strangers coming to the house. But for now, this was the only way that Linda could do the work that she was trained for.

There was a convent that specialised in helping bereaved people in the Walthamstow area of East London. Linda was asked if she would like to attend a course for people who wanted to act as support workers to the bereaved. Linda met with the Reverend Eric Porteous, a hospital chaplain at Whipps Cross, and they decided between them to jointly take the training course.

It wasn't long before Linda was introducing more new people to the course and giving them the confidence to go out and help the bereaved. Linda was also working as a cancer support worker to a group of people in Romford. So her life was extremely busy. She was now developing her counselling practice, doing the work for CareMatch, and starting to take biblical examinations as a local preacher.

There were some people who had very fine qualities to do the support work for the bereaved. One such lady was a Quaker by the name of Rosily. She was a very spiritual person and her faith meant a great deal to her. She ran a shop, dealing with healthcare products and complementary medicine. One person visited her shop asking if there was something that would help him to be calmer.

Ralph Boyce had lost his wife some six months earlier with cancer of the oesophagus, and he was devastated. All he could talk about was his wife, his children, and the company that he worked for, namely, Tate and Lyle Sugar

Refinery. Rosily had several visits from Ralph to her shop and found that she was getting out of her depth due to the way that he was struggling.

'I don't know if I'm qualified enough to help you,' she said to Ralph, 'But I know someone who is.'

She promptly gave him Linda's number. Several weeks went by then one day Linda's telephone rang but the person on the other end of the line immediately cancelled the call. This happened several times, then Linda realised that this person was incredibly nervous so on answering the call next time she said, 'I don't know who you are but I can hear by your breathing that you're struggling. Please speak to me and let me try and help you.'

Linda had many calls like this from counselling clients who were far too nervous but she waited on the line, not saying anything. Eventually, he said, 'Are you still there?'

'Of course I am,' Linda said, 'Please try and talk to me.'

The phone went down then and another two more times. Eventually, he called back and was extremely tentative with his questions. Linda arranged to give Ralph an appointment the next day. It is important not to keep people waiting after they have plucked up the courage to speak. They need someone to metaphorically hold their hand and give them a listening ear as soon as possible.

Ralph visited Linda for his first session. All he could talk about was Joan, his late wife, his children and grandchildren, and his beloved Tate and Lyle. He loved his work as an electrical planning engineer. His role was to maintain the big cranes in the dock, and to maintain electrical requirements on the factory floor. Thousands of tons of sugar would be held in huge silos and it was Ralph's job to change the lighting on the bands as the sugar went on a conveyer belt, eventually emerging packed into the familiar bags of sugar sold in every shop and supermarket.

Ralph's main asset was that he was great on punctuality. A clock could be set by him knowing that he would call dead on the stroke of eight o'clock and he would never allow himself to overrun, even if Linda gave him permission. On the first appointment, Alma opened the front door and showed him into Linda's consulting room.

No comments were made but Alma said later that he had the most beautiful eyes and that they were very kind and expressive. Obviously, having a counsellor who was totally blind was a bit of a shock but he soon settled down. Ralph had lost Joan six months earlier so he would eat his main meal in the Tate and Lyle canteen and when he got back home he would prepare something and eat it straight from the saucepan – he had no real interest in food.

As far as he was concerned, it was just something to keep his strength up. He talked and talked about Joan. They were married for thirty years and he could not envisage a life without her. At the end of the session, he said that he felt relieved to be able to talk to somebody. He was having panic attacks at night and would not go to bed. He just had two chairs, one that he sat in, and the other on which to put his feet. That was how he slept – extremely fitfully.

Linda and Ralph went for several weeks, going over the same ground, again and again. He talked about the need to move on but he was totally stuck in his bereavement. So Linda said to him, 'Do you want to spend the next thirty years being lonely?'

'Well, if you put it like that, then the answer is no,' he replied.

Linda said, 'We have to make a plan and get some more structure to your days and give you some purpose.'

He just could not function so they worked on a plan which charted blocks of an hour, working things through until the end of the day. One of Linda's first roles was to stop him eating his food out of the saucepan that he'd cooked it in.

Linda said, 'Lay the table and sit there until you have finished your food.'

His response was, 'It's so awful, coming back to an empty house.'

Linda said, 'I know, but remember what I said about thirty years hence? If you are to survive, things must change. Start making an effort now.'

The sessions went on and they had got to number eight. One day, when he arrived, Linda could smell aftershave and could hear the creaking of new shoes. She commented on the fact that he was obviously feeling better.

'How do you know that?' He said.

'Because of the aftershave and the new shoes.' said Linda. He was incredulous that Linda had picked that up about him. Linda went on, 'When we are talking about painful things, you turn your head right around to look at the bookcase behind you.'

'You're amazing,' he said, 'it's incredible that you know all these things?'

There was one funny incident when Linda had forgotten to turn the lights on, so they talked in the dark. But obviously, Linda did not realise this. Suddenly, outside, there was a very loud crash of thunder, followed by lightning. Linda jumped out of her skin and Ralph thought that this was highly amusing.

'That's what happens when you are blind,' Linda joked.

The sessions continued for a few more weeks then Ralph arrived, telling Linda that his mother had died of a stroke. He was very close to her but she had never lived with him and his late wife, Joan. Naturally, all this was a set-back to his progress because he now had to plan for his mother's funeral. Linda told him that she would be there to support him if he needed it, but that she had every confidence he would cope.

Linda was very aware that the sudden bereavement of his mother could put Ralph's progress back so she just continued to support him on a weekly basis but gave him permission to call if he needed to speak to someone. He never did, always being mindful of the work that Linda did, and never took advantage.

In November, Ralph suddenly announced that it was his birthday on the 10th. He said to Linda that, apart from his family, he had no one to share it with now, so would she allow him to take her out to dinner?

'That's very kind of you,' Linda said, 'but I'm afraid that it's not possible because a professional distance should be maintained between a counsellor and their client.'

Ralph said, 'I just wanted to thank you for all the help you have given me over these last few months and I thought that it would be a nice way of combining the two issues.' He was so polite and considerate that, in the end, Linda agreed to go. On the day of his birthday, he arrived looking extremely smart, wearing a laced, white shirt and a black bow tie with a dinner jacket.

Linda had her aunt and uncle visiting that day – their comment was, 'What a lovely, smart, young man you have taking you out.' Alma was not amused.

Ralph said to Linda, 'Show me how I need to help you when guiding you around.' He was very sensible and informed Linda of any obstacles that she might be facing. Linda was having kittens – How would she cope, and what would she do when she needed to go to the toilet? But, in the restaurant, when the starter arrived, Ralph asked what he should do to give assistance.

Linda said, 'By the clock face, put the main part of the course at twelve. Any salad and so on should be scattered around the plate with you telling me where it is, also by the clock face. The key thing to remember is not to make the pieces too large or too small – just make them bite-size.'

Linda was terribly nervous but she got through the meal very well.

'Your help was brilliant,' she said, 'You've taken to that like a duck to water.'

Ralph's response was, 'But it's not a problem, is it?'

'Some people find my disabilities very difficult to deal with,' said Linda.

Ralph replied, 'You are not disabled, you're just someone who needs a bit of help.'

What an understatement that was, but how great that he could see Linda in that way.

The main course of steak, and the dessert that followed, all went without a hitch.

Sadly, the pleasant evening that Linda had just had was about to be shattered. On arriving back home, as Linda's mother opened the front door, she said, 'Oh my God, you've been eating garlic!'

Linda said, 'Well I know they were a bit stronger than usual but they were extremely nice.' But Alma decided to make a big fuss over it by opening all the windows to 'let the smell of garlic out.' If this was designed to undermine Ralph and make him feel awkward, she succeeded.

Linda felt very angry how her mother had embarrassed her and undermined Ralph. Linda apologised to Ralph and thanked him for a lovely evening.

After Ralph had left, Alma said to Linda, 'What's been going on with you two?'

Linda said, 'Absolutely nothing, except having a very pleasant meal with a gentleman.' Linda just could not believe how well Ralph had handled her during the evening – nothing seemed too much trouble for him. She reflected on all that had happened that evening.

As Alma helped Linda into bed, she said to Linda, 'You look absolutely radiant.'

Linda just smiled. Alma was controlling the situation – right from day one.

Chapter 28

Ralph continued to go for his weekly counselling sessions. There were a couple of times when Linda had to ask him to change his appointment because she was doing other consultancy work with Dr Greengross. Ralph suddenly asked out of the blue one day, 'How do you get to these appointments, because you obviously don't drive?'

Linda joked, 'I'd be a bit of a public hazard if I did!'

'All I want to say is,' said Ralph, 'If ever you need wheels, I'd be only too happy to drive you because I think that the work that you are involved in is amazing and I have so much time on my hands that I don't know what to do with it.'

Linda and Ralph came to the end of their nineteen sessions and he thanked her profusely for her help and she said that it had been a very great pleasure to see him getting his life back together. Linda felt quite sad when he left, knowing that she would not be seeing him again.

Then in the early part of 1986, Linda was asked if she would go to a residential care home in Chigwell, Essex to teach someone how to read Braille. He couldn't pay for the taxi and Linda felt that she should not be out of pocket so she remembered Ralph's offer of driving her. She picked up the phone to ask if he could help. He readily agreed. They started four months of travelling to and from Chigwell to help Brian, a blind person, to read Braille. It was quite difficult because all Brian really wanted was companionship and he liked talking to Ralph.

Getting him to concentrate on the Braille was extremely frustrating but he could talk a hind leg off a donkey. Every time Ralph took Linda to the care home where Brian lived, there was always an appalling odour of incontinence – so bad that it made your eyes water. One day Ralph said, 'When we leave this place tonight, would you like to go for a drink to get the smell out of your nostrils?'

Linda said, 'Yes, that would be lovely.'

So from then on, each week they visited Brian, and then went on for a drink or a light supper afterwards.

All this time Linda was questioning herself and her feelings. She wondered what was going on. She knew that Ralph was extremely capable and sensible about helping her and she felt more comfortable in his presence than in any one else's. Alma was very good at guiding Linda around in public places, and she learnt what Mr Bolton had said when they were at Dorton House for the interview—'Follow the sound of my voice, Linda, and walk towards me.'

It worked very well in public places, like a noisy pub. However, it could be a little tricky with Ralph walking backwards, encouraging Linda to follow the sound of his voice, only to find someone coming up from the rear, trying not to spill any of their drinks.

One evening, Linda said to Ralph, 'I have to ask you a question. As you know, if you think that you may need counselling in the future, I would not be able to give it because I have already stepped over the line. But if you say that you don't need any further counselling and you would like our friendship to continue, then you must let me know.'

His immediate response was, 'I'll elect for the friendship.'

Well at least that was out of the way and now out in the open.

Sometimes when they came back from Brian's home, they'd call in to a very nice oldie-worldie pub, part of which was fourteenth-century. It was the Boar's Head, at Herongate, Essex. They liked the chicken Kievs or mushroom omelettes – with chips, of course! Ralph would have a great time using the big poker to stoke the open fire. He would describe all the shapes and colours – he loved looking deeply into the fire. One day, after they'd ordered their meal, the licensee said, 'Oh, you're in "nookie" corner!'

Linda's face was as red as a beetroot, but they both certainly laughed about it. Ralph was always wanting to take Linda out but as can be imagined, Alma did not approve.

'You're not going out again are you?' questioned Alma, 'And what time are you getting back?'

Linda felt very annoyed because after all, she was thirty-five – to have every move scrutinized was extremely frustrating. They carried on seeing each other and visiting Brian and then just generally enjoyed each other's company.

It was a beautiful spring day, so Ralph decided that he'd like to go for a walk in the country. He loved describing nature and the countryside to Linda. He would pick up leaves from the ground and tell her what trees they were from and he would show her the bark of many trees to let her see how different they could be. He was really trying to get into Linda's world and understand.

Any trips out like this annoyed Alma because she was more concerned about the marks on her carpet that were made by Linda's wheelchair on her return than any sense of enjoyment that might have been had by Linda. Alma would ask, 'What have you two been doing?'

Absolutely nothing was always the answer. That seemed to annoy Alma greatly.

They carried on with their walks in the country and playing some classical music at quite a loud volume as they drove through the country lanes.

Some months later, they were out on another such excursion, during which Ralph said, 'In view of the way your mother shouted and yelled about her carpets, I think that I ought to put a hose on your wheels and clean them with a wire brush and get you to check it.'

Ralph did this very carefully and Linda ran her hands over the wheels to feel if they were clean. She couldn't find anything wrong with them. But on her return home, Alma opened the door and exclaimed, 'You're not bringing that bloody thing over my carpet!'

Linda felt very embarrassed because she knew that there was nothing wrong with the wheels.

Ralph said, 'Don't worry, Alma, you won't have to think about it ever again.'

Linda wondered what was going to happen now. She soon found out. The next day, Ralph had gone to the local wheelchair company and bought the identical model of wheelchair. This man was incredible – nothing was going to stop him. He delighted in giving Linda pleasure. Linda thought that his attitude about the wheelchair was quite magnificent. Now one wheelchair would live in Ralph's car and the other in Linda's home. Alma was curious to know why Linda wasn't taking her wheelchair out when Ralph turned up to take her out.

He said to Alma, 'I told you, it would never happen again – and it won't because I have bought Lin the same model of chair which will be kept in my car.'

Alma was open-mouthed and just barely grunted her disapproval. Ralph hated the way she tried to take control of whatever Linda did. Rather than letting her enjoy things for their own sake. Linda just held all these things in her heart and thought that Ralph was just such a wonderful person.

Chapter 29

In November, Linda decided to start doing her Christmas shopping early. She wanted to give Ralph a Christmas present – but what should it be? She decided on a Philips Cafe Duo, a coffee-making machine. When it arrived in the post, Linda got the full "Spanish Inquisition" from Alma about why she should be giving "that man" a present. Linda said, 'Because he has been an exceptionally nice person and I just wanted to give him something small.'

Alma said, 'Twenty-odd quid is not something small! And I don't know why you have to do it?'

'I do it, because I choose to. Please don't keep telling me what I should do with my own money,' said Linda.

Alma just wouldn't let up about the way she perceived that Linda was irresponsible with money. In the end, Linda became so exasperated saying, 'If the present was for you, such as a nice new dress or a piece of jewellery, or anything else that you fancied, I am sure that I would be "allowed" to spend whatever you "permitted" me to spend. I am thirty-six years of age and I'm totally compos mentis. I know the value of money as you know only too well, and am totally sick of how you want to continually control every aspect of my life.'

Alma retorted, 'I don't care *what* you give that bleedin' bloke.' But it was clear that she did.

Linda gave Ralph the coffee machine a few days before Christmas. He was very touched by the kindness. He never expected to get anything, indeed, never wanted anything. He was a man who Linda felt needing spoiling once in a while, or at least, spoil himself occasionally.

But others' happiness was more important to him.

Ralph's daughter, Tina and her husband had established the tradition of having Christmas day on their own with their child, and then they were happy for other people to visit after that. Ralph kept in touch with Linda over Christmas.

He said, 'I must see you. I feel very lonely and I know that you are too. I'm going to visit my daughter on Boxing Day and then I would like us to meet up and go for a meal or some such.'

The day after Boxing Day, it was snowing hard. Ralph rang the front doorbell. When Alma saw Ralph at the door, she told him, 'She can't come out because she'll fall over.'

Ralph said, 'She won't, she'll be perfectly safe. I've sorted it.'

Ralph went to the boot of his car and took out a roll of red carpet which he rolled out from the front door step all the way to the passenger door of his car. He came back for Linda and said, 'Right Lin, it's perfectly safe for you to step out of your front door – just follow the sound of my voice.'

Ralph took hold of Linda and they walked to the car, and he helped Linda get into the car before rolling the carpet back up and popping it back into the boot. Linda just wanted to laugh but she knew that if she did, Alma would go absolutely mad. Ralph just said to Alma, 'We'll see you later,' and then turned to Linda and said, 'Blimey, she's got a face like thunder and it looks like you'll be in for it later.'

As they drove away, he and Linda burst into unrestrained laughter. But Linda knew that on her return home, she would "get it in the neck"—and she certainly did. But for now, she just wanted to enjoy a meal and the rest of the day with Ralph.

Linda was beginning to realise that this man would not be beaten. His "all because the lady loves Milk Tray" moment, showed Linda that he would stop at nothing to try and make somebody happy. All this time, there had never been any terms of affection between them or physical touch other than what was necessary to give Linda assistance – but she thought about it all the more. How dare she, as a multiply disabled person, even consider that this attractive, able-bodied man would remotely think of her as desirable, particularly when he could have the pick of a number of women?

Then, she thought to herself, '*How could I ever think of making a different life for myself, one that was not suffocated by control?*'

It was something that she had prayed about for years but Alma had always said, 'Don't get any dreams in your head about getting married or having a boyfriend – no one's going to look at *you*.' So Linda had been given negative messages all through her teenage years and now in adulthood too.

On returning from their day out, Linda got the "bullets" from Alma that she had expected. 'What do you think that you were playing at here today,' said Alma, 'Undermining my authority like that?'

Linda said, 'Oh, come on Mum, didn't you honestly have a little smile to yourself, thinking how ingenious he was?'

'No I fucking didn't,' replied Alma, 'And don't you dare do anything like that again.' Linda was always scared of the way that Alma flared at the least provocation.

Linda telephoned Ralph and suggested they might go to a concert at the Royal Festival Hall on the South Bank. It was a Raymond Gubbay Concert comprising, Tchaikovsky's Romeo and Juliet Suite, Rachmaninoff's Second Piano Concerto, and Ravel's Bolero – a piece that Linda was not fond of, but she thought that Ralph would probably like it. Ralph collected Linda at her home and they drove to the concert hall on a Saturday evening. This meant that Linda would be a little late home – shock horror!

On arriving at the concert hall, each lady in the audience was given a long-stemmed pink rose in a cellophane wrap. Ralph leaned over and said to Linda, 'You've set me up!'

Linda's face must have been a picture as she felt quite embarrassed knowing nothing about the ladies being given a single pink rose and said to Ralph, 'I truly had no idea and I hope that I didn't embarrass you?'

Ralph teased her and said, 'Oh, come on, you did know?' But Linda stuck firm to her original statement.

As the very romantic Rachmaninoff washed over her, Linda felt that she could hardly breathe. Whether it was the romantic music, or other feelings, or a combination of the two, she did not know, but what she was absolutely certain of, was that she was beginning to fall in love with this man. They had taken things very slowly. Linda ever-mindful of his bereavement and also frightened of "rocking the boat", running the risk of losing what was becoming a very special friendship. She questioned her feelings time and again, not daring to hope that it was true. She now realised that it was a make-or-break situation. She would have to come clean about her feelings in some way or other. It was a very enjoyable concert for them both.

On the way home, Linda felt that she ought to "check out" the situation. So, as Ralph was changing gear, she ventured her hand forward and touched his hand. All the while she was worrying about rejection but he took hold of her fingers and squeezed them lightly.

'*Ah, he does care*,' Linda thought to herself. They travelled a few more miles and Ralph pulled off the road onto the grass verge. Linda asked, 'Is there a problem with the car, Ralph?'

He said nothing, but turned in his seat to face her. She was aware that he was weeping. She just touched his arm and said, 'Joan would want you to be happy.'

His comment pleased and surprised Linda, 'I never felt, or should feel, that I could be happy ever again, but you have made me feel that I can be.'

He took Linda in his arms and kissed her very gently – the tears still streaming down his face.

Linda thought, '*Oh my God, this man has a moustache and I don't like them! Oh well, I'll just have to get on with it!*'

They became entwined very quickly, and it was wonderful.

Linda told him how much she cared for him but she found it hard to verbalise because she felt that no one would be interested in her. Ralph's response was, 'Well, I find you a most attractive woman. You are not disabled and will never be so in my eyes.'

Naturally, they just kept on responding to one another and the floodgate of emotion between them finally burst its banks.

50% funding available on selected holidays

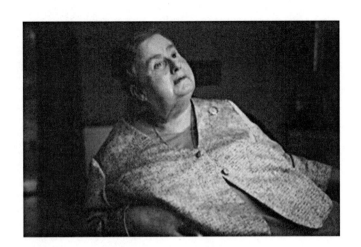

But there is one person there who isn't on the guest list.
It's Eamonn Andrews with a bookful of surprises which
begin when he tells you "Lin Berwick 'This Is Your Life'".

and of course your story couldn't begin without the people closest to
you, your mother and father Lina and George, and brothers George and John.

Many months of effort are rewarded when you take your very first steps, only
to make a devastating discovery, you are losing the little eyesight you have.
Undeterred you are determined to continue your education and become the first
disabled student to be admitted to Barton House School for the Blind.

Chapter 30

The following week, Ralph took Linda to the Royal Festival Hall again.

'Before you get out of the car,' he said, 'I have something for you. I can't do this every time but I wanted you to have this.'

He gave Linda a long-stemmed red rose in a cellophane wrap.

'How lovely,' Linda said, 'Red roses are my favourite flowers.'

The concert was good and they stopped on the way back to have a cuddle in the car. Linda said to Ralph, 'I'm not sure about the moustache because it tickles?' They were just delighting in each other's company.

Linda said to her mother, 'I won't be in for a meal this evening. I'm going out for a dinner with Ralph.'

'What? Again!' She exclaimed.

'Yes, it's great isn't it,' replied Linda, happily.

Alma snapped, 'No it bloody isn't! Don't think that he's ever going to care about *you* – he'll take whatever money you have, and leave you in the lurch.'

'Why can't you be less critical of the poor man? He's done nothing to you and he's given me a great deal of pleasure,' exclaimed Linda.

Alma said, 'Oh yes, I bet he has. What *is* going on with you two?'

Linda felt so frustrated that it wasn't worth speaking about it anymore because everything was turned into negative comments. Any time Alma referred to Ralph, he didn't have a name as far as she was concerned. He was either, "him", "that bloke", or "it". Linda just gave up.

Every Friday Ralph would give Linda a bunch of carnations – it was a very sweet and thoughtful thing to do but Alma was always disparaging saying, 'I don't know why he has to give you these every week, cluttering up the house?'

'I would love my house to be "cluttered" with flowers. You're only jealous,' Linda said. 'You could always ask Dad to buy flowers for you.'

'Do you think I fucking care?' Alma asked.

'Yes, I think you do,' said Linda. But Alma just snorted and went off in a huff. If it meant that much, Linda would have happily given her mother flowers every week.

One Monday evening, when Ralph came to collect Linda, he said, 'We're not going *out* for a meal this evening, we are having a meal at *my* house – it's been cooking on a timer since this afternoon.'

'*My God, here's another problem,*' thought Linda, '*I've never spent time with another man without other people being around.*' Linda felt rather nervous but realised that all she had to do was keep her mobile phone to hand. If this man proved to be the undesirable type, the type who might take advantage of her disability and her blindness, then she would be in trouble.

However, it was worth the risk. On arriving at Ralph's home, there were a few problems to surmount. He had such a high step up to his front door and there was no handrail for support.

'There's only one thing for it,' he said, 'I will have to pick you up.'

He carried Linda over the threshold and landed her on her tripods, guiding her to a nearby chair. 'I'll just get you a drink,' he said, 'I know that you like Brandy, so here's one for you.' It was a very cheap and nasty cooking brandy that was like drinking fire water.

Linda said, 'I'm sorry, but this is awful, I can't drink it.'

Ralph said, 'You're not getting my best brandy!'

'I better had,' she joked, 'Otherwise, I'm not coming back!'

Needless to say, the champagne Remy Martin Brandy was quickly brought and all was well.

He said, 'I'm just going to have a shower and change before dinner so you just enjoy your drink.' While she waited, all was well until Suki, the Siamese cat, who was very vocal, suddenly sprang onto Linda's lap without warning. She yelled and Ralph came running. He laughed seeing Suki on her lap but quickly realised that Linda wasn't amused. She was terrified of cats. That really could have been the end of their friendship but thankfully, there was so much more that they had now.

Everything had been taken extremely slowly and prayerfully. Up until now, nothing had been said to Linda's parents because she knew that there would be a further backlash. The evening meal passed without any problems until Ralph decided that he would put some music on. He chose Nat King Cole, who was his late wife's favourite singer, and promptly burst into tears.

Linda said to him, 'Why are you punishing yourself like this? What are you trying to prove?'

Ralph said, 'I've got to get over this. This is ridiculous.'

Linda said, 'It's not ridiculous. It's still relatively early days. Just take one step at a time. You cannot just shut out the memories and behave as though they never existed. You will do it eventually, but not now. When you want to make changes, and go to the next stage, I will be there for you, to help and support you.'

Ralph said, 'But I've done it all wrong. I never wanted to let my emotions get the better of me, and now, all I've done is to make it worse for you.'

'You are not making it worse,' said Linda, 'Just relax, and take your time.'

Ralph's response was, 'It's bloody good, this free counselling!'

Linda knew that he would never take advantage. He only ever had the utmost respect for the work that she did.

Linda decided that she would not tell her parents that she had been to Ralph's home that night because the consequences could be dire. All she knew was that Ralph was a thorough gentleman.

Linda said, 'May I give you a hug to say thank you for the meal this evening? It was extremely kind of you. Also, thank you for the flowers that you gave me when I arrived.'

'There will always be flowers in my home for you, so that you can smell the fragrance and know that I am holding you in my heart,' said Ralph.

Chapter 31

Linda visited Ralph's home the following week. On arrival, she found that there was an extra step put in, and a sturdy handrail to support her as she climbed the steps to his front door.

'*How wonderful,*' she thought, '*This man was not fazed by disability and he would do everything he could to help and ease the situation.*' She let him know how pleased she was. Ralph then took himself off to the bathroom to bathe and wash the "Tate and Lyle sugar" out of his hair. Linda was beginning to find her way around his home and as long as there were no steps, she knew that she'd be safe. However, what she hadn't bargain for was the rising butt hinges on the doors which made them self-close.

Linda would struggle up to the door, open it, and then have to find her tripod sticks to balance. Unfortunately, that was just enough time for the door to close on her. She tried again and again and again, becoming more and more frustrated. Ralph could hear her expletives from the bathroom and he was watching the proceedings very carefully – and with great amusement! But Linda did not find this funny.

Eventually, she managed to wedge her body against the door so it could not close, then pick up the tripods and walk through the doorway. She knew from the splashing in the bath, where Ralph was. She took the hose off the shower and aimed it full-blast at Ralph who was still sitting in the bath. The water was freezing cold; needless to say, he leapt out of the bath pretty quickly and threatened to give Linda a "hosing" too.

'Don't do that,' she said, 'Because it would be highly dangerous with tripods on a wet floor.' Ralph resisted the temptation and they had a good laugh about it.

Ralph said that he wanted to learn about some of the difficulties that Linda would have to face when trying to do some cooking and so on. Measuring liquid and dry ingredients was quite difficult for Linda to manage. At no time did Ralph ever get annoyed if she spilt something or found something too difficult to manage. Mostly, she was embarrassed because her mother would never let her do these things for fear of making a mess or cutting herself.

Ralph said, 'Well, what's the big deal? If you cut yourself, there's always a plaster?' This was music to Linda's ears. He really *wasn't* fazed.

They shared a meal and Linda did the washing up. Ralph couldn't believe how thorough she was, touching the surfaces of the plates to make sure that they were scrupulously clean.

Ralph said, 'I really enjoy watching you and admire your determination to get it right.'

As she took a plate out of the water, it slipped out of her hand, fell to the floor, and smashed. Linda felt terrible because it was the dinner service that Ralph and Joan had bought for their new kitchen. Sadly, Joan never got to see the kitchen completed.

Linda said, 'Oh my God, I'm so sorry. I know how much all this "Pool Pottery" meant to you both.'

'Don't think anything of it,' he said.

Linda said, 'But I do, I would not have wanted to break anything.'

Ralph said, 'There's an easy answer to all this.'

He took a plate off the draining board and threw it onto the floor, smashing it, next to the one that Linda had broken.

'What did you do that for?' Linda said.

'We are even now!' He replied. 'I broke one and so have you so now you can forget it.'

Linda was to learn that Ralph cared nothing for material things so long as the people that he loved were safe and happy. How different from her own parents – they had a home that looked like a furniture showroom with everything pristine and perfect but no love in it. All Ralph had was a rickety folding table, four chairs, and two G-Plan armchairs. For the most part, Suki, the cat, took ownership of the chairs. Ralph asked Linda what was the most comfortable position for her to be in, so that she could have a cuddle.

'Actually,' she said, 'The best position is to be on my side, lying down.'

He asked whether they could do that and Linda asked him whether he had bought a new bed since Joan died.

'No,' he said, 'This is the one that she died on.'

Linda felt extremely uneasy saying, 'I'm sorry Ralph, but I really couldn't lie on that bed. It would be far too distressing for me and it wouldn't feel right. What you do is one thing, but please don't expect me to comply because I really can't.'

'Oh right,' he said, 'Well it's probably about time that I got rid of this bed anyhow.'

On the next week's visit, Linda had a lovely new bed to greet her with new sheets, pillow cases, and a new duvet with cover to boot.

Linda thought, *'Bless this man for being so thoughtful and caring.'*

They Christened it together, having their first intimate cuddle. Of course, nothing *happened*. Linda would do nothing to run the risk of an unwanted pregnancy. But, the risk of pregnancy was never to be a problem because her hips and knees were so tight with Cerebral Palsy that the sexual act itself would be pretty nigh impossible to achieve.

Even in trying to be intimate and close, she always experienced severe pain, due to her hamstring transplants as well as Cerebral Palsy, and the potential partner, whoever they were, would have to be extremely patient, long-suffering, and kind. However, it was wonderful to be close to someone who Linda was beginning to love more and more. Ralph was facing more challenges than he could even begin to imagine but to hold each other, and be tender, loving, and close, was the most important thing to them both.

Linda said, 'I think we are getting to the stage where we should tell my parents and your family? And I know that the news won't go down too well with mine.'

Ralph said, 'Well the sooner we get it out of the way, the better.'

So, that evening, Ralph took Linda back home a little earlier than usual. Linda's father, George, was actually annoyed that they had arrived home early because he and Alma were watching something on the television. Ralph was offered a cup of tea and Linda got the usual, 'You don't want a drink, do you?' from Alma.

Linda did not respond and the offer of a drink wasn't ventured. Whilst the adverts were on, Ralph suddenly announced to Alma and George, 'I think I should tell you that Linda and I are becoming more than just friends.'

George said, 'Oh, I thought something bloody funny was going on when you shaved off your moustache. I know Lin doesn't like them.'

Linda couldn't help laughing at his observation. He was a man who didn't miss much – except people's feelings. He had no idea how to deal with them and most of the time they were never spoken about. Alma made no comment at all, except to say to Ralph, 'Do you realise what you're taking on?'

Ralph said he thought that he did. Ralph left soon after this conversation and Linda was ordered by her parents to, 'Get off to bed, now!' This was how they spoke to a thirty-six year-old woman!

Ralph always wanted to say goodnight to Linda, privately. Up until now, he had never been able to do that. Now it was out in the open, things might change, although Linda didn't bank on it. When the house settled down for sleep, Linda rang Ralph to say goodnight – after all, it was the business extension in her bedroom so it wouldn't be interfering with anyone. But Linda heard one of the other extensions "pick up" with her conversation to Ralph. Alma was obviously listening-in.

Both Ralph and Linda were aware that the line wasn't private and when they commented on it, they heard the "click" of the extension line being shut down!

Next, the door of Linda's bedroom opened suddenly, 'Haven't you had enough time with him already this evening?' Alma said, 'Get *off* that phone and go to sleep!'

'This is my own private line, and I want to say goodnight,' said Linda.

'Well *do* it then,' said Alma, 'And then go to *sleep!*'

Ralph and Linda had only shared their news some two hours previously and trouble was already starting. Sadly, it would continue for the next eighteen years.

Chapter 32

The next few weeks followed a familiar pattern. One day, Ralph told Linda that he loved her.

Her response was perhaps a little surprising. 'Don't say that,' she said, 'Unless you really mean it. I never want you to use that phrase glibly or flippantly. I want you to use it when you are absolutely sure of your feelings.'

Ralph said, 'I do love you but I am frightened of hurting you and wonder what your life would be like if I decided to finish our relationship?'

Linda said, 'I know you think of yourself as my knight in shining armour, but remember, it may not be *you* who leaves *me*, but *me* who leaves *you*. A marriage or a relationship based on pity would never work. I want you to help me take risk and enjoy doing so – I've been wrapped-up in cotton wool for far too long. I want us to have fun and delight in each other's company.'

That evening they went to the Boar's Head at Herongate for a meal. On the way back, they stopped in a country lane and had a cuddle in the car before returning home. Alma opened the front door, 'What bloody time do you call this?' She said.

'It's not even ten o'clock yet, Mum,' replied Linda.

Alma said, 'Don't cheek me – just get in here and do as you're told!'

Linda looked at Ralph with complete exasperation. Despite Alma's protestations, Linda and Ralph still said goodnight to each other; even so, Linda could feel the tension brewing.

The next morning, breakfast was a very frosty affair for Linda and Alma.

Alma said, 'I don't know why you have to keep going out, and I don't know why you have to waste your money on *him*?'

'His name is Ralph,' said Linda, 'And, I am not wasting my money because we always split the cost unless there's a special reason like a birthday or whatever. Anyway, what does it matter?'

'It matters to me,' said Alma.

Alma helped Linda to get her tights and shoes on, and when Linda didn't say thank you immediately, she got smashed in the face with Alma's fist, causing her to have a black eye and a bruising across her nose.

'What did your last fucking servant die of?' Alma said.

'I'm sorry,' said Linda, 'I was just thinking.'

Alma said, 'Oh yes, you're always just fucking thinking – thinking of *him*.'

However, in actuality, Linda was thinking, '*Please God, let me be free of all this.*'

Alma could see that the bruising around Linda's eye was getting quite bad. After all, when you've had an eye removed, the area around the prosthesis is always quite tender.

Alma said, 'Remember, if anyone asks you, you walked into the door – *right*?'

'Yes, Mum,' replied Linda, 'but what you are doing, is nothing short of abuse and if you continue to do this sort of thing, I will report you to the police or social services. I am a thirty-six-year-old woman and you do not have the right to abuse me in this way. I am heartily sick and your jealousy has to be seen to be believed.'

Alma said, 'I expect you'll tell *him* when you see him tonight?'

'I won't have to, he will see my black eye for himself – and he won't be happy,' said Linda.

Needless to say, it was the very first thing that Ralph noticed and he wondered what had gone on. Linda told him everything unequivocally and he was absolutely disgusted.

'You have got to get out of there before you get hurt,' he said, 'You remember our conversation last night? The first thing I want to say is, our relationship is not based on pity. Like you, I know that would never work. Our relationship is based on my love for you and my admiration for you. I am beginning to see that whatever decisions I make concerning my feelings toward you, have got to be absolutely rock-solid because if I walked away, you would never be allowed to make another decision.'

'She would exert total control over you. As for me seeing myself as your knight in shining armour, I guess that I did feel secure in terms of your feelings for me. When you said that it may not be *you* who leaves *me*, but the other way around, I must admit, you totally took the wind out of my sails. I suppose I had become too complacent in this relationship but I promise, I will never do that again, or take your feelings for granted. I'm telling you now that I *know* that I love you, and that I want us to spend our life together.'

He could not bring himself to utter those four magic words to Linda (Will you marry me?) but nevertheless, the barriers of doubt were breaking down nicely.

On returning home, the atmosphere was frosty once again. Ralph said that he was worried about leading Linda into the Lion's den. Linda called Ralph when he arrived back home to say their usual goodnights. Alma was hovering around outside Linda's bedroom door. Linda then settled down and went to sleep until the bedroom door crashed open at a force into the bedside cabinet. Alma was screaming, standing at the foot of Linda's bed.

'I used to be number one, and I'm not anymore,' cried Alma, sobbing.

Linda struggled to pull herself up onto her elbows – in those days she did not have a variable height bed. She said to Alma, 'Come here to me.'

Alma came forward and fell into Linda's arms, crying. Linda turned her round and sat her down slowly onto the bed and said, 'In terms of being my mother, you will always be my number one. What you have done over the years has been fantastic and I will never be able to thank you enough. But the love I have for you and the love I have for Ralph, are two different kinds of love. It doesn't mean that I love you any less. It is just different. Now, come on, dry your tears, and pull yourself together. You have nothing to be frightened of, indeed, you should be proud of all your achievements.'

Linda held her tightly and told her that she loved her. It was very hard to be jolted out of sleep in this way and of course, she lay there for hours after Alma left, wondering what it all meant and where it was going.

Chapter 33

It was Linda's birthday, and Ralph had taken a day's holiday from work so that they could be together. Alma realised that Linda had an infection in her left eye socket and she was preparing to clean it to make it more comfortable. Even though Linda didn't like having both prostheses removed at the same time, this was the way that Alma insisted on doing it. It didn't matter how much Linda protested – it had to be done Alma's way. There was a knock at the door – it was Ralph.

Ralph said, 'Where's Lin?'

Alma replied, 'Well, she's sitting on the toilet with her head over the hand basin and I am dealing with cleaning her eye sockets because she has an infection.'

Hearing Ralph's voice, Linda had an immediate sense of panic because he had never seen her with her artificial eyes out.

'*Oh my God!*' She thought, '*What do I do now?*' There was nowhere to hide. Linda felt that this could really blow the relationship wide open. She heard his footsteps approaching from the hallway into the bathroom, so she buried her head, looking down to the floor, and started to cry. By now, Ralph had come into the bathroom. He rolled up his sleeves and said to Alma, 'Show me what you do.' Alma said, 'No, there's time enough for that when you are married.'

'I don't think so,' he said firmly, 'I need to know, now.'

Linda was still turned sideways with her head toward the floor when Ralph said kindly, 'Lin, turn yourself round to face me.' But Linda would not. Ralph said, 'Come on, Lin, turn to face me.'

Linda was still weeping and reluctantly, she turned her body round to face him.

Ralph said, 'Now, raise your head up.' But she would not. Ralph took hold of her face in his hands and lifted her head up to face him, 'Now, open your eyes,' he said. The eyelids had dropped into the empty space and Linda felt terrible. He very gently lifted one of the eyelids, and then the other, saying, 'Well, that's not so bad.'

Linda was still crying. Ralph took hold of her, kissed her lightly on the face, and said, 'I love you just as much without them.'

Linda said, 'How can you say that?'

Ralph replied, 'Because it's all part of you.' They just held on tightly to each other.

Alma responded, 'I just can't make you two out? You've got me beat.' She then walked out of the room in a huff.

Linda and Ralph were embracing each other, passionately when Alma returned, 'I just don't get it,' she repeated.

Ralph said to Alma, 'Right – *now* show me what you do.' He scrubbed his hands and fingernails thoroughly with Hibiscrub, the substance that surgeons use before performing operations. It is a very strong antibacterial product with a very pungent, antiseptic odour. Whenever Linda used it, it transported her back to the days in Moorfields Eye Hospital when she had her eye operations which culminated in their removal.

Alma showed Ralph how to fit the eyes under the top lid, allowing the bottom to just drop into the space. It was quite an easy process but a bit daunting for the first time. As Ralph put the prosthesis, as it is correctly known, under Linda's top lid, allowing it to drop carefully into the bottom lid, she could feel him shaking. But he would not give in, and he certainly wouldn't let Alma know just how he was feeling.

When the job was done, he kissed Linda and ruffled her hair, 'That's good,' he said, 'At least I will know what to do under your instruction if it ever comes out in future. Now, I'll give you what I came round for.'

He went outside to his car and returned carrying a dozen, long-stemmed red roses and a birthday card. The roses were absolutely beautiful and Linda was very touched by his kindness. Alma pushed past them both, unceremoniously, and said nothing.

Later that day, Linda and Ralph went for a lovely ride in the car through the Essex countryside, playing their music loudly as they went. This was a day that would be a "Red Letter Day" as far as their relationship was concerned, – and it had survived. Indeed, it was doing much more than surviving, but thriving too. Ralph had said to Alma, 'If I can't do this for Lin, then the relationship will be over.' Linda knew that that was what Alma wanted to happen but mercifully, she was proven wrong. Linda knew that she loved Ralph with a passion, indeed, she absolutely adored him, and he revelled in the love he gave and received.

Chapter 34

Alma was following her usual pattern of disapproval at every turn. When Ralph bought Linda flowers on a Friday, she complained about having to "deal" with them, and the "mess" that they would create. Linda never told Ralph of her criticisms because she did not want to offend him. Ralph was showing Linda at every turn just how much he loved her.

Each time Linda went to Ralph's home, even if it may have been for purely innocent reasons, Alma was critical all the time. One night, when she helped Linda into bed, she took off Linda's underclothing and scrutinized it, saying, 'There's a funny smell about you, and you've got marks of sexual arousal in your underclothing.'

Linda said, 'Well at least it shows that I'm normal!'

'Don't be so fucking stupid,' said Alma, taking off Linda's knickers and rubbing them around Linda's face, calling her a slut and a whore, saying, 'Call yourself a preacher – you are disgusting! I have always put you on a pedestal and now, you are the lowest of the low.'

Linda was going red in the face as she said to Alma, 'What is the matter with you? You are looking for problems all the time and when you can't find them, you make them up. I have done nothing this evening apart from going round to Ralph's and making some lovely bread and rolls which I brought back for you to enjoy.'

'Well I *don't* enjoy anything that you and *him* get up to!' Alma said. 'I don't trust *you* and I don't trust *him*.'

Linda said, 'You don't trust anything that Ralph and I do together. If we go to a concert, you complain if I'm out past ten. If we go for a meal, you want to know what we've eaten and how much we spent – and so it goes on. I am getting extremely tired. I know that you want to wreck this relationship, but I pray to God that you don't. You know exactly what you are doing – it's all so calculated.'

Alma wailed, 'And what about all the things that I've done for you – all my life? I have sacrificed my life for you and now you just "up sticks" and go your own way and care nothing for me.'

Linda said, 'I will always be grateful for everything that you've done all these years. If I live to be a hundred, I could never repay you. But you are of an age now, where you should be grateful that someone has come into my life to make me happy.'

'Yes, but what about me?' She wailed again.

'When we have gone out to the shops or some such place, Ralph and I have invited you to come too but you always refuse. With what has happened here tonight, you should be ashamed of yourself, because you are taking your parental duties a bit too far and you are crossing the line once again.'

'If you found arousal in my underclothing, why couldn't you just smile and say, well at least they're happy, instead of wiping my underclothing around my face?—that is abuse in the extreme and goes well beyond parental duty—after all, I'm thirty-six-years of age and Ralph is a man in his early fifties with two adult children of his own. He should not be put through this at every turn. I would have far more respect for you if you picked up the clothing and put it straight into the washing machine and said nothing.'

Naturally, when Linda saw Ralph the following day she told him what had happened. His response was, 'I'm going to go round there and have it out with them.'

Linda pleaded, 'Please don't do that. It will only make matters far worse. When I'm out with you, or at your home, it feels like a breath of fresh air and I feel as though I can breathe. But when I go back to my home, I feel totally suffocated and trapped because there is no escape from her relentless targeting. I would love to be able to have some clothes so that I could change before we went out to dinner but I can't because she will query why I want to change my clothes.'

'Well, that's ok,' Ralph said, 'I'll buy you some clothes that you can keep here, and Julie, your best friend who makes clothes for you, could probably alter some clothing if we go to the shop and she helps us choose it.'

So, this was their plan of action. At least, if the clothing was clean and fresh, Linda wouldn't have to suffer that barrage of abuse from her mother. Julie understood the difficulties and she was very happy to be a partner in crime.

Ralph had bought Linda two lovely knitted jackets – they were very warm, heavy, and comforting. When Alma saw them, the only comment that she made was, 'They're not practical.'

'Why do they always have to be "practical",' said Linda, but got no response from her mother. Linda liked the clothing from Jacques Vert, they used to make larger sizes which were very helpful. Julie altered it for Linda's shape and the clothing looked lovely. Ralph would whisper into Linda's ear, 'And it's *not* practical!'

Julie, Ralph, and Linda laughed about this and took the shop assistant on board, 'You must come back and let us see you in the clothes once they have been altered,' said the assistant.

Linda and Ralph were happy to do that because they had been so marvellous in the shop. Linda was beginning to blossom and feel like a sensual woman. She loved Chanel No. 5 and lovely blouses, skirts, and jackets. She looked great.

Alma used to always knit Linda's jumpers and cardigans – she'd done a wonderful job making them all fit perfectly to Linda's shape, but Linda was, nevertheless, being dressed by her mother, which was unfortunately in the style of an unattractive, elderly woman. Alma would say again, 'Make no mistake, no one is going to look at *you*. *No one* is going to be bothered about you in the way that I have. I have sacrificed myself for you.'

Linda said, 'I am getting a little sick about your self-sacrifice. I don't need to be reminded of it every day. I didn't ask to come into this world and I have struggled ever since I did. All that I want now is some happiness, but you are trying to spoil even that. Nothing I or Ralph say or do ever pleases you. We can never do anything right and I'm getting to the point where I wish I were dead because all of all this bickering and criticism, day after day. It isn't serving any purpose whatsoever. It's just making me ill. If you can't say anything nice, then say nothing at all.'

Alma said, 'I can see that you tell him things because of the way that he looks at me and he sits at the table with his arms folded, giving me the "keep off" signals.'

Linda said, 'Well he's certainly not happy and I noticed that you always behave shittily, when Dad isn't here. If I have much more of this, I'm going to tell Dad.'

Linda didn't know whether telling her father would be a good move or not, but it couldn't carry on like this, day after day.

Chapter 35

Linda's relationship with Ralph was moving on at a pace, but they had to surmount one particular hurdle, namely, the meeting of Ralph's children. Ralph decided that they should take it one step at a time. So, one Saturday afternoon, by arrangement, Ralph took Linda to meet his daughter Tina, and granddaughter, Emma. Tina was warm and welcoming, and tried to make Linda feel at ease. Children are great at breaking the ice and Emma, at the age of two-and-a-half, was delightful.

Emma could not understand why Linda didn't respond when she tried to give her some of her toys. In fact, she became so exasperated that she would throw the toy in front of Linda and walk off in disgust. Tina tried to explain to Emma that Linda could not see her so she would have to put things into her hand. Emma soon got the idea and was eventually sitting on Linda's lap. It was lovely for Linda to be holding such a small child.

People didn't often share their children with someone like Linda who was disabled. They were often fearful and did not know how to respond. But Linda loved the opportunity to build a friendship, and to get close to a little child. Ralph was very good with Emma. He had this wonderful ability to get down to a child's level, and loved playing "chase" up the stairs and around the house.

Emma loved nothing more than to sit on Ralph's shoulders so that she could see the world from a great height and squeal with delight as Ralph ran up and down the stairs. He was incredibly patient. Linda couldn't help thinking that her own father had never played with her or her brothers in this way. Now, too many years had gone by.

The next week, Tina, her husband Vernon, and Emma, visited Ralph's home. Paul, Letia, and Tony, his six-year-old grandson, were also visiting. Ralph collected Linda from her home and on arriving outside his home, Paul and Letia came to the car and tried to greet Linda as she stepped out of the car. What people often failed to remember was that, if you need tripod sticks to walk with, it is necessary to keep hold of the sticks, or at least to hold on to the car door, in order to maintain balance.

However, in their desire to do the right thing, they took hold of Linda's hand so that she was balancing rather precariously. Ralph could see what was happening and instructed them to wait until Linda was seated. Linda was wheeled to the front door and climbed the steps into the house using the rail that Ralph had put up, acutely conscious that she was being watched by everyone. Conversation was somewhat stilted, but Paul was quite a jovial fellow. The problem was, he didn't seem to be able to judge when jokes were appropriate and when they were not. But overall, the meeting between everyone went very well.

When everyone left to go home, Ralph came to Linda and said, 'Well, I think that was mission-accomplished. I think the meeting went very well and I think you made a hit with them, but they were terrified that you were a preacher, a counsellor, and a writer.' But Linda thought that they should have seen her first and foremost as a human being. She hoped that it would get better.

April, 1986, was now upon them. The situation at home for Linda was just as bad as it ever was. Each day Linda prayed for the situation to be better and the relationship between Alma and Ralph to improve. Sadly, that never happened. Linda and Ralph spoke often about them sharing their lives together, 'That's all very well,' Linda said, 'But you've never looked after me. I want you to really know what it's like. I want you to truly understand how difficult that it can be, and for you to seriously think about whether you want to take it on – warts and all.'

'I want you to have the opportunity of trying out what it's like living with me for a weekend and then, if you find it all too much, you can walk away without any recriminations and say to yourself, that it was nice while it lasted, but I could never commit myself to someone like that in the long term. I want you to understand what it's really like living with a person with disabilities. I know that you always say that I'm not a disabled person, and that I just need a little help, but the reality is that I need a great deal of help and it is whether you could handle that.'

'For example, if I need to have a bowel movement and I don't have a closomat toilet available, or my artificial eye should come out in public and you need to clean it and put it back, or having to cope with the compression-therapy stockings, helping me into bed, and so on. If you then tell me that you want to

162

run with it, then we can obviously talk about our future life. Alma has the attitude that nobody does it better than her. That may be true, but the way you would help me would be different, and I need you to find out for yourself. I want you to experience these issues without anyone standing over you and breathing down your neck and making nasty comments, because it does take time to learn.'

'I don't want anything to spoil what we've had in these last few months – it has been so special and whatever happens, whether you choose to run with it, or walk away, I will always love you for what you did and the joy that you have given me. It is no good talking to Mum and Dad about this, they will put all the obstacles in the way and furthermore, they would watch you like a hawk and there would never be any margin for error. If you couldn't do it perfectly, then mother would never let you forget it.'

'So, what's your thinking,' Ralph asked.

'I would like us to go and visit my friends Jenny and Bruce, in Dorset for the weekend,' said Linda, 'They are two very busy business people but they are really lovely human beings and I am sure that they would give you a warm, Dorset welcome.'

Linda spoke to Jenny and it was agreed that they would visit. Alma did not approve and she mused to herself out loud, 'What the hell is going on?'

'Absolutely nothing,' Linda said on hearing her mumbled musings, 'We just want a lovely weekend, with lovely people in the quiet Dorset countryside.'

So, one Friday afternoon, Ralph and Linda set off on the one-hundred-and-forty-two mile trip to Verwood in Dorset. Linda's heart was really happy. She was going to have Ralph to herself for a whole weekend without someone commenting about why she wanted to go out and why she wanted to do something. She really felt that she could at last breathe. They talked for most of the journey and were both really happy.

On arrival in Dorset, Jenny and Bruce gave their customary welcome. Ralph felt instantly relaxed with them both and they seemed to really warm to him too.

Ralph said, 'I can't believe the difference between the welcome I have received here compared with the frosty atmosphere of your parents' home.'

Linda said, 'Sadly, you will never be able to compare it.'

During dinner, it was a case of Jenny and Bruce getting to know Ralph. That evening Jenny and Bruce had arranged to go to a fancy-dress party. Just as they were about to leave the home, Bruce took some money out of his wallet and stuffed it into his pocket. He then threw his wallet over to Ralph and asked him to look after it until he got back. As he threw the wallet, its contents spilled out all over the floor. Ralph hastily picked up everything and stuffed it back into the wallet.

Ralph said, 'I can't believe he's just done that. He trusts me enough to give me his wallet and I am a complete stranger to him? What amazing people they are.'

Linda had known Jenny since 1964 when Jenny became Linda's flute teacher. She had qualified in piano, flute, and voice at the Guildhall School of Music and Drama in London. She was a volunteer for the Wingfield Music Trust for the Disabled. Linda revelled in their musical times together. Indeed, Linda took her flute down to Jenny so that they could make music together. Ralph loved listening to the two of them making music.

Jenny had a Beckstein grand piano and the tone was beautiful. It was wonderful to hear Jenny singing as she sat at the piano, accompanying herself. As Jenny and Bruce left to go out for the evening, they told Linda and Ralph to help themselves to anything that they wanted, including the alcohol in the wine cabinet. In all the time that Ralph had known Linda, he had never experienced such kindness – especially from people that he didn't even know.

Linda and Ralph sat out in the garden with the lovely sound of the water fountain, splashing over the rocks. Later they went inside and sat in front of a wonderful log fire. Ralph did as he always did when he saw a real fire – picked up the poker, and changed the shape of the coals, describing the colours and shapes that he created to Linda. They just delighted in each other's company, listening to various pieces of music and having a quiet cuddle on the sofa.

Jenny and Bruce returned feeling quite merry after their evening out. Fortunately, they were not the sort of people who went to bed early so they spent quite a while chatting. Jenny gave Ralph a set of house keys saying, 'Here are the keys to the house – come and go as you wish. If you want help just ask for it, otherwise, we will leave you to get on with it.'

When it came to bedtime, Jenny said to Linda and Ralph, 'What type of bed would you like – a double, or two singles?'

Linda looked over towards Ralph for him to decide what to do. Of course, he said, 'I'll leave it up to you, Lin?'

Linda said that she would like the double bed. Without any hesitation, the bed was rearranged and it wasn't long before they were left to their own devices. Linda was very nervous because she was being quite bold in making that decision. Whatever happened, she wanted to have the opportunity of lying close to someone that she loved and waking with them the next morning – so important to be close at the start of the day.

Linda got up in the morning and Ralph helped her with all of her personal care needs.

He said, 'This wouldn't be my number one job, helping to clean you without your specialized closomat toilet, but if it means, for the sake of five minutes help, we can lead a normal life, then where's the problem?'

Linda loved him for his attitude. After breakfast, they drove to the Poole Potteries. After they'd purchased some items in the pottery, Ralph said, 'Would you like to go to the Priory at Christchurch?'

'Well actually, no,' Linda said. 'I'm freezing cold and desperate to go to the toilet.'

Ralph said, 'But I thought that you liked churches?'

'I do,' said Linda, 'But I'm desperate for the loo.'

So they drove back to Verwood. Linda made herself comfortable and went into the bedroom to tidy herself up. The door closed behind her and Ralph came over to her and said, 'Well, I've coped with all your bodily needs and functions and I haven't been fazed by them. So, I want to ask you to marry me.'

Linda was quite overcome, and she said to Ralph, 'I would be deeply honoured.'

They held each other tightly. They then went back into the kitchen to join Jenny and Bruce. Ralph invited Jenny and Bruce to lunch, but at first, they declined, saying that they were far too busy.

Ralph said, 'Oh, that's disappointing because I've just asked Lin to marry me and she has accepted. And I am ecstatically happy.'

'Well, in that case,' they said, 'We're coming! And the champagne is on us!'

They drove to Lin's favourite restaurant in Dorset, La Fosse, in Cranborne. From the outside, it was a very ordinary-looking restaurant, not fancy at all – but the food was to die for. They had driven there in Bruce's new Range Rover – a very high four-by-four vehicle. It was quite difficult for Lin to get up onto the high seat, but with lots of pushing and shoving, it was achieved. The meal was superb and the champagne was ice-cold and lovely. On coming out of the restaurant, Linda was talking to Bruce about what it means to go "off-road". They were almost back at Jenny and Bruce's home when Bruce reversed the vehicle and said, 'I'll show you what I mean.'

They hadn't gone very far when the vehicle sank up to its wheel arches in deep, wet mud.

Bruce and Ralph tried everything to shift the vehicle, but it was stuck fast.

Bruce said, 'I think that I'd better go and seek the help of some of my friends in the village.' It was pouring with rain and Ralph was in his best suit. They had to walk back several miles to the village to enlist the help. It was some three-quarters-of-an-hour since they had left the restaurant and, surprise-surprise, Linda said to Jenny in the car, 'God, I hope that they're not too long because I don't half need the toilet.'

It took almost another hour for pieces of carpet, a boat hawser tow-cable, and planks of wood, fitted under the wheels to give purchase, before they were free and out of the mud in the New Forest! Bruce was never allowed to forget this incident by his friends in the village and for months, the carpet and bits of wood remained in situ in the forest. Ralph and Linda used to "salute" the spot each time they went past. Ralph and Linda had a truly magical weekend and they did not want to go home, partly because, they knew that the "inquisition" would start.

On their return to Linda's home, they went in and told Alma their news. Her words said one thing, but her voice said another.

'I'm very happy for you both,' Alma said, 'But are you sure that you know what you are taking on,' she said to Ralph.

'I think so,' he said.

Alma replied, 'This is not something that you say, "I think so" to? Do you realise that you're giving yourself a lifetime of caring? She is never going to be looked after by you in the way that I have looked after her.'

Linda thought to herself, '*Oh Blimey! Here we go again – the "nobody does it better than me routine"*!'

Ralph was jolted out of his thoughts by Alma's next comment.

'I suppose you slept together?' She said.

Linda replied, 'If you don't want to know the answer, don't ask the question.'

'Well, I *do* want to know the fucking *answer*!' Alma screamed, 'Just *fucking* tell me!'

Linda said, 'Well, if you really must know – yes, we did.'

Alma said, 'I am going to phone Jenny Porter and tell her exactly what I think—more importantly, you wait until your father gets home, you slut, you filthy whore—call yourself a preacher—you are disgusting!'

Linda said, 'Why do you have to bring things down to such a low level? Why can't you say, "Congratulations!"?'

'There is no need to *congratulate* you,' replied Alma and stomped out of the room.

Ralph came over to Linda and held her tightly, saying, 'I'm so sorry darling, that she has to behave like this. We did nothing that was sordid. You are thirty-six years of age, and I couldn't be happier that we are going to be together and spend the rest of our lives with one another.'

Later that evening, Linda was sitting in the living room by herself. Her father came into the room and said, 'Your mother has just told me about you and Ralph and what you did.'

Linda said, 'Before you say anything, Dad, let me just say a couple of things. Firstly, all we did was lie together and be close. I am still a virgin and will probably always be so, due to my Cerebral Palsy. And secondly, by the time you were thirty-six, you had three children. I wanted the opportunity of being close to someone, even if that was my first and only time – surely you can understand that?'

George just grunted, 'I will never speak to you on this subject ever again. But I want you to know that whatever happens, there will always be a place for you in this home – and please don't forget it.'

Linda said, 'Thanks Dad, I really appreciate that.' And no more was ever said on the subject.

Chapter 36

The next week, Ralph decided to buy Linda an engagement ring. Linda said to Ralph, 'It might be nice to ask Mum if she would like to come with us to give me a female perspective on the ring?'

'Do we have to?' Ralph said, exasperatedly.

Linda said, 'We don't *have* to, but I would *like* to.' Linda had had a week of clipped, frosty, sarcastic comments from Alma at every turn. She was heartily sick of this response, feeling very worn-down by it all. On the Saturday morning at breakfast, Linda asked Alma to go with them to help choose the ring.

Alma said, 'No, I won't. I don't want to and I'm not interested in anything that you two get up to, and when you get back, you will find me with my head in the gas oven because this is what you've brought me down to – after everything I've done for you.'

Linda was absolutely exasperated by this continuing melodrama and although Linda should not have said what she did, she was now losing patience – big-time.

'Well, Mum, make sure that you tell me which way you are going to lie on the floor by the oven, so that I can make sure that I can step over you on my return.'

Alma was absolutely furious, and all thoughts of her putting her head in the gas oven evaporated in the barrage of abuse that she rained down upon Linda.

Linda would never have said that under normal circumstances but, now that Ralph had declared his intentions, Alma was beginning to realise that this was real, and she just could not cope with it. Linda quickly called Ralph from her bedroom and said, 'It's all gone pear-shaped. I need you to come as soon as possible and get me out of here. I don't want anything else to spoil this very special moment in our lives.'

Ralph arrived about twenty-minutes later. They went to the local shopping centre and chose a very discreet, simple ring – one single solitaire diamond set on gold raised shoulders. Linda would not let Ralph pay a lot of money just in case it all went wrong. The cost was not important anyway – it was more the sentiment behind it.

Ralph decided that he would not have a ring himself because of the nature of the work that he did. He was worried that he would catch it when he was climbing ladders and ropes during the course of his work at Tate and Lyle. They had a lovely time choosing the ring, and of course, they were both extremely happy. Linda was able to take her ring straight home because it fitted perfectly.

On her return home, the atmosphere on walking through the door was not just frosty, but more like a freezer with the door open! Linda could sense it immediately.

George said to her, 'Don't come into the kitchen because the floor is like a swimming pool. Your mother has had another of her bloody outbursts and I am just sick of the way she goes on about you two.'

'So what's happened?' said Linda.

George said, 'Well, she prepared the vegetables for dinner, put the water in the pans, and put the lids on. Then, when she was going on and on about you and Ralph, I said to her "For Christ's sake, why don't you leave those poor people alone to enjoy their lives?" Well, that was the key to light the blue touch paper and stand back.'

'So,' said Linda, 'What did she do?'

'Well, she took off the lids on the saucepans and poured the contents, including all the vegetables, straight over my head.'

Linda said, 'And what then?'

George said, 'I just filled all the saucepans back up full of ice-cold water and tipped them all over *her* head, including all the vegetables – hence the kitchen being covered in water, carrots, and everything else!'

Linda said, 'So what was her reaction to that?'

'She was furious, but it did stop her screaming,' said George, 'She is like a bloody madwoman – totally flipping her lid, and I'm telling you now, babe, I'm bloody sick of it. I don't know why she can't just leave you two alone?'

That evening, Ralph was invited over by Alma and George to spend the evening with them because Linda's aunts and uncles were coming to visit – Alma had put on some supper for the occasion. It wasn't exactly an engagement party, but it was her way of trying to acknowledge it. Linda's aunts and uncles made all the right noises, congratulating them both and asking to see the ring.

After supper, all the relatives took their plates into the kitchen and closed the door behind them, leaving Linda and Ralph by themselves. Alma was obviously winding herself up like a clock-spring, and they were trying to console her saying, 'Look, don't worry, it's never going to happen, is it? He's never going to look after her as you have? You have been absolutely marvellous and he will never cope like you.'

Linda was sitting next to Ralph on the sofa and they could hear everything that was being said. The relatives' attitude was completely hypocritical – congratulating them to their faces on the one hand, yet saying behind their backs to Alma, that it would never work.

Ralph just held Linda tight and said, 'They don't know what we're like and how much we love each other. We're going to be together until death parts us. I can't stand the way they are all talking behind our backs. Why don't they just ask me a direct question about my feelings for you? I would have far more respect for them if they did that. But instead, they stay in the kitchen, assuring Alma that it's never going to happen and never going to work.'

Instead of appeasing Alma, the relatives could have helped the situation far more by making positive noises about the relationship, perhaps telling Alma just to give it a chance and see what happened. When they came out of the kitchen and Alma showed them to the front door, she was still in floods of tears, and all Linda could think was, What the hell was it going to be like on her wedding day?

Chapter 37

Linda and Ralph started to try out various restaurants to find out which ones they liked the best for their wedding reception. They wanted the reception to be held at a restaurant in Essex. One that they frequently visited was some distance from Linda's home but they enjoyed the food very much and they knew that it would make a really special occasion.

Because it was somewhat out of the way, and in the countryside, Ralph thought that the best option would be to bus people to the restaurant by coach. At least, that way they would all arrive together and make it easier for the staff in the restaurant. The Rolls Royce was to be driven by Ralph's brother, Fred, and the coach by another member of the transport company.

However, when Alma and George heard about the plan, their immediate response was, 'Well, if you do that, we're not coming to the wedding.' Linda and Ralph couldn't see what difference it made because all the people would be dropped off back at their homes in the evening. Try, as Linda and Ralph did to persuade them, they would have none of it – already, Alma and George were controlling what was to happen on the wedding day, but they were adamant, and of course, Linda wanted them to attend.

In the end, they chose Mary Green Manor at Brentwood in Essex. It was a sixteenth-century moat house – a lovely venue and very regal in its setting with lots of panelled woodwork and good food. They were advised by the Reverend Ronald E Kemp to find the venue first and then finalise the date. The date was set for Independence Day – the fourth of July, 1987.

Once the venue had been chosen for the reception, it was time to look for somewhere for Linda and Ralph to set up home. Initially, Linda's parents said, 'Well you could buy our place.' But Ralph said he didn't want to. 'What's wrong with it?' they said.

Ralph said, 'There's nothing wrong with your home but I wouldn't want to live alongside the busy A127 because it's noisy and very smelly with the traffic fumes.'

Alma saw this as a personal affront and she said, 'How dare he say, that my house isn't good enough.'

Linda said, 'He didn't say that. He just said that he wouldn't want to live on a main road with all the exhaust fumes.'

Now that the date for the wedding was set, it was time to sort out some of the practical issues such as, wedding invitations, hymns, flowers, wedding-dress material and so on. Once the invitations were written, there was a further argument about the allocation of seats at the reception. There were fifty-three places at the reception – the bulk of which Alma was to be given the authority to allocate to whom she wished and to sit where she wished. Ralph had a total of nineteen places for his family and close friends.

Of course, Alma wasn't happy – she wanted more. When she couldn't have more she became annoyed. Linda gave her the names and addresses of key people and she asked her to make sure that her Uncle Norman got his invitation because as Alma well knew, Norman was Linda's favourite uncle.

Alma said to Linda one day, 'I've had a response from your Uncle Norman, and he and Jan will not be coming to your wedding. They are disgusted at the way you've treated me and feel that you have been most unfair to the person who has done so much for you.'

Linda said, 'Give me his telephone number so that I can speak to him.'

Alma refused and Linda never knew his address, certainly not the postcode. She knew it was somewhere in Canvey Island, but that was it. So, as far as she knew, Norman would not be coming. She was heartbroken – after all, she had been the bridesmaid at *his* wedding. It wasn't until some thirty years later that Norman expressed his sadness to Linda just before he died about how bitterly disappointed he had been that he did not receive an invitation to her wedding. When Linda explained to Norman that this was yet another way of Alma ruining her special day, he was utterly disgusted and very sad.

It was April, 1987. Ralph had to go to Scarborough for a conference to do with Tate and Lyle. When Ralph and his brother, Fred, parted, Fred said to Ralph, 'Come back as soon as you can and don't stay away too long.'

Ralph said to Linda, 'Only call me if you have a problem, otherwise I will call you every evening.'

Linda was sitting at the dining table with her parents, having an evening meal. Suddenly, the telephone rang and it was Barbara, Fred's wife. Her voice sounded strange—she blurted out, 'Fred is dead—get Ralph!'

Linda told her parents and George went into a panic, 'What are you going to do?' He said.

Linda said, 'I'm going to call Ralph, obviously.'

George said, 'Yes, but how are you going to tell him?'

'I'm going to tell him exactly what's happened. There is no point in pretending otherwise. If I didn't tell him the truth, he would only come home at full speed and I don't want him to do that because he will obviously be in a state of shock.'

Linda called the hotel where Ralph was staying. He was most surprised that the call was for him and he realised that something must be up.

Linda said, 'I don't know how to tell you this news darling, but I think that the only way is to come straight out with it.'

Ralph was staggered, shocked, and very upset saying to Linda, 'I will come home immediately and we'll go and see Barbara.'

Linda said to Alma and George, 'When Ralph gets here, I will be going with him to Barbara's, and obviously I am not sure what time I will be back?'

'You don't want to do that,' they said, 'You don't want to get in the way or interfere. Death is a private matter and you shouldn't be there.'

Linda said, 'I hear what you say, but I will do whatever Ralph wants.'

Ralph's friends at the Tate and Lyle conference were very kind to him, arranging for sandwiches and flasks of tea for his journey back – they also offered to drive him as they knew that he was in a state of shock, but he said that he would be better off on his own.

It seemed no time at all before he was knocking on the front door of Linda's home. Alma commented to Ralph about Linda, 'She shouldn't be coming, it's not her place to be there and she'll only get in the way.'

Ralph said, 'She's coming. I want her with me. She will never get in the way. She is part of my life now, so she's coming.'

When Linda and Ralph got into the car, Ralph said, 'I just don't understand your parents. You will never get in my way. You are not the sort of person who pushes in where they are not wanted. You have always been deeply respectful and I know that that is never going to change. When we reach Barbara's home, perhaps I should spend some time with her on my own.'

Linda thought that this would be a good idea but within what seemed like seconds of Ralph departing the car to meet Barbara, he was back, saying to Linda, 'Barbara wants you to come in now because you're family.' Linda really had a sense of belonging – perhaps for the first time in her life.

On returning from Barbara's, Linda and Ralph still had a cuddle before they went back in to Linda's home. Their reception by Alma and George was again frosty, being a total rerun of all the things that had been said earlier. The issue was nothing to do with Ralph and his brother, it was all about the late hour that Linda was getting to bed – never mind giving someone much-needed support. Linda would not have minded whether she stayed up with Ralph all night if it was necessary, as long as he was more settled.

The next day, Linda had a phone call from Barbara to say that she and her daughter had decided that they wanted her to conduct Fred's funeral service. Linda was incredulous, '*What an honour,*' she thought to herself.

Mr Kemp decided that he would assist Linda by coming to the crematorium so that the right buttons would be pressed – and Linda could just imagine that Fred would have found this highly amusing, especially if she'd pressed the wrong ones!

On the day of the funeral, some of Ralph's distant relatives queried Linda with comments like, 'What are the likes of you doing here?'

Linda thought that this was an imposition on their part because she had as much right to be there as anyone. Ralph was aware of what was going on. He stood at Linda's side and said, 'This is my fiancée, and, she is taking Fred's funeral service.'

The relatives were speechless, 'But she's in a wheelchair,' they said.

'Yes, she maybe in a wheelchair,' said Ralph, 'But her brains are not in her backside!' At that point, Ralph got into the car with Barbara, her daughter and her husband, and Linda was to meet up with them after the service.

Fred, was a confessed atheist, and Barbara, a committed Christian. Linda joked with the congregation and said, 'Well Fred, just in case you've got it wrong, we're hedging our bets!' This broke the tension and created some well-needed smiles. Linda was only too happy to leave Mr Kemp to press the right buttons and it may well have been all too much for her to contend with under such difficult circumstances.

Everything was fine until Mr Kemp said, 'We'll go to the door now and meet the mourners.' The tension of the afternoon absolutely shot Linda's emotions to pieces. As she reached Ralph, they collapsed into each other's arms, and sobbed, consoling each other. Fred had been very dear to Ralph, and had become very special to Linda, and for him to lose his life in this way was so unexpected and pointless.

At the wake, Fred's daughter, Sue, came to Linda and said, 'Mum and I would like to congratulate you on a marvellous service. You obviously studied Dad very well and got him down to a tee.'

Chapter 38

Ralph had an offer from June Taylor, the wife of his best friend Ron. She made beautiful wedding cakes and wanted to give one to Ralph and Linda as a wedding present. They were going over to Ralph's and Linda was also going to visit in order to discuss the creation of the cake. Linda asked Alma whether she would like to come and help her choose the design.

Alma refused, giving her usual reply, 'I'm not bloody interested in *anything* that you and "*him*" do.'

Linda said, 'Can't you be interested for once about my wedding?'

'No I can't,' Alma said, 'Because I'm *not*!' So it was then up to Linda and Ralph to make their own decisions about the cake. The outcome was in fact, magnificent – three tiers of different flavours and Linda and Ralph's initials on small shields around the cake.

Betty, the lady that helped Linda with her paperwork for CareMatch, said to Alma, 'You really ought to think about the dress material.' Linda said that she would like to go with them to choose it.

Alma said to Betty and Linda, 'I don't want you there. I'm quite capable of choosing the material myself.'

Linda said, 'But I would like to choose a lovely silk or satin fabric because it's going to be a lovely day in July and hopefully it will be hot.'

Alma said, 'You'll *get*, what I *say* you'll *get*! And it's not *your* choice, it's *mine*!'

Linda could not believe that even on the subject of her own wedding dress, she had no choice in the matter. Betty told Linda later that she was absolutely disgusted with Alma's attitude and felt that Linda should have been there. Alma and Betty went off to choose the fabric.

By now, Linda felt completely rejected and by and large, disinterested. If she couldn't have a say in what she wanted, then what was the point? Alma and Betty came back with a roll of fabric and some suit material. The suit material was a heavyweight light grey. She had also chosen a red lining for the suit – Betty had tried to get her to choose something more appropriate for a wedding but with no success. She had purchased a blue and white shirt from Marks and Spencer with a little red tie attached to the shirt.

None of this would have been Linda's choice. Although the suit fabric was a lovely quality, it certainly wasn't at all summery – it was chosen with a grey feeling that seemed to match the grey fabric! So Linda was stuck with it all. Ralph was extremely annoyed and said to Linda, 'We'll go out so that you can choose the fabric yourself and *I* will pay for it.'

'You can't do that,' said Linda, 'Because it's all got to be a surprise – I want to look lovely for you on our special day.'

Ralph said, 'You would look lovely whatever you wore and I wouldn't care.'

Linda thought, '*Bless his heart – he just wants to make me feel better about the situation.*' Sadly however, she did not.

Linda's friend, Julie (the lady that altered her clothes), was scheduled to make the dress and the headdress but sadly, she was rushed into hospital and had to have an ileostomy, the removal of the lower and upper bowel, which was so serious that she almost died, twice. So Julie arranged for a friend of hers to make the dress instead. The fabric was a slightly raised pattern on a cream background of "Lily-of the-Valley" flowers. The headdress was pretty but not too fussy with flowers threaded through it.

Julie managed to attend the wedding, even though she was still very seriously ill. Linda felt it to be an absolute privilege that she was there. Whilst Julie was in hospital, Ralph and Linda visited her and Alma rowed with them both about intruding in Julie's life at such a difficult time. They naturally checked with the doctors and nurses first and were assured by Julie that she would love to see them both. But Alma took it upon herself to say that this wasn't right.

With just three months to go before the wedding, the search was on in earnest for a new home. They decided to try and keep to the Hornchurch area as it would be central for Linda to visit her parents and close for Ralph to visit his daughter who lived in Wickford.

Many properties were rejected on either the size of the rooms according to wheelchair access and whether suitable adaptations could be made such as in the bathroom and so on, or the accessibility of the outdoor patio area. A plan was drawn up to build a patio that came from the living room area with level access, leading down a ramp to the street area. The plan was that Ralph would build a structure of bars, rather like the shape of a boxing ring, so that if Linda overbalanced on her tripod sticks, she would not be able to fall off of the patio.

Any possibility of falling would be cushioned by plants all the way along thereby taking off the starkness of the metal bars. The kitchen was very small but manageable, and Ralph didn't want to rush the decision about the kitchen design so for a long time they used a microwave oven and a table-top Tefal oven until one of Linda's uncles gave them a Baby Belling cooker which helped the situation enormously. Alma and George's reaction was to say, 'You could rip out the kitchen and make it suitable for an able-bodied person.' Keeping the disability "under wraps".

But Ralph wanted to get it right and not be rushed.

The first hurdle was to sort out the mortgage. Linda's bank allowed them to have a twenty-five-year mortgage on the property. It was decided that Linda would pay the mortgage, put in a specialist Parker Sovereign bath – that is a bath that raises and lowers a seat over the side of the bath so that a person can easily transfer from the bath onto sticks or a chair. When getting into the water, the bath mechanism raises-up so that the legs could be turned and placed into the water with ease.

It also had a gyrating spa bath attachment which was lovely with all the bubbles. There had not been many times in Linda's life when she could have a relaxing bath, so this was a real treat. The plan was that Ralph would move in six weeks before the wedding so that he could oversee the work on the building of the patio and how he wanted it to be achieved. One day, Ralph noticed on arriving home, that the workman were under huge umbrellas to try and get the work completed on time.

Moving-in day for Ralph was difficult as Alma and George were there watching everything. They were giving Linda a blow-by-blow commentary of every item that Ralph brought to the property. As has already been mentioned, Ralph cared nothing for material things. He was now moving into a much larger property and so his furniture was swamped. But it didn't matter because things would be changing anyway.

When Alma saw the patio, all she said was, 'It looks like a bloody boxing ring. And why did you have to choose black rails?'

George said, 'Well, I think that it's brilliant. He's really thought about the issues and she will be safe – it doesn't matter what you think about it.'

After an afternoon of "comings and goings", Ralph came in and gave Linda her first set of keys to the house – she had never been given her own keys before and she was now thirty-seven!

Alma said, 'What are you giving *those* to *her* for? She will obviously lose them.'

'Well,' Ralph said, 'If she does, I'll just change the locks.'

Linda was absolutely thrilled with this moment. This property was now theirs.

Alma said to Linda, 'Come on, we'll get you out of all this chaos and take you home.'

Linda didn't want to go home. She wanted to be with Ralph.

Ralph said, 'I want her to stay and I'll bring her back later. Don't worry about a meal – we're eating out and celebrating our new home.'

Alma was not amused and slammed the door in a huff on her way out.

Linda and Ralph breathed a sigh of relief as the door slammed shut behind Alma. She had given Linda a barrage of comments, most of them negative and hardly complementary about Ralph. They both just rejoiced in the fact that they had got their new home. Linda was so happy. It didn't matter about the "chaos" and the boxes all piled-up, they just had a cuddle, lying on the carpet – how important that was.

The next step was to visit Margaret, Ralph's florist, whom he visited every week in order to buy Lin flowers. She and Linda got on extremely well. Linda told her that she wanted a very fragrant bouquet and it must include roses. Margaret decided upon orange tea-roses, white Stephanotis, and very fragrant, multi-coloured Sweet Peas. Some ribbons would be placed in the bouquet so it could be tied to the handles of Linda's tripod sticks so that when she walked back down the aisle with Ralph at her side, it would look as though she was carrying her own bouquet.

The principal guests would have carnations. The men, a corsage of red carnations, and Alma, a corsage of fragrant orchids. Jean Thomas, Lin's Matron of Honour, would have a bouquet of roses and mixed flowers. That, being decided, they had the next momentous problem to overcome – Alma suddenly announced, 'What are you doing about my mortgage?'

Linda said, 'I'm not doing anything, because it *isn't* your mortgage? I have paid it for six-and-a-half-years and I gave you five-hundred pounds when you bought the house in Poplar.'

Alma said, 'Well, you can get your dirty, stinking, rotten hands off my mortgage – and you can go to your solicitor and sign it over to me and I am going to make sure that I'm there to see you do it.'

Ralph had previously spoken to Alma and George about the possibility of Linda continuing to pay the mortgage of Alma and George's home in Hornchurch for the rest of their lives, so that they could have a trouble-free mortgage pathway in return for all the help that they had given to Linda. In return, Linda then should have the house when both her parents had died.

When Ralph mooted this idea, Linda said that it would never work and they would never agree to it because they'd be worried about the boys, George and John, getting their share and indeed, that was the response that Ralph got.

An appointment was made to see Linda's solicitor. He was a long-standing friend of hers and he was aware of how the mortgage had been set up with The Commonwealth Trading Bank of Australia as he was Linda's solicitor at the time. On reaching the solicitor's office, Alma started to push herself forward, telling Linda to *sit* down, *shut up*, and to keep quiet. The solicitor annoyed Alma tremendously by saying, 'I will see Linda first.'

All the time that Linda was talking to him, Alma was shouting and banging on the door saying, 'get her dirty, stinking, rotten hands off my mortgage.'

It was most embarrassing. The other clients in the solicitors wondered what the hell was going on. Linda's solicitor said to her, 'Look, you have paid this mortgage for six-and-a-half years and through the gift of a five-hundred pounds you also gave your parents towards a deposit in 1972 on the original house in Poplar, you have a legal percentage claim of whatever they make on the house in Hornchurch if they were to sell it. So I strongly urge you not to pass on the mortgage to your mother, otherwise, you won't get what is rightfully yours, especially when I hear the way that she is carrying on outside.'

Linda said, 'I'm not really worried. I am happy with Ralph and I really need to be free of this barrage from her. I will always be eternally grateful to her for everything that she has done throughout my life, and if I am to have some kind of relationship with her in the future, I feel I have to let it go because I do not want us to have a permanent barrier.'

He said, 'I really don't think that you should be doing this but if you insist, I will make it clear to your mother without you being there.'

When Linda left the office, Alma was so fired-up that she pushed her way in, slamming the door. Linda had already signed the mortgage over to her mother so she had got what she wanted, even though she was shouting and yelling at her.

When they got home Alma said to Linda, 'And you can sign that account that we have in joint names over to me because this is my money.'

Linda said, 'Don't you remember, Mum, that I put some money in that account too because you said that it would be for my future?'

'Well, it's not,' said Alma, 'it's mine, and I want it, and what's more, I'm going to get it.' Linda signed the form because it wasn't worth the arguments. She felt too tired and too exhausted to argue.

So Alma took the remaining twelve-thousand-pounds cash out of the account, and paid it to The Commonwealth Trading Bank of Australia, completely clearing the mortgage so she had no payments and no debts. But she told people that Ralph and Linda had impoverished her, and that she would now have to take out a new mortgage. This was a total pack of lies and Linda felt quite ashamed and disgusted with her mother.

Chapter 39

Members of the Harold Wood Methodist Church had decided to help out with some of the costs of Linda and Ralph's wedding. The organist gave his services free of charge, the Reverend E Ronald Kemp also gave of his services without charge, and all of the choir members made no charge, which was wonderful. Margaret Palmer was usually in charge of flower rosters and general floral duties. She got her team of people together and consulted Ralph and Linda about what flowers they might like.

The only stipulation that Linda and Ralph requested was that there should be a wonderful fragrance of flowers as people came in to the church and that there should be no freesias because they were Ralph's late wife Joan's favourite flowers – Linda and Ralph didn't want Ralph's children to be upset.

There was to be a beautiful arrangement of flowers at the communion table and flowers tied with ribbons at the end of every pew. People were to be invited to take them as a memento when they left, leaving the main floral arrangements in place for the following day's services. Everything was now in place in terms of structure – it would be a highly-fragrant occasion, and look very beautiful.

One morning, as Alma and Linda ate breakfast together, Alma questioned, 'You're not having a joint bank account with *him*, are you?'

Linda said, 'I have already had this discussion with Ralph and he knows that I want my total independence to decide where I should put my money, and how I should spend it, as it is totally my decision. That is one of the jobs I've still got to do, so I will be arranging to have Braille bank statements so that I can see what is happening for myself.'

At this, Alma went ballistic, 'What do you want Braille bank statements for?' She screamed, 'Don't you trust me? Do you think that I'm stealing your money or something?' At which point Linda was smashed hard in the face once again.

Linda said, 'What the hell's the matter with you? It doesn't seem to matter what the discussion is about, you have to turn everything into negativity and the use of fists.'

Alma said, 'I don't know what you mean?'

Linda said, 'I'm sure you do, and I'm not accusing you of doing anything with my money.'

'Well, don't think there's any money for your wedding,' said Alma, 'Because we haven't got any, and you are not getting anything out of me.'

Linda said, 'Well you gave money to the boys when they got married, helping them with the evening reception costs and so on, and so I was hoping that you might at least make a contribution for your only daughter's wedding – especially as you and I never thought that it would ever happen?'

Alma said, 'Well, you're out of luck. There's nothing here for *you*. We are going to have a marquee here in the garden and you will be expected to attend – so *that's that!'*

Linda said, 'Ralph and I have already told you that we will be leaving the wedding reception at six o'clock, heading for our honeymoon. So, we cannot attend, neither do we wish to attend any reception that you might choose to put on in view of the way that you are treating us. And, furthermore, if I get any more smashes in the face, you will be reported because I've had quite enough and I cannot take any more because I am not prepared to – enough is enough.'

Linda and Alma left the dining table in an angry, frosty silence.

That evening when Linda met with Ralph, she told him what had happened. His reaction was, 'I don't care what you do, but you have got to get out of there because you are just not safe. Her anger about losing control over you is getting completely out of proportion. It has not been healthy in all the time that we have been together. I remember when I sold my home in Harold Wood and had nowhere to live, and Bill and Dolly put me up.'

'Your parents could have invited me over so that I didn't have to travel every day to Dartford, leaving at just after six in the morning because of the traffic. They could have invited me into their home and watched how I was with you but they did nothing. All your mother did was to pile-up all of your possessions – Braille books, equipment, and give it to me by the box-load before I'd even moved in. It was only your father who told her to "pack it in".'

'As you know, I just accepted every box that she threw at me without a word. But of course, I wondered where the hell I was going to put it all before I moved.

That is why I had so many boxes when I moved into our new home and heard Alma and George talking all the time about the number of boxes that were being piled into the garage and so on. I had nowhere else to put them all.'

Linda said, 'I know, darling, you were absolutely wonderful and I thank you so much for your patience. I must say, I am beginning to lose mine. I know how hard it is for her to "let go" but I will never understand why she couldn't be happy for me – after all, my parents are now getting elderly and if anything happened to either of them before I moved out, life would be very difficult for us.'

'So, Alma in particular, ought to be thanking God for you coming into my life when you did, believing it to be an answer to prayer but sadly, she cannot see or doesn't want to see that God has answered our prayers. All she can see is the relinquishing of control and the loss of money that would have been hers had I died, which is awful. Surely my life is worth more than the money that she would have had in her bank account? I was taking a huge leap of faith – faith in you, because I knew that you loved me and wanted us to be together.'

Ralph replied, 'When Alma says that there is nothing for your wedding, I am sure that you feel hurt by that, but don't let her control you in this way. What she's doing isn't kind, and it isn't loving. She just wants to rule. Well, our honeymoon departure is not going to be delayed by a reception that I don't want anyway, and I'm sure you don't either after everything that has gone on?'

Linda said, 'As regards to leaving the family home before the wedding, I can't do that.'

Ralph said, 'Yes you can because, if you had come to me, then she would have said that we were living together and made everything look sordid, but if you put yourself into a residential care home and brought the wedding forward as much as possible, she would find it very difficult telling people that the reason you had left home was because you couldn't stand the strain and the aggression anymore.'

But Linda felt that she just had to stick it out for the sake of public relations and to save face.

When Ralph returned Linda to her home, he explained to Alma, 'We have already told you that we are leaving for our honeymoon immediately after the reception. We will *not* be attending any function that you might choose to hold. You have not requested us to attend – you've just told Linda that you will be there after the reception and that's not on. You should at least respect our wishes.

So, we will definitely not be there because our arrangements have already been made. We have a long journey to make—over two hundred miles—and Linda will have already had an exciting but exhausting day. We just want to relax and be together. Don't worry about the cost of the wedding either, as Linda and I are paying for it ourselves so you won't have to bother.'

Ralph told Linda later that Alma's face was a picture – she had an expression like thunder because for once, Linda had got someone who would stand up for her, fight her corner for what was right, and Alma didn't like it one bit.

Chapter 40

The progress towards the wedding day was accelerating ever more. There never seemed to be enough hours in the day to do all the things that Linda and Ralph wanted to do. Ralph had to purchase his suit for the wedding and his son, Paul, was going to be one of the main witnesses – so he, too, sported out on a new suit. This was something that Paul rarely had – he was more a "jeans and T-shirt" man. So, all this formality was a bit much for him.

Three weeks before the wedding, Ralph came to Linda and said, 'I'm having a bit of a problem with the words of the wedding service?'

'What's that?' Linda asked.

'I can't say, "according to God's Holy Law?" Because I don't believe in it?' said Ralph, 'I want us to get married in a registry office. What do you think of that idea?'

Linda said, 'I can't do that – I'm a preacher in training? It would go against everything that I believe in, especially when you put it to me about a registry office wedding. I want our family and friends to be there and bless what we do together.'

Ralph said, 'Are you telling me that if I told you that I couldn't go through with it, it would all be off?'

Linda said, 'Oh for goodness sake, don't put me in that position.'

Ralph said, 'But are you telling me that if I ask you to choose, you wouldn't do what I wanted?'

Linda replied, 'I cannot compromise my faith. Please don't ask me to make a choice.'

Ralph said, 'Well I am asking you to make a choice.'

'If you force the issue,' said Linda, 'It won't be you who wins.'

Ralph said, 'Are you telling me that your faith is more important than I am?'

Linda said, 'Oh please, I told you, don't ask me to make that choice. I can't.'

Ralph said, 'But you are asking *me* to choose aren't you?'

Linda replied, 'I think that the best thing you can do is to make an appointment to see Mr Kemp.'

Linda went with Ralph and explained Ralph's dilemma to Mr Kemp.

Mr Kemp said to Ralph, 'You knew that Linda was a committed Christian when you asked her to marry you and you also know that preaching is a life-long commitment.'

The three of them spent a couple of hours talking around the problem.

Linda said to Ralph, 'I think that it would be far better if you could speak to Mr Kemp on your own. I shouldn't be influencing your decision. So, further meetings were arranged and for now, everything was in the balance, just hanging by a thread – which way would Ralph jump?'

On returning from Mr Kemp's, Alma asked Linda what was the matter. Linda told her mother the problem.

Alma said, 'Oh, I thought he'd never see it through – I thought he would want to duck-out and find any excuse that he could to leave you in the lurch.'

Linda said, 'It isn't like that. He is genuinely struggling about the whole Christian commitment thing and he finds those words "according to God's Holy Law" extremely hard as a confessed atheist.'

Alma said, 'It was obvious, he was going to take your money and run, and leave us to pick up the pieces.'

Linda said, 'It's got nothing to do with money.'

'Oh yes it has,' said Alma, 'He will take half the house and any money that you have as well.'

Nothing Linda could say or do would convince Alma of Ralph's genuine intentions. Linda hoped that perhaps it was purely nerves and that it would all come right in the end.

There were two more meetings between Ralph and Mr Kemp. On the third day, Ralph said to Linda after his meeting with Mr Kemp, 'Mr Kemp advises me that many people don't take the words of the marriage service nearly seriously enough, and that he was sure that God would bless this relationship.'

Mr Kemp was convinced that God hadn't brought Ralph this far, only to fail because God wanted them to be happy. His advice was to say the words as best you can and he was sure that God would bless them both. So, still struggling, Ralph came to Linda and told her what Mr Kemp had said. Ralph went on to say to Linda, 'I'll go through with it, because I love you, but please don't ask me to believe in it.'

Linda said, 'I'll just be grateful that you are there.'

But of course, Alma was revelling in the latest difficulty. She said, 'I told you, nobody would ever look after you like I have done—*nobody* does it better than *me*—you couldn't even *expect* them to. Nobody in their right mind would want to take you on.'

By now, Linda was feeling absolutely terrible. She had been so sure of Ralph, and of his feelings for her, and every level of commitment that they had made together so far. Now it was all up in the air. Linda prayed, 'Please God, don't get me this far, only to have my life shattered – I just couldn't bear it. Life has been so difficult and Ralph has been the only thing that has made all this pressure palatable.'

'It really didn't help for people to have their two pennyworths and to prod and poke at the situation. So, although it was calmer, there was still an air of tension. Would he, or would he not, say those words respecting Linda's calling as a preacher?'

For now, all she could do was to wait and see.

Chapter 41

Linda was sitting at home, waiting for Ralph to arrive, when Alma walked into the room and, with no provocation at all, grabbed hold of Linda by the throat with one hand, and started punching her on the head and face, with the other.

'What the hell is going on?' Linda struggled to ask.

Alma said, 'You don't care about me. I would have had *that money* that you're giving to *him* and now it's all going to be wasted.'

Alma continued punching Linda, still holding her by the throat and shaking her head violently.

Linda said, 'Mum, Stop! What do you think you're doing?'

The punches continued. Linda was terrified and raised her hands up to try and fend off the onslaught.

Alma said, 'Don't you put your hands up to me, you saucy bastard.'

Linda said, 'I'm just trying to protect my head. What about all the operations I've had? And you are smashing me in the eyes and nose? I was just sitting here, minding my own business, and you started crashing in on me.'

Alma said, 'I just don't want anything to do with that bastard future husband of yours.'

While the punches were still coming at a pace, Linda said, 'Well it doesn't matter whether you like him or not, it's going to happen.'

At that point, Linda heard Ralph and her father coming into the house. Ralph could obviously hear what was going on. He ran into the room, grabbed hold of Alma, and pulled her off Linda, asking Alma, 'What the hell's the matter with you? This has got to stop now!'

Naturally, Alma did not like being found out as to the kind of things that she was doing.

Ralph turned to George and said, 'George, this has got to stop, and you have got to do something before someone gets seriously hurt.'

George's frightened response was, 'Yeah, I know.' And he walked off, shaking his head, not saying another word.

Ralph grabbed hold of Linda and said, 'We are leaving right now.'

Alma said later that Ralph gave her one of his angry stares – if the truth be told, Ralph had just had enough and he was furious with her. Linda was really shaken and felt as though she did not want to stay in the presence of her mother for a moment longer, but she felt that she had to do the conventional thing and stick it out for the sake of the wedding, even though she felt terrified.

Linda said, 'I just cannot understand the complete irrationality of all this. She is not thinking of my happiness, she is only thinking of the finances that she will lose when I leave home and it is absolutely disgusting. I love her deeply and I would do anything to help her and to make her happy but whatever I say or do is wrong, and I am becoming an absolute nervous wreck. Every time I am in her presence, she finds something to start an argument about – I just don't know what to do anymore?' Linda sobbed on Ralph's shoulder.

Ralph said, 'You know, you could give all of this up and just get married quietly.'

Linda said, 'I have thought about a day like this all my adult life, not ever daring to dream that it may happen. Too often, I have been told that no one is going to look at me and no one cares about you except your mother – and of course, I believed it. Then, you came along and changed my life immeasurably to the point that I now have the means of escaping from all this. I love and bless you for the way that you've responded to me and coped with Alma's nastiness.'

'Most men would have either have told her where to go, or got out because her grip was far too tight. She cannot help herself, and now she has become, I believe, seriously mentally ill – the antidepressants that the doctors prescribed are obviously not working. She cannot imagine a life without me and hates the loss of control, and cannot bear just "existing" with Dad because they've never really had any kind of life together, just on their own.'

Linda spent a blissful few hours with Ralph but she was terrified about returning home. On arrival, George opened the front door, 'How are you babe,' he said.

Linda said, 'To be honest, Dad, I don't feel very well. The incident earlier has just made me even more of a nervous wreck.'

George said, 'You know what she's like, she goes like a bloody mad woman and you just can't do anything with her.'

Linda said, 'Yes, I know, but *you've* got to help her deal with the wedding and what's coming after.'

Two weeks before the wedding, George started to decorate the living room. It all looked very smart. Alma wanted it looking nice for any photographs that might be taken on the big day.

Linda had been out with Ralph and on returning Alma said, 'You owe your dad sixty-seven pounds for some wood.'

Linda said, 'What's that for then?'

Alma said, 'He is renewing some of the woodwork around the living room patio doors.'

Linda said, 'Well, that's not my problem. I am already paying two mortgages at the moment – this one, and the one that Ralph and I will be moving to. And you have planned it so that you have made me pay right up to one day before the wedding. You couldn't even let me get away with a week's worth of mortgage payments.'

Alma said, 'And by the way, you haven't given me this month's treat yet?'

Linda said, 'No, I know that I haven't.'

Linda had given Alma twenty-pounds-a-month for her to spend on whatever she wished because she now wouldn't be having a weekly wage from the bank. Linda had paid it, along with all the other household bills for some four years or so, since August 1983, when they both left the bank.

Alma said, 'So are you telling me that you're not giving it to me then?'

'No, I think that I've paid out quite enough,' said Linda, 'And I won't be giving you a twenty-pound treat on a regular basis anymore, and, I'm not paying for the wood around the patio doors to be repaired either.'

Alma was not happy. Linda thought her whole life revolved around money and Alma put the screws on her as tightly as she could.

One morning, Alma announced that she was not coming to the wedding.

'But why not?' Linda asked.

'Your father and I are just not coming,' said Alma, 'You can make any excuse that you like – that we are ill, or anything that you choose to say.'

Linda said, 'What I choose to say is that your places are set at the head of the table and they have been booked and paid for, and if you don't turn up, I will tell people the exact reason why you are not there. It has nothing to do with illness but everything to do with your reasons about Ralph and me. You are doing exactly the same kind of thing that Grandma would have done – she went to hardly any of her sons' marriages which I think was appalling. So, I am not making any changes. You will take your places at the table and I hope, you'll behave with dignity and decorum.'

The matter was left like that. Linda was determined that if Alma and George failed to show, then the rest of the wedding party would be left in no uncertain terms as to what had actually happened. Linda had just had enough and the day was pretty much spoilt anyhow. But she was determined that nothing was going to spoil this special moment for her and Ralph.

Then, on the day before the wedding, a new carpet was fitted in the living room. A beautiful green leather three-piece suite arrived, followed by an L-shaped sideboard with many cupboards, to fit in the corner of the room. It all looked absolutely beautiful but of course, there was no money for Linda's wedding! Any spare cash had been frittered away on the furniture and carpets and Alma was determined that she was not going to ease Linda's financial burden.

Linda felt extremely hurt but on the other hand, why shouldn't Alma have what she wanted, after all, Linda wouldn't be there anymore? So she could do what she liked. All this luscious carpeting, furniture, and woodwork made Linda feel hurt but also a little envious as it had been done so pointedly – Alma almost "wagging a finger" at Linda at what she could achieve.

Linda didn't feel that it was her father's doing because there was absolutely nothing wrong with the furniture that they had – the house already looked like a furniture showroom anyhow. But there was nothing that Linda could do. Alma had got her mortgage cleared, extra money in the bank, and everything that she wanted – except, of course, Linda.

On the day of the wedding, Alma came into Linda's bedroom at six in the morning. Linda had been lying awake for hours, wondering how Ralph was feeling and whether he had any major misgivings about the church service.

Alma said, 'Well, have you got any regrets?'

Linda said, 'None whatsoever. I can't wait.'

Alma said, as she was putting Linda into the bath, 'You have no regrets at all then?'

'I've already told you, I can't wait,' was Linda's reply.

Linda had had enough of the last couple of years and just couldn't wait to be free—free to breathe—free to make her own choices—free to make mistakes, and free to love Ralph with all the love, passion, and respect that she could muster.

At the breakfast table, George had prepared Linda's favourite breakfast – crispy bacon and fried tomatoes with bread and butter. He was obviously doing his best but the bacon was more "cremated" than cooked! However, she ate it and said nothing. Gradually, people started to arrive. Vernon, Ralph's Son-in Law, had been asked to take the wedding photographs.

Linda and Ralph did not want formal pictures, partly because they would be so expensive.

Linda always told people, 'Please don't ask me to pose for photographs – just take them when the facial expression is right as it is quite difficult for a blind person to pose correctly for photographs.'

As people were brought into the living room, they all commented on how smart everything was. This pleased Alma enormously. After the hairdresser had tinkered with the hair, Linda was helped to get dressed and to put the headdress on. She had photographs taken with Jean Thomas, her best friend who was to be her Matron of Honour, and her mother and father along with other family members.

When the Rolls Royce arrived outside the front door, the neighbours started to come out and look. As Alma walked Linda to the car, George said, 'Oh bloody hell, the bleedin' neighbours are watching now.'

Alma's response was, 'Fuck the neighbours,' And she proceeded to help Linda into the car. Linda sat in the front seat next to the driver but she was determined that on the return journey from the church to the reception, she would get in the back of the car and travel with her husband as any other couple would have done. Alma followed behind in the family car so that she could assist Linda with arranging her dress and flowers before going into the church.

George got out Linda's wheelchair from the boot of the car and when everything was ready, he wheeled her into the church. Linda kept telling him, 'Slow down, Dad, we don't want to reach the altar before anybody else.' But because George refused to attend the dress rehearsal, it all had to be done on the day.

As Alma had had no part in the arrangements for the wedding, she was totally shocked when she walked inside the church – it all looked magnificent. Alma put on her fixed smile which never left her for the whole of the day. One lovely moment was at the end of the service.

George passed Linda over to Ralph and said, 'She's yours now.'

Linda felt so proud as she made her wedding vows and even though Ralph struggled with the words of the service, he did partially say, 'according to God's Holy Law.' Linda just gently squeezed his hand because she knew that it was a difficult issue for him. The church was full and like all good Methodists, the singing was loud and clear, although not from Ralph's side of the family or other family members from Linda's side. Once the register had been signed and the songs had been sung, it was time for Linda to take centre stage with Ralph and walk with him holding her arm, down the aisle.

Many people could not contain their delight and applauded. This was a moment worth the struggle to walk, and to stand with Ralph outside the church, greeting friends and family. Linda felt quite exhausted by the time she got back into the Rolls Royce. Ralph knew that Linda did not want people to take lots of photographs as she struggled to get up onto the high seat of the car.

He said, 'Don't worry, Lin, no one can take photos. I am standing in front of you.' They then had that special moment in the back of the car with everyone cheering as they drove off to the reception at Mary Green Manor, the sixteenth-century Moathouse in Brentwood, Essex.

Chapter 42

In Mary Green Manor, Linda's father was dishing out his usual critical comments. Firstly, he didn't think much of the melon starter. Then, it was the roast beef that wasn't "done" enough. The roast potatoes weren't crispy enough, and he'd never eaten such a funny-looking dessert as Baked Alaska. Linda felt furious. In the end, she said to him, 'Did you pay anything for this wedding?'

He answered, 'No, I bleedin' didn't.'

Linda said, 'Well just shut up and eat then – without complaint, preferably!'

After the first course, Linda had to ask Ralph to take her to the bathroom. As she rose from the table, there were anxious comments as to whether she was alright.

Ralph said, 'I'll give you three guesses but you'll only need one!'

This caused much laughter and helped break the tense atmosphere. Everything about the reception went like clockwork including the announcement of the guests by the hotel manager, Mr Luigi, as he called out the names as they came up the red carpet to the bride and groom. This was done so that Linda would know who was coming to her in advance. But Alma felt that this was, "bloody ridiculous".

Linda could never understand why everything that she and Ralph had arranged was regarded as bloody ridiculous by her parents. It was really tiring. Mr Luigi used a full-sized sword to cut the cake – somewhat hairy for Linda when she couldn't see just how sharp the blade was.

With the "cutting-of-the-cake" ceremony over, everyone retired to the garden for coffee and wedding cake, and a chance to meet and greet all the guests properly.

Alma said to Ralph, 'You go and talk to your friends, and I'll guide Linda around.' Ralph ignored this comment and stuck to Linda like glue. They stayed in the gardens until around five-thirty in the afternoon when Linda was taken to one of the bedrooms to change into her, "going away" outfit. Tina, Ralph's daughter, was there to lend a hand. Paul, Ralph's son, suddenly announced to Tina that he had found the car that Ralph had carefully hidden. Within half an hour the good old Ford Escort was decked out with balloons, ribbons, cans and bottles along with writing all over the windscreen.

Just as Linda and Ralph got into the car, Linda's Aunt Pat threw a whole box of confetti into the car at once – it was a real pain for months afterwards, trying to get the small pieces of paper out of the air conditioning and other inaccessible parts of the car. Everyone was quite happy as Linda and Ralph drove away up the motorway. People were honking their horns and shouting "Good Luck" messages as they progressed.

Ralph pulled into a lay-by and took a bottle of water to wipe off the lipstick from the windscreen. It was an awful mess but eventually they got it clear. Alma had tried to persuade them to stay for the party in the evening at her house but Ralph was adamant that he was not going to, especially in view of the weeks of aggravation that he had encountered. He just felt that he couldn't take any more and wanted to get "the hell out of there"!

Later that evening, Linda and Ralph discovered that not a single member of Ralph's family was invited to Alma's evening do in her marquee. Much food was wasted which she wasn't happy about, but then if she'd invited those members of Ralph's family, it wouldn't have happened. Linda and Ralph had done their level best to make everything lovely for Alma. Linda presented her mother and father with a coach trip holiday to Scotland.

Alma had always wanted to go to Scotland and Linda used that to say that now they had the chance to spoil each other and to go on some nice trips or holidays, relaxing in each other's company. But all Alma and George could do was to complain about their first venue in Carlisle before moving on to Scotland the next day.

Linda and Ralph wanted time on their own to prepare Linda for managing by herself. That would be a pretty scary time as Linda had never spent a day by herself before. On the first night of their honeymoon, they arrived at their first stop in Stafford.

Ralph's first comment was, 'If you could see what I can see now, you would be most annoyed.' Linda discovered by Ralph placing her hands in such a way that she could detect that there were two single beds in the room – with a large gap between them!

Linda said, 'I'm not having any of that.'

She rang the hotel manager and had the single beds replaced by a king-size. The manager said, 'I suppose you're just married or something?'

Linda's annoyed response was, 'You can forget the "or something", we are just married.' This hotel was not of the standard that Ralph and Linda would have wanted. The room was stiflingly hot and the window could only be opened by a couple of inches. Ralph tossed and turned most of the night and they could not wait to get to the English Heritage Hotel in York the next day.

The English Heritage Hotel in York was an altogether different kettle of fish. The hotel staff was excellent, the food beautifully presented, and the atmosphere was just right. The king size bed was beautifully comfortable and best of all, Ralph was able to open a window! At breakfast the next morning, Linda met Nancy, the head waiter, for the breakfasts, who enquired whether they, she and Ralph, were newly-weds?

Linda was surprised that it was so obvious. Nancy ascertained what Linda wanted for breakfast. Her wish was for mostly fruit with a crusty bread roll. Once Nancy heard this, an array of fresh fruit arrived at Linda's breakfast table every morning – each day seeming to surpass the one before. Linda thought that it was some kind of competition as to who could outdo the other but the service was so kind and friendly, that Linda and Ralph went back for several years of visits, sometimes they attended the hotel for lunch on the day of their anniversary, the fourth of July.

There was so much to do in York and the Yorkshire people were very warm and welcoming wherever they went. Linda and Ralph decided to visit York Minster. The hotel concierge said that getting parked in York was difficult, even with a Blue Badge. So, if they spoke nicely to the policeman and offered a tip, he would probably find a parking space for them. They had no sooner got settled in the cathedral when somebody came along asking everyone to leave with an "everybody out"! Linda and Ralph tried to ascertain the reason and were eventually told that there was a special church function going on that morning.

Linda said, 'Well, if it's a service, I would like to stay?'

'Oh no, you can't do that madam,' said one of the church officials.

Linda said, 'Well, you cannot stop me from staying in God's house, so I'm not leaving.' Eventually, Bishop John Hapgood, was summoned and he responded to the situation by saying, 'If the lady wants to stay in God's house, of course she can stay.'

Ralph and Linda just wanted to merge into the background and listen to the proceedings. This service was to celebrate the bicentenary of the Ecclesiastical Insurance Company. The men wore top hats and morning suits, and the women were in their finery. Unfortunately, Linda and Ralph were placed right at the front of the proceedings, even though their wish was to fade into the background. They were neatly dressed but obviously they were holidaymakers and looked quite inappropriate for the occasion.

Nevertheless, the singing of the choir and the organ playing was magnificent. At the end of the service, the organist played the famous music of Widor's Toccata from his Organ Symphony Number Five (the music used for the occasion of many Royal Weddings). The sound was truly splendid and the tears streamed from Linda's eyes. Ralph anxiously asked if she was alright.

'Well, darling,' she said, 'This is the highlight of my honeymoon so far.'

Ralph said, laughing, 'Well thanks very much for that!'

They visited many other attractions in York during that week, including the Treasury House with a personal guided tour given by the curator which came about as a result of him asking if Linda had enjoyed the tour.

'Not really,' she said, 'Because everything is roped-off, and as a blind person, I am not being allowed to touch anything.'

'Oh, I'll sort that out,' he said, taking many of the ropes away and showing Linda things individually and at close quarters. At one point he said, 'Here, cop hold of this.'

It turned out to be a priceless Ming vase. When Linda realised what she was holding, she was terrified that she might drop it. But he was confident enough to allow her to hold it safely by herself. A lot of the American tourists soon realised what was happening and followed behind in the wake of Linda's tour, getting much more information than they otherwise would have. It was just wonderful, for example, feeling the tortoiseshell and brass work on a huge chest.

The curator invited Linda to open it and lift the lid back – there was a wonderful fragrance of sandalwood and Ralph said that the colours of the woodwork were superb. Linda would not have normally had the opportunity of seeing things at such close quarters. He invited her to place her hands in the chest – it had a beautiful plush velvet lining.

Everywhere that Linda and Ralph visited on that week's honeymoon, they had fantastic cooperation. Linda was able to touch some of the huge trains in the railway museum and some wonderful old horse-drawn buses from the transport museum. They also went to an interactive exhibition that takes you back in time to the days of the Vikings.

It was a very realistic presentation, including all the smells of the towns of the time, which were not very pleasant. It made Linda realise just how great a thing it was that the streets had been cleaned up and how people could appreciate better sanitation. All these trips out were interesting but, in Linda's opinion, there was nothing more wonderful than sitting in the Yorkshire Dales with a picnic of sandwiches, cakes, fruit, and Champagne for two, provided by the hotel, which was all the more magical because she was with the person that she loved most and knew that she would spend the rest of her life with him, however long, or short, that might be.

Chapter 43

Linda and Ralph didn't want this happy week to end but now it was back to the hard grind of getting to know the new house well – Linda had one week with Ralph watching and guiding, to familiarise herself with everything in the house. When examining the post, Ralph found a two-hundred-and-fifty-pound cheque in a folded envelope accompanied by a small note which read 'Lin, here is your wedding present, Love Mum.'

There was no mention of Ralph of course, and no sign of the two-hundred-and-fifty-pound contribution from George – Linda was told initially that she would be given a five-hundred-pound cheque towards a dining table and six chairs from both of them (it wasn't until some three-weeks later that Alma turned up with George's contribution). This made Linda and Ralph feel very unhappy, and it also did nothing for the confidence-building that Linda would need in the days ahead. What was it about Alma? She just couldn't bear to acknowledge Ralph – in any shape or form. Linda just could not understand it and felt hurt and angry all at the same time.

Ralph's response was, 'Don't worry about it, I don't respect them after the way you have been treated, therefore I have no need to like them either. I have really tried in the two-and-a-half years that we have known each other but my patience is wearing a bit thin. I just wish that you could cut your losses and forget them.'

Linda said, 'I can't do that, Ralph, because I remember all the years of struggle, challenge, and sacrifices that they have both made for me.'

Ralph said, 'Yes, but surely you don't have to carry that kind of gratitude for the rest of your life?'

Linda said that she would always have a burden of gratitude, how could she not due to the way that she had affected their lives right from the moment that she was born?

Ralph said, 'As a parent, you never stop being concerned about your children but you should just love, watch, and let go, leaving them to fly the nest, but also to be there when needed.' On that Sunday evening, Linda lay awake all night, terrified of the coming day. She was sure that she would make many errors but all she could promise Ralph was that she would do her best to make him proud of her.

Ralph said, 'If you didn't do another thing, I would always be proud of you but I know that you are a fighter and you won't give in easily.'

Linda prepared the evening meal but, because it was a small Baby Belling cooker, she was worried about getting it into the oven. She had many difficulties coping as the kitchen was not adapted for a blind, disabled person. The only one new piece of disability equipment for the kitchen was the talking microwave. This was a great help when making a hot drink. On that first day when Ralph had to leave Linda on her own, she was absolutely terrified and frequently shed tears. Linda's frustration was always that her mother had never let her do things in the kitchen using knives and so on with her usual refrain, 'You might cut yourself.'

Ralph's attitude to all of this was quite different, 'Well, if you cut yourself,' he said, 'I'll make sure that you can reach the sticking plasters!' His attitude was far healthier and he gave her the confidence to try.

When Linda walked out onto the patio for a breath of fresh air, she was always relieved to come into contact with the handrails. It was not so easy walking back into the house because there were no rails to guide her in. In all the years that Linda and Ralph were married, Ralph never got angry if Linda dropped or spilt anything, and Ralph would just have to help clear things up when he came home.

Linda was sure that there must have been times when Ralph wondered what he'd taken on. He could have had a much simpler life had his partner been able-bodied. Linda was never happier than when she heard the sound of Ralph's key opening the door and calling out. Those first few minutes were such a relief to Linda – all the emotion that had been pent up that day just flowed. There were frequent tears. She began to wonder whether she would ever accomplish things but gradually, as the weeks and months went on, she became more proficient at the daily tasks.

On that first Monday evening, Ralph went to pick up Alma and George from the coach station in Romford where they had just returned from their Scottish holiday. There was no enthusiasm from Alma and little more from George who bleated, 'Nice Holiday – all we saw was, sheep, sheep, and more bloody sheep!'

Linda said, 'Well surely, there must have been some things that you enjoyed – like the scenery?'

'Not much,' said George.

Linda just couldn't believe this. She would have given anything to see the pictures of places like Loch Lomond and Inverness, and many more. Because they only had a small oven, it was decided to do quiche, new potatoes, and salad for George and Alma. Of course, George was not impressed.

'Why don't you get this bloody kitchen sorted?' He said.

Ralph said, 'We are saving up for it and then, it will be brilliant with all the things that Lin needs.'

The kitchen was obviously a bone of contention on Alma and George's part and Alma said very sarcastically and disparagingly, 'Of course, you two would live in the garden shed as long as you were together, wouldn't you?' Linda of course, readily agreed.

Linda was still familiarising herself with everything in the bungalow. They had quite a large sitting room and Alma and George had given them an old Chesterfield sofa and a couple of winged-back leather chairs. So Linda would come in at the door and tap her tripod along to the other end of the sofa and move to the hi-fi and television.

Using exactly the same technique, Linda had to find the remaining wall space until she came up against the sliding door which led into the kitchen. Then it was a straight walk until she came level with the kitchen sink. On the outward journey from the kitchen, Linda turned right to find the patio door and the handrails leading down to the street level. Linda practised and practised, from Saturday afternoon until late Sunday evening.

It was fine until Linda had to take her hands off the tripod sticks to do something, and then the frustration came when she had to feel for the stick, which invariably fell over so that she had to struggle to pick it up before she could walk again. Many times, she knocked into furniture and was constantly bruising her head as the tripod sticks had to be so far out in front of her, which on one level was helpful, but on another, made her feel off-balance because she had to lean forward in order to find things.

On the second day, Linda was trying to do some hand-washing. She quickly realised that this was an absolutely thankless task because she couldn't always tell which bits were clean and which bits weren't so she resolved that either the home help had to help with the hand washing or it was to be sent away to the washing and ironing service.

So on that morning, Linda had been working on her Bible studies for her preaching exams and decided that she would come out and make a hot chocolate. The hot chocolate boiled over into the tray and Linda was trying to clean it up. At that point, Alma knocked at the door. Betty, George, and Alma walked in.

'Oh my God,' Alma exclaimed, 'Look at the bloody mess you're in. You're bloody useless. Get out of my way and I'll sort it.'

Linda told her not to worry because *she* was sorting it – hence the kitchen paper in the bin.

'You'll never cope,' said Alma, 'And I'm going to tell *him* exactly what I think when he gets home.'

'I wouldn't do that,' Linda said, 'Otherwise he might just give you your answer because you wanted to keep me as your possession, having complete control. And it has served you well to do so. Once you knew that I intended to marry Ralph, you should have used the two-and-a half years to work out the problems, to decide the things that I could achieve, and help me make the decision as to what I would need to get other people to do – such as the hand-washing and Ralph's shirts.'

'But you have not done one single thing to prepare me for this day and your constant gloating and criticism is almost too much to bear and I am sure that if you ring Ralph and tell him what you think, he will in no uncertain terms tell you what he thinks!'

Needless to say, the telephone call didn't happen. Alma never rang Ralph at any stage. All she did was to be critical about everything and it drove Linda completely mad because she was trying to do her best.

Linda and Ralph had a discussion regarding the kitchen design. It was such a small kitchen that it didn't require much working out. The difficulty was getting the right equipment within the small space. They sought the help of a kitchen designer based in Walthamstow, London. He liked Gaggenau kitchen equipment so they had a Halogen Hob, a microwave oven with a drop-down front rather like a roller door which aided Linda and her disabilities.

A huge Gaggenau Butler sink was fitted which was the length of one of the walls – it was so large that a full-size oven tray could be placed in to it without any difficulty. The oven was below the microwave, sitting on a Ropox Unit, a special disability device where cupboards are mounted on a frame and then handles are turned to rotate the cupboards either up or down so that the top cupboards could be lowered in order for them to be a "reachable" height from a wheelchair or raised for an able-bodied person.

It was somewhat disconcerting to visitors when Linda and Ralph showed them how the cupboards could be raised or lowered and people could watch the cupboards move up and down the wall – not the sort of thing to experience if they'd had one too many drinks! The cupboards under the window were raised off the floor to give a better turning-circle for Linda's wheelchair so that she could get her feet under the cupboard area in order to maximise the space within the kitchen.

The kitchen flooring was a brilliant non-slip German design which was so good that, even if water had been spilt, it was still perfectly safe. They had beautiful Pogennpohl kitchen cupboards and work surfaces with all sorts of space for kitchen accessories such as utensils and rubbish bin holder and so on – the whole kitchen was extremely expensive and looked absolutely brilliant, with its suspended ceiling giving it a wonderful finishing touch.

When this was completed, at least Alma and George had nothing more to say regarding criticism. They had saved their money, bought wisely, and the end result was both aesthetically pleasing and highly suitable for a person with disability.

As a result of the newly-designed kitchen, Linda became proficient at food preparation for the first time in her life and she absolutely loved it. She would put chopping boards over the glass of the hob, then wind the cupboard up to her level, slide the saucepans to one side to the draining board, then lift the pots with the vegetables in to the sink, filling them with water, and then reversing the process as she transferred the pots to the hob. It all worked incredibly well and. Linda loved to keep it spotlessly clean by standing herself up and leaning her body into the corner for support as she did so.

Ralph was so proud of all her efforts. There were times when there were more things on the floor than on the work surfaces but he never got angry and just laughed about it saying, 'If I were in your position, I wouldn't be managing half as well.'

He loved it when he came home from work and the dinner was almost ready with his coffee poured out and his favourite music was playing on the hi-fi with a lovely tumbler of whisky waiting for him to sit down and enjoy. He said,

'You'll never know how wonderful it is to come home and have all these things prepared, and receive a lovely welcome from you.'

Linda was just doing her level best to make him happy because she could never quite believe that he would want to spend the rest of his life with her. Of course, Alma was always totally disparaging when she knew that Linda had tried to do things to make life pleasant for Ralph.

In Linda's mind, she just wanted Ralph to be happy. People would say that they loved visiting them because they could tell how much that they loved each other and they just wanted to share in their joy.

Chapter 44

Linda and Ralph's life together was going on quite nicely with no major hiccups. Linda was developing her counselling service from home and the extra income was most welcome. It was a bit of a shock when Dr Wendy Greengross visited and informed Linda that she had to make her redundant from the position of counsellor with CareMatch.

For Linda, it was a case of wondering what she could turn her talents to next. It felt that it was time to develop lecturing and writing on issues relating to disability. So, Linda set up a disability consultancy service. She lectured for Havering Social Services and also applied for work with the London Boroughs Training Centre where she worked with other colleagues, relating to disability and general care matters.

In 1988, Linda became a fully-accredited Methodist Local Preacher. This was a great victory and a great sense of work well done. Although her father, George, when told of her success with her, "B" and "C" passes equal to candidating for the Methodist Ministry should she wish to do so, said, 'I thought you *knew* the bloody subject?'

Linda was absolutely incredulous that seven years of hard work could be dismissed without so much as a bye your leave.

Linda's work was beginning to be recognised by important members of society. She had been approached to be a counsellor for the disabled on the BBC Television "One in Four" disability programme. At this time, it was not uncommon for Ralph to come home from work to find television technicians and lighting crew recording in their home.

The neighbours found it quite interesting when they saw windows being blacked-out or changing colour in order to depict say, a sunny day, when in fact it was actually pouring with rain outside. It was all very exciting.

Linda and Ralph had been asked to appear on the programme "The Time, The Place" with John Stapelton, but the programme was filmed in Bristol, so they were put up in a five-star hotel that was supposed to be wheelchair-friendly. But it turned out not to be, in fact it was extremely difficult to manage. Linda and Ralph decided to spend a few extra days in Bristol at their own expense, just to see more of the area and to enjoy the surrounding countryside.

On returning home, they both felt quite exhausted. Linda announced to Ralph that, when she died, she wanted money to be put aside to adapt hotel bedrooms to make the life of people with disability much easier to manage. Ralph thought that this would be a good idea so they went to see their solicitor.

His response was, 'I can set up a charitable trust fund but why the hell don't you do this in your lifetime, overseeing the work yourselves, and using your own expertise?'

Linda and Ralph thought that this would be a good idea. So they sought out a group of Christian friends, each with their own particular skills, to oversee the work. That night they put in a total of eleven-hundred-and-fifty pounds between them, to become a registered charity and, on the 18th of August, 1989, "The Lin Berwick Trust" was born.

The trust's purpose was to build self-catering holiday accommodation for the most profoundly disabled people, their families, and their carers. Little did Linda and Ralph realise that their dedication and commitment to the work would become an obsession for more than twenty years.

One year later, in 1990, Linda completed her second book, "Inner Vision", published by Arthur James Ltd. Her first book, "Undefeated", was published by the Epworth Press, ten years earlier in 1980. All of these incidents were helping to mould Linda and assist her with the development of her work.

There were redundancies mentioned by long-term employees of Tate and Lyle Sugar. Linda was struggling to manage at home due to intense back pain and Sciatica. Coping on her own from five-thirty in the morning until Ralph arrived home at around five in the evening, was proving to be a great struggle for Linda.

So Ralph wondered whether it might be the time for him to take early retirement. He discussed terms with his manager and he and Linda looked at the figures to work out whether they would be able to manage financially. As Linda's work was developing with the consultancy, it was thought that they would cope very well. So, it was agreed that early retirement procedures should commence.

Linda had been preaching on a regular basis for some eighteen months and Ralph had taken her to church and coped with getting everything ready for the services very well. Ralph had regularly attended church on a weekly basis since they married in 1987, and they now preferred to worship at Upminster Methodist Church with the Reverend Alan Barker.

Each time they had Holy Communion, Alan would bring bread and wine to the pew where they were sitting. Ralph always shook his head in refusal, so that Reverend Barker then moved on to Linda. One day after Communion, Alan said to Linda, 'Wasn't it wonderful that Ralph took Holy Communion today?'

Linda was incredulous. This man who blatantly announced that he was an atheist had suddenly accepted Christ into his life. She was amazed, 'Why on earth,' she said to Ralph, 'Did you not tell me that you were going to do it? I have prayed every week that you would take Holy Communion and find the Lord and that it would be something that we could both share and rejoice in. But you cut me out.'

Ralph said, 'This was something between me and God.' This of course, Linda respected. Reverend Barker asked Ralph whether he would like to attend membership classes to become a member of the Methodist Church. At first, Ralph refused but later said that he would like to join. He attended the meetings for some six weeks.

The Membership Service would be on the 31st of March, 1991 – a truly Red Letter Day for them both. Members of both their families would attend. In the meantime, it was worked out that Ralph should retire on that actual weekend – all in all, it was a momentous occasion.

Reverend Barker had already asked Ralph if he would like to say something at the service.

'Not on your life!' Ralph said, 'No way! I am not going to make a speech in front of all those people.'

Reverend Barker quite accepted this. But on the day, Ralph suddenly announced that he wanted to say something. He told the congregation how Linda had never forced him into the church. It was his sole decision. He said that he was very grateful for the fact that church had become so much a part of his and Linda's life together. He had come to the church because he felt welcome and now he was no longer on the edge of things but felt fully engaged.

Reverend Barker gave him a huge hug of delight. It was a lovely occasion for all to share but Alma didn't even say congratulations to Ralph – so this icy war was still continuing, even though they had now been married for four years.

Fundraising for the Lin Berwick Trust was continuing in earnest. The "Buy a Brick" campaign took off. There were money boxes in the shape of a house to raise funds for this campaign and it was hard work but progressing, albeit slowly. Indeed, too slowly! After two years of not hard, but consistent campaigning, they had only raised eight-thousand pounds.

The then treasurer wanted to shut down the charity because they weren't raising money fast enough. However, they all decided, except the treasurer, that they wanted to continue.

Reverend Denis Duncan, the charity's vice president, decided that they should organise some prestigious events. The first was lunch on a river boat by the name of "The Silver Sturgeon" on the river Thames, where they held a three-course lunch for seventy-six people. It was a lovely afternoon and everyone enjoyed it, especially those people with disabilities, because they felt that, as the charity was for people with disability, it was right that the people with the disabilities had a high profile to others who also shared in the day, along with the press.

Denis also started to use the profile of the charity as an awareness campaign. On one occasion, he featured Linda's work in the Saturday Telegraph "Meditations", where he just happened to squeeze in Linda's name and address.

Eight-thousand pounds dropped through her letterbox, some of it wrapped in newspaper, which then had to be opened in the presence of either a trusted neighbour or a member of the committee. When people do charitable work, they have to be above board and "squeaky clean". That time when the letters came rolling in was extremely exciting.

Sometimes they'd have as many as forty letters in one day and it enhanced the charity's bank account enormously. Money was raised both on "The Silver Sturgeon" and from the Saturday Telegraph Meditations to the extent that it wasn't too long before they could look for a suitable plot of land. They found it in the village of East Harling in Norfolk.

They had to find twenty-six-and-a-half thousand pounds to buy the plot and it sat there until they could raise enough funds to engage an architect. At this point, the treasurer resigned because he thought that they were being irresponsible. Linda could never understand why he regarded it as irresponsible just to have the land sitting there. As the weeks and months passed by, more and more donations came in, and an architect was duly engaged – she naturally had her own ideas, but Linda and Ralph showed her how they wanted it to be.

Everything was mapped-out by using paper to illustrate things, such as turning circles for the wheelchairs, wide doorways, and the like. The end result was amazing – a bedroom and bathroom that was thirty-seven feet long by fourteen-feet wide to allow for easy access so that a disabled person could be supported by two people if necessary when getting on or off the toilet, or in and out of the bath or shower and so on – the principle being, at least three feet between every item of disability equipment.

There was much discussion as to the type of disability equipment that was needed. Linda said that they must have an overhead ceiling track hoist. Many thought that this was Linda going "over the top" but in the end, they could see her reasoning. In the years since the property was opened in 1997, the overhead ceiling track hoist has had ninety-eight percent usage out of all the specialist items. It was something that Ralph and Linda were deeply proud of and they treasured their time with the charity whilst achieving their goals.

In 1994, Linda was voted one of the RADAR people of the year. Others on that occasion included Dame Vera Lynn who enjoyed the high profile of the occasion. On the afternoon of the presentations, Linda was asked to go to Thames Television and speak about the award – it was completely unexpected but she was becoming more known and every event helped to further the vision of The Lin Berwick Trust and what it was achieving.

By now, Linda and Ralph were working together with the London Boroughs Training Centre to speak about the issues of providing suitable packages of care where the carer is being fully supported by the local authority so that if the carer should leave the client unexpectedly, or die, then the person with disability would receive more support, not less.

Linda was able to show through her work that if you realistically support carers, then they can function much better. But if they become so exhausted that they cannot function, then no one benefits, least of all, the person with the disability.

The building of Berwick Cottage progressed slowly but purposefully. There were some six weeks to go before the official opening but the charity was fifteen-thousand pounds short to complete the project. An appeal was made by Linda through their newsletter and the fifteen thousand pounds arrived within a fortnight. The final touches could now be completed.

Chapter 45

As Berwick Cottage was coming to its victorious conclusion, it was not without an unfolding personal tragedy for Linda and Ralph. Ralph had been struggling with symptoms of anxiety and panic attacks for a number of years. Linda awoke one morning to hear terrible screaming noises emanating from Ralph beside her in bed, along with a sound as though he was blowing bubbles. Linda knew that there was something seriously wrong. She first ascertained whether he could hear her. He made further screeching noises to let her know that he could.

She tried to get out of bed to phone for an ambulance but unfortunately, as she did so, she overbalanced and fell to the floor. She pulled the telephone towards her and dialled nine-nine-nine. When she asked for the ambulance service, she got an extremely helpful young woman on the line. With the tension of the moment, one of her artificial eyes catapulted out, falling several feet away on the carpet and, obviously, Linda couldn't tell where it was.

Linda explained on the telephone to the ambulance controller what had happened while still continuing to relate the details about what was going on with Ralph. Linda could also hear the controller speaking to Ralph's daughter, and to George and Alma, and later, as she explained to the ambulance control centre that this was a genuine call.

Linda asked the controller to emphasise to Alma and George that they should come as soon as possible as she needed help to put her eye back in, and to get washed and dressed in order to go to the hospital with Ralph.

A policeman spoke on the entry phone and Linda released the door and he came into the bedroom with the ambulance staff and helped them get Linda back into her wheelchair. The ambulance staff then took Ralph off to hospital.

As Ralph was being taken away, Linda said to him, 'Don't worry, Darling. I will be with you as soon as I can.' Eventually, Alma called to say that she still hadn't completed her breakfast, or showered, and she was not able to hurry – she said that she would get there "in her own time". She arrived at ten forty-five in the morning. Her first task was to put the eye back in and then help Linda to dress.

They reached Harold Wood Hospital at eleven-fifteen. Linda was champing at the bit because she had no idea what she would find. She found Paul, Ralph's son, sitting in the corridor, crying, saying that his father was going to be disabled now. Tina, Ralph's daughter, was talking to the registrar but she couldn't supply him with any medical records or any medical information other than the fact that Ralph had been suffering from depression.

Linda took the situation in hand and told the doctors how he had been over the intervening months. By now, he was totally conscious and able to speak normally. He asked Paul to leave them so that he and Linda could be alone. When Linda reached his bedside, they just fell into each other's arms and sobbed. He said that he was so frightened because he had no idea what was happening and yes, he could hear Linda speaking to him earlier at the house, but he had been unable to respond. He went through a series of blood tests and general medical examinations, followed by a CT scan. The anxious wait was palpable. Paul kept talking about Ralph being disabled.

Linda said, 'For God's sake, he undoubtedly has a problem but you've already written him off. Why don't *you* just grow up and keep calm?'

Tina said nothing to Linda, except for: 'You were amazing, giving the doctors the low-down about everything. I don't know how you did it?'

'Years of practise,' Linda said.

All the tests came back negative, but he did have postural hypertension causing low blood pressure when he stood up. This would need to be referred back to his GP. By three o'clock that afternoon, Ralph was told that he could go home. Linda was on a knife-edge after what she had experienced and a friend offered to stay the night in case anything else should happen. Linda was very thankful for this practical help and took her friend up on the offer.

But Linda and Ralph were still extremely anxious, and it called into question what was going on, and the fear that they both shared about how they should deal with their lives in the future?

Several months went by. The work was still progressing with the trust and the great day of the official opening was looming, but, before that day, Ralph had another visit to the hospital. Linda said that she was not leaving the hospital until they had been seen by a neurologist to find out what exactly was going on. They had already been seen by several medics over the intervening months but

Linda said to the doctors, 'We have come armed with sandwiches and a flask of coffee. And we are not leaving this hospital until we get some definitive answers.' At first, the doctors said that there was nothing wrong with Ralph.

'Well, I think there *is*?' Linda said.

'Oh, *you* think that you know all the medical answers do you?' The doctors said to Linda in a very disparaging way.

Linda said, 'Well I think that he's got Parkinson's.'

'Oh you do, do you?' The doctors said sarcastically.

Linda said, 'He's shaking, crying, feels depressed, he's right-handed but it's his left hand that shakes, he doesn't smile any more, he cannot whistle, and he's unable to catch up with his own feet when trying to walk.'

The doctors said again, 'Oh you think that you know these things, do you?'

'Yes, I do, and I'm not leaving this hospital until we've seen a neurologist so you might as well sort it out now,' said Linda.

The doctors knew that to try and push them out of the door would be hopeless. Linda wasn't going anywhere. Eventually, a neurologist, a Mr Rudy Capildeo, was summoned. Ralph said to him, 'I've got trouble with my hip and knees. That is why I'm walking strangely.'

Mr Capildeo said to Ralph, 'I don't want you to talk to me, I just want you to walk up and down the room and then come back to me.' Mr Capildeo said to his assistant, 'He's got good heel and toe movement but watch him when he turns.'

Then he told Ralph to stand as he went behind him saying, 'I'm just going to pull you backwards and I will be deliberately taking you off balance – but I won't let you fall. I want you to then pull yourself forward and get yourself into a proper standing position.'

Ralph could not achieve this. Then Mr Capildeo asked Ralph to raise and lower his hands, and move his fingers independently. He examined them very carefully and got his assistant to feel the movement in Ralph's hands. He asked his assistant if she could feel anything. She spoke about the movement in Ralph's wrists. Then he asked Ralph and Linda to come to his desk.

Mr Capildeo said, 'Well, what was it you wanted to speak to me about, Mr Boyce?'

Ralph said, 'I just wanted to tell you about the problems that I'm having with my hips and knees.'

Mr Capildeo said, 'It has nothing to do with your hips. I'm afraid that you have Parkinson's disease which may cause you problems with movement, problems with walking, problems with speech, and may even render you incapable of walking at all, and put you in a wheelchair. I would suggest to you to do whatever you want to do now in life, otherwise it may be too late.'

Linda just felt as though the ceiling had met the floor and everything was closing in. She just yelled, 'Oh God no, not Ralph. Why are you doing this to us, Lord? We have dedicated our lives to You, and this is how You repay us?'

Linda started to cry. Ralph's response was laughter, 'You're not so clever now, are you?'

He said, 'Remember how you got angry with me on Sunday morning about the way we were arguing when I told you that my legs were hurting every minute?'

Linda was just too shattered to care but all she kept doing was apologising to Ralph and thinking that he's at the other side of the desk and she couldn't even reach him.

Mr Capildeo said, 'You've had Parkinson's disease for several years now and I am going to put you on some medication. After three weeks, you will be back where you were some three years ago, and you will be able to function well. But we will book you in for a CT scan and an MRI scan to see the extent of the damage caused by the Parkinson's.'

Linda and Ralph were totally shattered. They went down the hospital corridor without saying a word until they got into the car. Then they just sat holding each other, and sobbed.

Chapter 46

On returning from the hospital, Linda and Ralph were in something of a daze. Linda was terrified about the implications, and what their future might hold – it all looked very bleak.

Linda and Ralph's individual approaches to the Parkinson's diagnosis were completely different to each other's. Linda needed to tell people in order to get the fear out of her system, whereas Ralph never wanted a single person to be told – he just went further and further into his shell. If anyone had visited their home at that time, they would have felt that there was something going very wrong with their relationship.

Alma was not talking to Linda at this time. Linda desperately wanted to tell Alma, but Ralph would not have approved. Linda spoke to Betty, her secretarial help, and asked her to tell Alma and George about Ralph's diagnosis.

The following week, Linda asked Betty what had happened when she told them, 'Nothing at all, dear Lin,' was Betty's response, 'And I am absolutely disgusted that given such a difficult time, she still can't acknowledge Ralph, or your marriage. I cannot understand why she behaves in this way. It is absolutely appalling. You and Ralph have done nothing wrong apart from to fall in love with one another. That love is plain for all to see and speaking personally, I really love being with you both.'

Linda gave Betty a hug and told her how grateful she was for her friendship and how much it meant to Ralph too. Betty said, 'I know you have been really decent to your mother, but she has been nothing short of abusive, such as, when you sent her flowers on Valentine's Day and Easter. And all she did was to swear at you and put the phone down saying, "Thanks for the flowers, but I don't know why you fucking bother?"'

Linda said to Betty, 'I know, and when Mum speaks like that, I don't know why I bother either? I just told her that I didn't have to come down to her level. I then got another torrent of abuse; "You saucy bastard, don't you bloody talk to me like that." I just can't win,' said Linda, 'Mum and Dad have been sent invitations to the open day of Berwick Cottage. Firstly, they denied receiving them so I sent another copy, but I still haven't had any response. It really pains me that they cannot even acknowledge this wonderful achievement.'

When Linda and Ralph got the news about Ralph's condition, they were surrounded by packing cases as they were about to move to Sudbury in Suffolk. Ralph queried what they should do now. Linda's answer was, 'Well, if you are possibly going to end up in a wheelchair, then this property will be too small so it is right that we move to Sudbury although I don't know how we are going to cope with such an enormous garden if you don't want to, or can't physically do it? Then, I don't know how we would manage financially, paying for things like a gardener.'

Ralph had also expressed how much he wanted to move away from Hornchurch because of the pressure that Linda was under with her mother. He asked Philip Richardson, the builder of Berwick Cottage, who lived in Sudbury himself, to look for a suitable property for him and Linda. This was duly found and Philip also got the planning permission to build an extension on the property and because there was a problem with adaptations to the property, Reverend Denis Duncan lent Linda and Ralph forty thousand pounds as an interim deposit to give to the previous owner so that they could be allowed to take up residence earlier. Then the major work could be done.

The removal date was the 1st of May 1997 – the day when Tony Blair swept triumphantly into Downing Street. Linda and Ralph were quite excited about this, having been Labour supporters all of their lives. But when Philip and his wife, Beverley, visited the property, Linda commented about Tony Blair, 'What a victory!'

But Philip and Beverley's response was, 'What a disaster!'

Lin and Ralph felt that their working-class roots were on display for all to see.

Sudbury folk didn't take to incomers readily. Indeed, there was a saying that you were not accepted in Sudbury until you had lived there for more than twenty years. In fact, people were often quite unfriendly and very reserved, unlike the people that Linda and Ralph grew up with in London and Essex. Linda and Ralph held a house-warming party for the neighbours to attend. It was a kind of "get-to-know-you" session.

Linda explained that because of her blindness, there was no point in people just smiling and waving at her because she would not be able to acknowledge them. However, since that day, no one ever did what Linda had asked. They instead, just kept themselves to themselves and carried on in their "comfortable" reservedness, which led Linda to always use the phrase that she was not here to comfort the afflicted, but to "afflict" the comfortable! Which summed up the situation very well.

The only problem was, that with the onset of Ralph's Parkinson's, their life was becoming more insular and lonely. The church does not do long-term illness very well. The church is fine for a short-term problem but when there are disabilities involved, such as Linda's and Ralph's, their friends have to realise that if they want to stay friendly with them both, they have to be in for the long-haul. There is no short-term about it.

Two really great people in this regard, were Stan and Jonquil Johnson. Linda and Ralph had met them when Linda preached at an evening service for blind people – there were some thirty guide dogs in attendance too. Stan and Jonquil were the son and daughter-in-law of Arthur and Dorothy Johnson, who made the very first donation to The Lin Berwick Trust once it became a registered charity. Stan always seemed to be on hand, especially for Ralph.

Linda would frequently call him and tell him that Ralph had had to go to hospital because of yet another urinary infection. Stan would frequently tell Linda not to chase to the hospital because he would get there and wait with Ralph until he was admitted to a ward. That was such a tremendous help because Linda was often at her wits end, wondering just *how* she would cope.

The official opening of Berwick Cottage, the first holiday home of The Lin Berwick Trust, was presided over by its president, Lin Berwick, and its vice president, Sue MacGregor CBE, from Radio 4's "Today Programme" and "The Reunion". Sue cut the blue ribbon and declared, 'Berwick Cottage is now open.'

There were more than one hundred people present at the ceremony with speeches, photographs, and more importantly, a speech from Ralph, who basically never spoke publicly if he didn't have to, largely because Linda was the mouthpiece of the organisation. Ralph said that this was one of the greatest highlights of his life. He was so proud of everything that the trust had achieved and that the charity could not have done it without its supporters. He wanted to thank all of them for this momentous day.

There were one or two special tiles placed on the roof of Berwick Cottage, containing the signatures of those dignitaries who were there on that day. Sue Macgregor put her signature and her good wishes on the tile for posterity. It was the fervent wish that this property would go on to develop an even greater meaning. When Linda said to those gathered that she was not stopping at one cottage, there was an audible collective gasp.

They all knew that Linda would never be satisfied with just one property because the need for more, specialised accommodation was imperative. The charity was to build two further cottages, one in Scotland, the other in Cornwall. These cottages were like the children that Linda and Ralph would have had, had she been able-bodied. When Ralph climbed the ladder to put the final tile on the roof, there were just five people at the ceremony that day who knew the real situation regarding his diagnosis. Linda and Ralph returned home feeling very proud, and elated, but also, extremely sad.

Chapter 47

Alma's birthday was in August and Linda was pondering what she should do about it because Alma had been ignoring all of her phone calls. Linda had even left a message concerning Ralph's diagnosis, which she also ignored. Linda asked Ralph what he thought they should do about Alma's birthday.

'Well, I don't think that it would be helpful to have a meal here,' said Ralph, 'Because she will have too much time to be critical. I think that it would be better if we invited them both out for a meal at the Mill Hotel here in Sudbury – it will be a neutral place and that way, she won't have too much time to complain.' Ralph was always very thoughtful like this, trying to ease the tension for Linda.

The day dawned and George and Alma duly arrived up from Hornchurch to Suffolk at the hotel for lunch. It was a most attractive place which had a working waterwheel set behind a glass screen right in the centre of the hotel restaurant – George was fascinated by this, as he loved to see working machinery. Alma made very little comment and the conversation was difficult and rather stilted. But at least it became more relaxed as the meal went on. It was terrible for Linda to feel this level of anxiety with her own mother.

With the meal over and birthday presents in hand, Alma and George decided to go back to Linda and Ralph's home. After a while, Ralph found an excuse and asked George to come outside to see if he could hear what Ralph thought might be a problem noise in the engine of his car. This left Alma and Linda on their own for the first time in months.

After a while, Alma said, 'I've been ill you know. The doctor made me go for counselling. Of course, it was all about *you* and "*him*". Linda felt like making a comment or two but decided to keep quiet.'

Eventually Alma said, 'Me and the counsellor spent hours talking about you two, and we were going round and round the houses, not getting very far. Then the counsellor asked me if you two were happy. I told him, God help us, yes – they're as happy as a pig in shit.'

'So what was the counsellor's reaction to that?' Linda asked.

'He said, if that is the case, why don't you let them get on with their lives and leave them alone?'

Linda said, 'Ok, what else did you say?'

'I admitted to the counsellor that I would never accept the marriage and hoped it would fail,' said Alma.

'How sad is that!' Linda said.

Alma said, 'the counsellor asked what was the likelihood of that happening? And I told him in no uncertain terms, no bloody chance!'

'And so, what did he say to that?' Linda asked.

'He said, well you've just got to learn to let go and leave them to get on with their lives if they are so obviously happy. Then they will come back to you.'

That little episode over, Linda waited for the next "pearl of wisdom" to be dropped. There was an awkward silence. Then Alma suddenly said, 'I'm sorry to hear about your husband, but that's what you get for marrying an older man.'

Linda felt absolutely furious. She said to Alma, 'Why does everything you say have to have a sting in the tail? Ralph's illness has nothing to do with his age. Yes, older people get Parkinson's and die, but Parkinson's hits young people too.'

Alma said, 'No it doesn't.'

'Well what about Michael J Fox, the actor?' asked Linda, 'He was diagnosed at twenty-six, and there are many other examples. You have no idea of the pressure that we have been under and how much it hurt me that you never even bothered to pick up the phone when Betty told you what had happened to Ralph. I think your lack of concern for us both was appalling.'

Alma said, 'I thought your news would give me another life of caring. I didn't want it and couldn't cope with it.'

Linda said, 'I can understand your feelings totally, but obviously at your age you would never have been asked to fulfil that role again. I could not have put that kind of responsibility on your shoulders, neither would I ever wish to do so.'

Linda was fighting back the tears but Alma never touched her or made any comforting noises or gestures towards her whatsoever. It was so like the isolation that Linda felt when she had to have her second eye removed. It was a stiff-upper-lip mentality at all times – emotion never came into it. George and Ralph came back in to the living room and as George and Alma were preparing to leave, they both thanked Linda and Ralph for the nice day and the presents. George said, 'I love this bloody house that you've got, I'd move here tomorrow if I had the chance.'

Linda thought to herself, '*I hope you never get that chance,*' selfishly needing to protect her and Ralph's interests.

It had been such a relief to move to Suffolk, away from the constant criticism and bickering that had already gone on for ten years since their marriage. This was not helped by Linda's brother John, who had always been jealous of the attention given to Linda by her parents. He used every opportunity to stir the pot and create as much mischief and discontentment as possible. At every turn, he would criticise Linda and Ralph, and what they did with their lives.

Chapter 48

Life was moving on at a fairly even pace. Ralph said to Linda, 'In view of the circumstances regarding your parents, I am not keen to go round there at Christmas, playing happy families and for us all to pretend to be Bon Ami. So I think that we will book up at our favourite hotel in York and have a musical Christmas.'

All the arrangements were made so Linda telephoned her parents on Christmas Eve to ask whether they could drop off the Christmas presents to them before they were to go off to the hotel. George said, 'Your mother doesn't want you here because we have just shampooed the hall carpet and she doesn't want your chair "wheeling" all over it.'

Linda said, 'I've heard some excuses, but this takes the biscuit!'

So as requested, Ralph put the presents outside George and Alma's front door. Linda was really choked-up as they drove away to York.

Alma and George were probably not having a happy time. Linda and Ralph had a very special Christmas with Champagne and music, and a visit to York Minster where the choir were singing. It was just wonderful, drinking in the atmosphere and having some lovely experiences with cocktails as well as some beautiful food. Although all this was very special, Linda still felt sad – Alma could still influence proceedings when she was hundreds of miles away!

On returning to Sudbury, they received a telephone call from Alma. Linda thought that she might get an apology, but no such luck. So, Linda was surprised to hear from her mother who said, 'I'm phoning because your father wants to move to Sudbury.'

'Sudbury!' Linda exclaimed, 'Why does he want to move here?'

'He wants to move,' Alma said, 'Because he misses you.'

'I can't tell you where you should move to,' Linda said as Ralph groaned audibly in the corner of the room. 'I can't tell you where to move to, Mum, but if you want to move here then we must draw a line under all that's gone on in the past and try to begin again. Only then, would I tell you to move. If you don't want to put an end to this terrible atmosphere, then don't bother to come because there has got to be some change. You never refer to Ralph by his name, except to call him, "him" which is not very nice.'

Alma said, 'You can't tell me where I should or shouldn't live.'

'I don't,' Linda said, 'But if you're not going to make an effort, what's the point?'

On returning from the Christmas hotel trip, Linda heard rumours that Alma was telling people that she and George weren't wanted in Sudbury. The next thing that Linda and Ralph heard was that Alma and George had purchased a property in Haverhill, a small market town some thirty-minutes' drive from Sudbury. This property was most unfriendly when it came to managing with a wheelchair. Ralph struggled to get Linda inside the house but it wasn't easy.

George and Alma came over from their new home in Haverhill to visit Linda and Ralph and told them that they had sold their Hornchurch home, making ninety-three-thousand pounds profit. Although Linda had done much to help them financially in the past, all they gave her was five-hundred pounds towards a new wheelchair. Linda understood that they didn't really know the cost of disability equipment and they thought that they were being generous, which was a joke, given what had gone on in previous years.

So it was 1999 and Linda's life was moving on regardless of her parents. She had just been appointed to the BBC Listeners Advisory Council which would take up some considerable time over the next three years. The very next year she was accepted as a Member of the Chartered Institute of Journalists – Linda was absolutely thrilled about this as she loved anything to do with broadcasting and writing.

The completion of Berwick Cottage, together with its success, fired Linda and the committee to continue working towards the next holiday home project. The trust had had a couple of false starts with a new project and they were seriously wondering how and where the next piece of land would reveal itself. The Reverend Denis Duncan and the Community Affairs Department of the Ford Motor Company, decided that they would be very ambitious and have an event on The Royal Yacht Britannia for ninety-six people. This would be a very prestigious occasion – black tie for the gentlemen and evening dress for the ladies. There would be a guided tour around the boat, a Champagne reception, and a three-course meal.

There would be many celebrities in attendance with the principal guests being, The Duke and Duchess of Hamilton, known to Linda and Ralph later, as Kay and Angus. Kay was a wonderful person who had spent much of her life as a Macmillan Nurse, and she had also worked in the hospice movement. She put Linda at her ease immediately and was also very solicitous as to the level of help that she would need during the meal.

All Kay wanted to do was to talk to Linda about her ambitions for the work and generally get to know her. The dining room was particularly beautiful on the Royal Yacht with its twenty-six feet of solid walnut dining table with all its beautiful cut-glass and silver cutlery – a very grand affair. At the end of the evening, Linda gave a passionate speech about how she wanted another holiday home, ideally in the North.

With that wonderful occasion over, it was time to regroup and wonder where this occasion might take them. Three days later, the Duke of Hamilton telephoned Linda and said that he and Kay were so impressed with her speech on The Royal Yacht that Kay thought that they had to do something to help Linda fulfil her dream.

The Duke of Hamilton said to Linda, 'Kay and I walked around our estate to see if there was a place where you could site a property and we think that we have found the perfect spot. We want you to come back up to Scotland next weekend to see what you and Ralph think of it.'

Linda said, 'Whoa! Hold on a moment. How much is all of this going to cost?'

He said, 'What about a peppercorn rent of one-thousand pounds a year for ninety-nine years? We know that you will need at least half an acre.'

Naturally, Linda and Ralph could not make these decisions on their own. They would need to talk to the other trustees and be fully involved when making the decision as to the property. But for now, Linda and Ralph would return to Scotland.

On reaching Direlton, near Edinburgh, it was freezing cold and snowing – December is not the best time to look at land in Scotland. However, the spot that Angus and Kay chose was absolutely beautiful – woodland, grass, and masses of birdsong were its key features. Linda and Ralph were also introduced to an architect, Fred Giffen, selected by the Duke of Hamilton. Fred had completed other building projects on The Duke's estate and he wanted anything that the trust might build, to be in keeping with his other properties on the estate.

Once the trust agreed, the project commenced. The plan showed that it was going to be a most impressive building, incredibly spacious, with a wonderful garden area and conservatory. Once the plans were finalised and it went for planning in the local council, opposition was made by the local residents. Angus and Kay were very aware what was being said.

It was felt that Linda and Ralph, and the Reverend Denis Duncan, should go to the planning meeting to address the fears of the residents. This was duly done. On taking the temperature of the meeting, it was found that seventy-percent of the people represented there did not want the building to be accepted and only thirty-percent thought that it would be a beneficial thing to do. Linda knew that she had her work cut out to convince these people. What they were dealing with was the "nimby" factor (not in my back yard).

They were worried that "these kinds of people" would be running amuck all over their gardens and making a nuisance of themselves and damaging their properties. Linda assured them that this kind of fear was unfounded. Most of the trust people were profoundly disabled and they would be incapable of achieving what the meeting feared. There were many questions about the facilities in the proposed property such as, why would an overhead track hoist be needed, surely just helping them into bed would suffice?

Linda explained that it wasn't as simple as that and she made one firm point by saying, 'Your attitude towards a disabled person today, might be someone else's attitude towards you tomorrow because one never knows from minute to minute, how one's life can suddenly change in a heartbeat – being able-bodied one minute, and profoundly disabled and incapacitated the next.'

She also told them about her life and her difficulties, and how her life had been altered by the loss of her sight. Then, a further vote was taken, and to Linda's utter amazement, the temperature in the room had totally changed – it was now seventy-percent for the project, and thirty-percent against. But, at the point of leaving the meeting, Linda and Ralph had no idea whether planning permission had been granted or not.

Chapter 49

After the Council meeting, Linda and Ralph arrived back at the hotel and tried to have an early night because they knew that it would be difficult travelling the next day. Just how difficult they were to find out to Linda's cost, and Ralph's extreme anxiety. They were told to check in for their flight at Edinburgh Airport by eleven in the morning. The flight was due to take off at one-fifteen.

It was the policy that Linda would board the plane before the other passengers to give her enough time to manage the journey down the plane's aisle and get herself seated. On boarding the plane, Ralph noticed that the seat configuration was different to that of the flight that they had arrived on. Linda always sat in the area designated for "mothers with nursing babies". It normally allowed for more leg room at the front of the plane as it allowed mothers with nursing babies to be comfortable.

However, the gap between the bulkhead and the first row of seats had been narrowed down to accommodate a small serving area for teas, coffees and so on. Ralph told the crew that Linda would not be able to sit in the seat allocated to her because she wouldn't be able to get past the gap using her tripod sticks. Because of the way that she leant forward, her head would touch the overhead lockers before she could turn to get into the seat.

The crew member said, 'Don't be silly, of course you can get in. The space is not too tight.'

Ralph insisted, but it was to no avail. The crew members started pushing Linda into the gap between the seats. Due to Linda's Cerebral Palsy Quadriplegia, any sudden movement which is not expected, caused her muscles to become rigid, causing spasms, rendering her unable to move. Linda asked them not to push but they continued. The more the crew members pushed, the more Linda's body went into spasm, and she could not move.

Eventually, her knees started to buckle, with her feet now pointing in opposite directions. Linda's knees were collapsing more and more. Ralph was trying to support her by taking her weight and holding her off the floor but unfortunately, the pain was so severe that she just fell into a heap with her legs trapped under the seating. The crew members tried to get her up, but it was proving impossible. Linda was now wedged and could not move.

In the end, the crew members came into the seat behind, and dragged Linda out from underneath the seat by her knickers, into the gap between the next row of seats – some of the passengers then joined in, also trying to drag her out by her clothing. Linda was crying both from the pain, and the embarrassment. She hated the indignity of what they were doing but her body was still wedged tightly.

As a result of the commotion, the plane lost its take-off slot and the passengers and crew were not happy. Eventually, Linda was dragged into the central aisle. Crew members put her arms above her head and bent her knees towards her chest. As Linda had had a hamstring transplant on both of her legs she could not bend them more than thirty degrees – that is, until the crew decided to "bend" them for her. She was in screaming agony and Ralph was asking the crew to leave her alone so that he could try and get her up from the floor.

Eventually, Linda was landed on a seat by the exit doors. Ralph asked the Captain whether he would allow Linda to stay there but he refused because passengers with disability were not permitted to sit by the exit. The Captain said that she could not remain there and that she would have to be taken off the plane. Linda looked as though she had just crawled out of a dustbin.

The beautiful new suit that she wore for the Council meeting looked totally dishevelled. Her skirt buttons were undone, her blouse was undone, and her jacket was undone. Her hair was all over the place, looking as though she had been pulled through a hedge backwards. Linda was crying as she was carried off the plane. Just at that point, somebody ran up to her and said, 'Miss Berwick, Miss Berwick,' to which a crew member replied to the person, 'No, mate, you've got the wrong person. This lady's name is not Berwick.'

Linda replied to the crew member, 'It's alright, professionally I am known as Lin Berwick.'

The stranger then said, 'I was one of the Council members that you met at the meeting a couple of days ago. I want you to know that we granted you your planning permission. We thought that your presentation was marvellous.'

Linda was thrilled to hear this but at that moment she didn't really care. All she was experiencing was terrible pains in her legs, back, and arms. Because the plane had missed the slot for take-off, they now had to wait until three o'clock in the afternoon. The airline offered Linda and Ralph some vouchers so that they could have something to eat and drink.

When trying to get on the next plane, Linda and Ralph were told that because they were now officially "stand-by" passengers, as their original seats could not be taken, they would have to sit in the second row of seats. This was terrible because the space between this row of seats was even narrower than that of the row on the first plane.

The only difference now was that Linda was in total agony and her knees had started to swell. The Go Airlines crew boarded Linda in her wheelchair from the rear of the plane from the trolley platform, and then she was asked to get out of her chair and walk to the seat. This was almost impossible. She was in so much pain that she knew that as soon as she had to negotiate getting her tripod sticks and her body in the very narrow gap between the seats, it would fail.

Sure enough, within three steps, her knees gave way again, and she fell to the floor like before. Crew members dragged her to her feet. Two of them held her by the shoulders, and another tried to pull her over the top of the seat in front. Naturally, with this harsh treatment, she just fell to the floor like a sack of potatoes. The crew proceeded to drag her out yet again, one pulling her arms above her head, the other bending her legs and dragging her body across the floor.

As the plane's intercom was linked to the airline desk, Linda's cries and screams could be heard over the speakers in the terminal building. On hearing this, one of the staff came rushing over from the terminal building and got onto the plane, shouting, 'What the hell are you doing to this poor passenger, we know from her medical records that she has spinal difficulties, has had back surgery, and a hamstring transplant on both of her legs.'

She knelt down on the floor and said to Linda, 'All I can say to you, my dear, is that I humbly apologise. My husband has spinal injury so I know something of the pain that you must be in.'

Linda was carried unceremoniously off the plane yet again and had missed yet another take-off slot! It was now a quarter-to-four in the afternoon. Linda and Ralph were then told that they would have to wait until twenty-past-ten before they could board another plane. Linda's knees were continuing to swell. She had no idea as to the extent of the damage but what she did know was that she hurt like hell.

There was a discussion as to whether Go Airlines should provide a car and drive her from Edinburgh to Sudbury in Suffolk. But Linda felt that she couldn't face a seven-hour journey on top of what she'd already been through. They decided to stick it out and wait for the next plane.

Ralph said to the airport staff, 'This time, I'm setting my conditions. I want to come to the plane and see exactly where you are putting Lin, and she must be boarded before all the other passengers. She cannot cope with crowds of people pushing and shoving, trying to get past.'

Ralph went with a member of the airport staff to look at the seat that Linda was going to be put in. Ralph came back and said, 'I think you'll manage it, Lin.'

Linda was boarded in her chair for the third time. It was the same pilot as the first flight that they tried to take earlier that afternoon! He apologised to Linda and said that he knew what had gone on and he was extremely sorry and that he would be writing a full report. Ralph said to him, 'Please let me handle Lin myself.'

Ralph asked Linda to stand and walk towards him using her sticks. She was in agonising pain and could barely reach the seat, and almost fell into it. But at least, she now knew that she would be going home.

On reaching Stansted Airport, Linda and Ralph found to their dismay that the man who helped take off wheelchair users with his specially adapted truck, had gone home and there was no means of getting Linda down the steps. The reason for this was that she'd had two flight cancellations. When the other passengers had alighted, Ralph was looking out of the window of the plane, 'Lin,' he said, 'If you could see what I can see, you just wouldn't believe it?'

They delivered to the plane, a fire engine with a turntable ladder, together with twenty fire crew members. Four of them bounded up the steps of the plane and one of them said, 'Well, who's this woman that can't get out of her seat then?'

Ralph said, 'It's my wife. Who's in charge here?'

But no one answered him. Ralph pointed to each of them individually and said, 'I'm just about fed up with what has gone on here today. It is disgusting. Now,' he said pointing to each one individually, '*You, you, you* and *you*, get your hands off of my wife, and leave *me* to put her in her chair and then *you* can carry her down the steps between you.' This was duly carried out and they landed Linda safely onto the tarmac.

As they got into the terminal building, Linda and Ralph were told that their luggage had been lost between the three planes – this was the straw that broke the camel's back. Linda and Ralph were utterly dismayed. They had to wait until the luggage was found, then they were allowed to leave.

They reached home at one-fifteen on Monday morning. Linda just managed to stand then collapse onto her bed, but the next day she couldn't move. She called the doctor and she was given strong pain-killers. She had photographs taken of the bruising on her back, knees, and legs. The following week she went to meet her physiotherapist who said, 'My God, what have they done to you? Your spine is so twisted that I don't know where to start!'

His immediate response was to slap a full bin-liner of ice down Linda's back to bring out the bruising and more on her knees to reduce the swelling. Go Airlines refunded the cost of the flights and sent Linda the biggest bouquet of flowers that she had ever seen. It was truly massive. Linda telephoned Go Airlines and thanked them for the flowers and the refund but told them that they would be hearing from her lawyer. The lady at the other end of the phone said, 'Yes, I thought we would.'

That legal consultation started what was to be a four-and-a-half-year battle which was finally resolved out of court. The settlement totalled one-hundred-and-forty-thousand-pounds. Forty-thousand pounds was for incurring public humiliation, and one-hundred-and-seventy thousand was awarded to cover Linda's care costs for six years. The reason why Linda didn't have a better pay-out was because they said that due to her husband Ralph's Parkinson's disease, she would have needed care within the next ten years because he would have died anyway.

Actually, one-hundred-and-seventy-thousand pounds for the level of pain and suffering, and the fact that Linda could no longer walk after this incident, was insulting. Her care needs should have been covered until she died but now, she was to struggle for the rest of her life, enduring the now increased incalculable costs for care, not forgetting the increased pain and suffering which far exceeded the one-hundred-and-seventy-thousand pounds settlement.

She also had to undergo post-traumatic stress counselling because she found the experience so traumatic. She was asked by the counsellor what she could see on that day as she lay on the floor of the aircraft. Linda said, 'Well I can't see anything, can I?'

He replied, 'Yes, you can, you know exactly what happened on that floor, and how *you* felt.'

Linda said, 'Well, I was in so much pain that I thought that I was having a heart attack.'

'So what colour did you see?' The counsellor asked.

Linda said, 'Everything was black and grey and due to the pain that I had in my chest, muscles, back, and knees, I was absolutely convinced I *was* having a heart attack.'

The irony was that Linda had gone to Scotland to seek planning permission for a new holiday home which would help hundreds of people with disabilities in the future, but, due to her injury, her own life was irrevocably changed forever, even though she had only striven to help others in need.

When Linda and Ralph told Alma and George what had happened, Alma said, 'Well that's what you get for doing stupid things like getting planning permission for a house that is never going to happen. And don't think you'll ever get a response from Go Airlines – you won't stand a chance.'

Linda said, 'Well it was so awful that I think I ought to.'

Alma said, 'Mark my words, you *won't* succeed!'

But of course, she was proved wrong.

Chapter 50

After the Go Airlines accident the previous year, Linda hoped that things would get better in 2002, even though she was still in tremendous pain from the incident, and was already feeling incredibly stressed with all the legal implications. Linda was nominated for the "Health and Social Care Awards" in the category of "Outstanding Achiever" in the field of social care.

Linda was presented with the runner-up prize of two-thousand pounds for her work with The Lin Berwick Trust by His Royal Highness, The Prince of Wales. In that same year, Linda was also nominated for "Woman of the Year"—the reception was to be held at the Savoy Hotel in London. Linda needed help from a carer because Ralph would not be allowed to attend as it was a women-only event.

The carer was in a panic as to what she should wear as she normally lived in jeans and a T-shirt. So Linda paid for an outfit to be made which the carer chose and absolutely loved. Unfortunately, Linda's nomination only came within the first ten nominees, so she didn't get an official award. The winner was the athlete Paula Radcliffe, who was currently in America so the award was received by Paula's mother.

In July, Linda received a letter informing her that she had been nominated for an Honorary Doctorate in Civil Law by the University of East Anglia and Suffolk College. This would necessitate the usual wearing of "Cap and Gown" which would obviously present a great many problems for Linda. All her clothes had to be specially made due to her body shape. So, Suffolk College arranged for a Mr Ron Brooks from the ceremonial gown-makers "Ede & Ravenscroft" to go and speak to Linda and measure her for this very prestigious gown.

Marilyn Watsham, the deputy director of Suffolk College, was to propose Linda's nomination. She would speak to the public on the day of Linda's nomination and there would be a special reception just for Linda for some forty-five guests. It was all very nerve-wracking but splendid. After the reception, Linda was asked to go into the robing room to change into the doctorate gown.

It looked amazing – navy blue with a beautiful silk, magenta-coloured hood, together with a strange black velvet hat, adorned with gold tassels. As Linda came out of the robing room, the guests at her private reception started to cheer and applaud. Alma came up to Linda and said, 'If you don't mind my saying so, you look bloody ridiculous in that hat.'

Linda responded, 'I probably do, Mum, but you know, I don't care one little bit. I just feel so proud that there is so much love and respect from Suffolk College and from all of the people here.'

The awards assembly hall was full of people – all very happy and excited that their own family members were to receive a degree that day.

Marilyn had previously asked Linda what would be the most important thing that she could do to make her feel better about the ceremony. Linda said that she wanted to receive her degree certificate on the stage in the same way as all the other participants. Marilyn took Linda's request to heart and arranged for a hydraulic platform to bring Linda from the floor to the stage level in her wheelchair.

Linda then had to reply to Marilyn's nomination for fifteen minutes – for this, she received a standing ovation from the hundreds of people in attendance. It was daunting because she had to read her script from the Braille text that she had created herself. Linda received her honorary doctorate from the Vice Chancellor of Norwich University before she responded to Marilyn's nomination.

In her speech, Linda told how she struggled with her early education and how she'd had to fight to gain employment. She talked of the prejudice that so many people with disability faced and how important it was to break down the barriers of the perceived disability as most people do not expect those with disability to 'achieve.' Linda said how much she would have wished to have the joy of a university education herself and how important it was for those present to make the most of every opportunity.

She also said how proud she was to receive an honorary doctorate in civil law and thanked everyone for all their help, especially Marilyn Watsham, in enabling this day to be such a success and for being a wonderful friend in the intervening years. The degree recipients were very responsive and indeed, Ralph, who was sitting next to Linda on the platform, arranged that as others came up to receive their degree, those who wished to shake hands with Linda, could do so as Ralph gave Linda a "tap" in the middle of her back so that she put her hand out at the right moment to shake the hand of the other participants.

There were some one-hundred-and-twenty-three degree scrolls handed out that afternoon and Linda shook the hand of all but two. It all went without a hitch, thanks to Ralph. At the end, more photographs were taken and Linda also had a picture taken as she signed the register for her degree.

There was a reception in a huge marquee for everyone to enjoy. Alma came up to Linda and said, 'I suppose I should congratulate you?'

Linda said, 'Please yourself.'

Alma said, 'I suppose I better give you this,' handing Linda a gift of a gold chain, 'But your speech was far too long.'

Linda replied, 'I was asked to reply for exactly fifteen minutes and that was exactly what I did – fifteen minutes, on the button. And from the response I got, I don't think there was a problem?'

Bev and Brian, Linda's friends from Cheshire, had come down just for the occasion. They had decided to pick Alma up from her home, bring her to the college, and then take her back home afterwards. They told Linda later that from the moment she got into the car, until the moment she returned home, her comments were pure vitriol. She did nothing but complain saying that Linda's aspiration to build a home in Scotland was a complete waste of time and that the doctorate ceremony with all of its pomp was utterly stupid and another complete waste of time.

Linda found this extremely hurtful but as far as she was concerned, it detracted nothing from the very special occasion. George had been left behind to look after their King Charles Spaniel – she was a sweet little dog but she hated being left so George would spend hours cuddling her on his lap. When Alma came back home, he only had her comments to judge Linda's occasion and sadly, all she could do was to find fault.

Chapter 51

In February, 2003, Ralph and Linda received an invitation from Babergh District Council in Suffolk to say that they were recipients of the Babergh District Council Community Achievement Awards in recognition of service to the local community. There would be a reception at which their awards would be jointly given, along with other community achievers.

Linda was so pleased about this because Ralph had worked tirelessly with her for many years but with special emphasis from 1987 when he chaired The Lin Berwick Trust. He did this until Parkinson's disease got the better of him and he was forced to resign. The Babergh awards ceremony was a lovely occasion for both of them. There was a very pleasant reception with Mark Murphy from BBC Radio Suffolk in attendance, accompanied by his wife, Lesley Dolphin, also a broadcaster from Radio Suffolk.

In May, a letter arrived for Linda – its postal address was 10, Downing Street, London. It was signed by Tony Blair, the then Prime Minister, saying that Her Majesty The Queen wished to honour Linda with an MBE in recognition of services to the disabled.

As Ralph read this falteringly, Linda said with absolute incredulity in her voice, 'What did you say?' She made him start the letter from the beginning. They were both laughing and crying at the same time.

Linda said, 'I'm sad that the award couldn't be given jointly because you have been amazing, giving so much time to the cause and the work of The Lin Berwick Trust.'

The first problem that Linda had to deal with was filling out the form, stating her acceptance, because it had to be done in complete confidentiality. Liz Bell, Linda's part-time carer, would be visiting that day and starting a period of work so she was sworn to secrecy, and then Linda put her signature to the letter. Linda said to Ralph, 'We must celebrate this.'

'How?' Ralph said, 'When we cannot tell anyone until the 13th of June at nine in the evening, just before the listing goes to the London Gazette and The Times, which is the formal announcement of the event.'

Linda said, 'All we have to do is to organise a party and when people ask what it's for, we tell them it's a surprise, and we don't deviate from that.'

Later, Linda found out that it was the Reverend Denis Duncan who had done all the behind the scenes work in order for her to get the recognition. Naturally, Linda rang the Reverend Denis Duncan because she knew that he had made these approaches to the office and many people had supported him in this endeavour – some sixty-six letters of nomination were sent in support of Linda. When Linda was told of the final listings she was amazed, because there were so many people who were highly influential and prestigious.

The Methodist Church was a great supporter of this application. Denis was absolutely thrilled because it had taken eight years from start to finish before the award was finally given. In fact, Jillian Tallon, Denis's partner, had been awarded an MBE some years earlier so Linda, Ralph, and Liz Bell set about working out a guest list and how they could deal with the logistical problems of putting on a surprise party.

The first problem was Linda and Ralph's garden. It was mostly wilderness – bits of work had been done here and there, but Linda and Ralph could never catch up with it, even though they had thrown quite a bit of money at it. Some so-called gardeners were not always honest. One such female gardener, told Linda that she had worked four hours a week over a number of months, but Linda later confronted this woman because people had frequently asked her when her gardener was coming!

Linda would say that she had already been. Once Linda confronted the gardener, she admitted that she hadn't been doing the garden but she had just taken the money every week anyhow. She realised that she had been totally dishonest, and so returned the money to Linda. This did nothing to help Linda's confidence in human nature. Indeed, she was extremely disappointed that people could behave in this way to a blind person.

Sadly, this kind of thing happens quite frequently when a person is seen as a vulnerable adult. It is pretty soul-destroying when some people think that because a person is sat in a wheelchair, their brains are in their backside when the reality is, that nothing could be further from the truth. Linda spoke to a landscape gardener friend of hers who offered to tidy up a large portion of the garden by putting a marquee on it and decorating it with flowers and plants on the inside, and pot plants on the outside. Then the wilderness of the garden didn't seem nearly so bad.

Linda and Ralph had made provision for sixty-six guests to share in a buffet-style sit-down meal. Liz was instrumental in organising the food with a friend of hers who happened to be a chef. Linda then booked the caterers and it was all systems go for a lovely evening on the 14th of June, 2003. On the day before, once it reached nine in the evening, Linda was legally allowed to tell people about her MBE. The first people she rang were her parents.

She rang and Alma answered the phone, 'Can you and Dad get to separate telephone extensions so that you can both hear me properly at the same time?' said Linda.

Once they were both on the line, she said to them, 'You know the surprise party that we're having tomorrow? Well, it *is* for a special reason. Her Majesty The Queen has chosen to make me a Member of the British Empire, so I will now be, Dr Lin Berwick MBE.'

Alma said, 'Oh darling, that's wonderful,' as she was laughing and crying at the same time. Then George, who was quite hard of hearing said, 'Isn't that the lowest award that you can get?'

Lin replied exasperatedly, 'Yes, Dad, it *is* the lowest. But you know, I'm still bloody proud of it. I thought that at the very least, you would have offered me your congratulations?'

George replied, 'Of course I'm bloody proud of you, you silly cow!'

Linda just couldn't believe it. All George seemed interested in was what the food was going to be like at the party the next day. When Linda told him that it was roast beef, roast chicken, and salmon, together with all kinds of side dishes and desserts, he said, 'Oh, that's alright then.'

Linda felt amazed at his lack of enthusiasm with not a word of congratulation. She found it terrible that when she'd striven to do so well and be successful with all sorts of achievements, it was obvious that nobody really cared.

On the morning of the party, the local press were knocking at Linda's front door at eight in the morning because the local journalist had been given the story after nine o'clock the previous evening. So they wanted to arrange a time for a reporter and a photographer to carry the story in the East Anglian Daily Times, The Sudbury Mercury, and The Suffolk Free Press. They were arranging when each of them could take photos. Then, Anglia Television arrived with an outside broadcasting unit and Linda was interviewed by one of their usual presenters. So there was much going on.

More and more items of food and decoration were arriving at the marquee, and then the alcohol turned up, not that Linda drank a great deal, but it was the height of summer so it would be quite hot and drinks would be welcome. Around five-thirty to six, the guests started to arrive, some had already guessed what the surprise party was for because they got onto the internet to see whether Linda's name was in the list of honours, and of course, it was.

Alma and George arrived with their dog, Lucy, who constantly stayed on George's lap – she would frequently be given tasty morsels of food which she devoured greedily. Judy, a former publican and Linda's current trusted cleaner, was in charge of the bar. A board was put over the king-size bed and all the alcoholic drinks were served through the window in what was the carer's bedroom.

Other friends brought musical entertainment. Everyone had a lovely time. Indeed, there was so much food left over, that many turned up the next day for a cold lunch. It all seemed rather dull when everything was dismantled and taken away. Linda would have loved to have kept the marquee so that she could sit in the shade on a hot day.

There were quite a few speeches made and Linda presented Alma with a lovely basket of flowers to say thank you for all the effort that she had put in over the years. However, Linda got no response from Alma whatsoever, and people told her sometime later, that Alma was quite miserable with a fixed-smile the whole evening, and never really joined in.

Chapter 52

Linda and Ralph were now experiencing huge financial difficulties regarding the paying for care and having resources that were pretty near depleted. The legal wrangling went on with Go Airlines and the stress levels for both Linda and Ralph were huge. At one point, Ralph said that he needed help to have something that would pick Linda up off the floor to help with the standing and getting her into her wheelchair.

Linda went to a mobility assessment centre and tried some disability aids but she found the experience far too painful and also too emotionally distressing. She did not want to have to be hoisted – for her, that would be the beginning of the end and life would have no purpose. There were many medical tests and various examinations on behalf of Go Airlines. One person on Linda's side, specialised in Cerebral Palsy. She visited Linda and Ralph, and spent most of the day with them, looking at every aspect of their lives and their struggles.

Linda was totally worn out with the struggle and let the specialist know that, in no uncertain terms. The specialist tested muscle strength, watched Linda trying to stand and walk, and this was an almost impossible task without Linda being in total agony. The specialist's suggestion was that Linda ought to be referred to a pain-control clinic.

She told Linda and Ralph that there was now some wonderful equipment where the medication could be controlled down the telephone line into a device which was fitted into Linda's back. It all sounded pretty drastic and what Linda was more concerned about was the effect of the drugs that were disadvantaged by the side-effects and nausea from them.

But perhaps one of the most important pieces of information that she gave Linda was that her pain level could be helped dramatically by having a dog. Linda and Ralph said it would be wonderful but, with Ralph's deterioration of his Parkinson's, how could that be achieved?

The specialist told them of an organisation called The Cinnamon Trust. The Cinnamon Trust walk the dogs and can also arrange to look after them if the owners either cannot do it for themselves, or their circumstances are such that they cannot look after their animals for the short or the long term for any number of reasons, such as hospitalisation and the like.

Linda and Ralph thought that The Cinnamon Trust was a tremendous organisation because it was plugging a well-needed gap and still giving people the companionship of the animals that they loved so much. Although Linda and Ralph thought that this would be fantastic, they felt that with everything else that was going on, they couldn't contemplate having a dog.

However, life takes some very strange twists and turns, sometimes in the most unexpected ways. Linda was still doing her counselling on a regular basis, despite all the other pressures that she was under.

One day, a person came to her who had lost three members of her family in very close succession. Linda spent several weeks talking to her about her sadness. Then, one week, she told Linda that she had got a chocolate Cocker Spaniel puppy. Harvey was eight-weeks old and absolutely beautiful. A couple of weeks later she told Linda that she was struggling with her asthma, due to Harvey's puppy-fur.

Eventually, the doctor told her that either her health would suffer, or the dog would have to go. She was heartbroken. In view of what the specialist had told Linda about The Cinnamon Trust, Linda wondered whether she and Ralph might take Harvey on. By now, he had been put in the local kennels because of this lady's asthma. Linda felt so sad for Harvey. On Easter Monday, 2004, Harvey was brought round to Linda and Ralph by the owner to see if they could manage him.

They asked the owner if they could give him a ten-day trial which would then help her pay for the kennel fees and establish whether Harvey could adjust to Linda and Ralph. At the time, Linda and Ralph had visitors – Alma and George, and other friends who were all sitting in the garden. As soon as they saw Harvey, they were all immediately smitten, and all wanted a cuddle! Linda waited in the house to receive him quietly. Even though it was only to be a ten-day trial, Linda and Ralph had purchased a puppy basket, drinking and feeding bowls, and some doggie-toys along with some puppy food. Ralph bought Harvey in to Linda and she was able to have a little cuddle.

He snuggled-up to her really closely and put his head around her neck. It was wonderful, for Linda had not had this joy since she got her poodle in 1962, some forty-two years previously.

Harvey was altogether different. He was such a gentle little soul. Eventually, Ralph put Harvey down on the floor and he started to explore his new surroundings. In the end, he did four agitated circuits of the kitchen, and then went under Linda's wheelchair and stayed there for a couple of hours. He was obviously quite nervous with all the initial attention that he had had on his arrival.

Eventually, Ralph coaxed him out from under Linda's wheelchair and gave him a drink which was lovely and cold – Linda loved hearing him happily lapping it up. A little later, Ralph gave him some food. Then it was time to put him into his new basket and settle him down for the night. Linda and Ralph put a hot water bottle into his basket to keep him warm. Ralph looked in on him several times during the night and he happily hopped out of the basket and onto Ralph's lap. The problem was, he did not want to go back into the basket, but Ralph insisted, as this too, was part of his new training programme.

It was wonderful to have this gorgeous little creature padding around. He was so tiny and looked as though his ears and his feet were too big for his tiny body. He looked as though he had carpet slippers on, where he'd got ten-weeks of puppy-fur on them. It was wonderful for Linda to hold him, and to make a fuss of this lovely little dog.

Harvey could be quite quick at gobbling his food down and Ralph was worried that he would eat it too quickly and possibly choke, so he started by lifting his food bowl off the floor, and putting it on the side for a few minutes, then making Harvey sit, before telling him to go forward for his food. This particular lunchtime, Linda and Ralph put Harvey in the kitchen and were having lunch with their guests. The next thing that they heard was a whimpering and a scratching at the door.

Ralph suddenly threw open the door, only to find Harvey standing there. Ralph said to Harvey, 'What do you think you're doing?'

Of course, everyone in the room were cooing at Harvey telling him how beautiful he was and picking him up for a cuddle.

The next day Linda and Ralph took Harvey out in the car, wondering how he'd travel. They needn't have worried because he absolutely loved it – just sitting in his basket as good as gold.

By now, Linda and Ralph had already said that they would love to keep him. He learnt very quickly and was soon toilet-trained. Some weeks later, Ralph took Harvey for a walk, but Harvey was so boisterous that he pulled Ralph over and Ralph fell to the ground into oncoming traffic. The people stopped their cars and helped Ralph back up onto his feet, but it obviously frightened him. He wasn't worried for himself, but only for Harvey.

He said to Linda later, 'I don't know whether I'll be able to do this because as he gets bigger, he will also get stronger, and he will probably cause me to overbalance again.'

This is where Linda suggested an approach to The Cinnamon Trust. Linda thought that they might reproach her for having a dog but they were quite marvellous about it. Eventually, a lady from the trust called Vivienne Hazel, came to meet Harvey. She instantly fell in love with him and it wasn't long before that love affair became mutual – Harvey absolutely adored her right up until the time he had to be put to sleep in 2019.

Linda and Ralph had a large fish pond with Koi carp. It also had a fountain, lots of water lilies, lighting, and ultra-violet filters for the water. Suddenly, Harvey became interested and it wasn't long before he came in to the house, totally bedraggled. Ralph would say, 'Oh the poor little thing, he's absolutely soaked, he must have fallen into the pond?' He would dry him with a large bath towel. And almost every time Harvey went outside, he came back soaked to the skin.

Linda said to Ralph, 'I would suggest that you stand in the shadows outside and watch, because I think Harvey is doing it deliberately.'

Ralph did this and found that Harvey would back himself up against the wall, then take a running leap into the middle of the pond, swim around, and then get himself out to go back indoors, absolutely soaking wet!

'You little devil!' Ralph said to Harvey. But they could never really be cross with Harvey because he was so loving and gorgeous. Ralph said, 'Well, the question is now, what do we do with the pond?'

Linda knew what she wanted to do with it because the pond was absolutely no use to her. She couldn't see the fish and was worried that she might go too close to the edge and fall into the pond herself. It was difficult because Linda had bought all the equipment for the pond, paid someone to dig it all out and put the pond liner in along with all the other bits and pieces to make it look attractive.

So, although Linda would have been quite happy to get rid of it, it had to be Ralph's decision because he loved it. He asked Linda what she thought.

She said, 'Well, I know that you love the pond, but for me, it's pointless. And I think that you and I would benefit far more from a living, responsive animal like Harvey, to that of a fish.' So it was decided to fill in the pond. Harvey was mystified and kept wandering around where the pond used to be. Eventually, it was all put back to normal. Linda was hoping that the pond would get rid of a great deal of the garden area, solving some of the problems of garden maintenance, but it wasn't to be.

Ralph did what little he could in this vast garden. He loved growing his runner beans, tomatoes, and he had bought some asparagus plants a couple of years earlier so they were now established. He had noticed one morning that the asparagus tips were just poking through the netting. He discovered that all of his asparagus tips had been lovingly devoured by Harvey! Ralph was utterly dismayed. He took Harvey over to the plants saying, 'What did you do, you bad boy?'

But Harvey was obviously more content with the tasty morsels he had in his tummy. A few weeks later, Linda and Ralph had gone again to the local garden centre and purchased a clump of carnation plants.

On returning home, Ralph said, 'I'll just water these well before lunch and then we'll put them in.' However, Harvey had other ideas. When Linda and Ralph were in the house having their lunch, Harvey happily ate forty-nine of the carnation plants, leaving just one!

Again, Ralph was incredulous, but Harvey obviously had a stomach ache because he pulled off a large sprig of Lavender, then sat at Linda's feet where she couldn't reach him, and ate it. It smelled beautiful but the consequences might have been disastrous.

All Harvey ever wanted to do was play – if he could get involved with something, he was happy. Linda had a carer who had a Jack Russell that she insisted on bringing to the home. Taffy and Harvey got on extremely well. It was obvious that Taffy was the leader. If there was any mischief to be had, Taffy was there. At one time, they started digging together – Taffy was encouraging Harvey to dig under the fencing.

When they had dug down sufficiently so that they could escape, they went missing. Harvey was found in one of the gardens further along the road, but Taffy did not return for several hours. He had this ability to climb up on his hind legs and knock the door knocker in order to be let in. Linda found this highly amusing but he was quite naughty. Harvey was incredibly good with his toys, never damaging them but when Taffy was on the scene, the squeaky toys were suddenly punctured and Harvey was somewhat bewildered that they then didn't make the usual sounds anymore.

Unfortunately, the carer never bothered to replace them.

Another time, Harvey went out into the garden and picked runner beans off the plants and sat and ate them too. Ever since he was small, he always loved runner beans, but only if they were thinly-sliced by his doting mummy!

Harvey was such a happy little dog and he was into everything. If anyone was sitting outside in the garden and Harvey didn't get enough attention, he would put one of his balls in the bucket, then take hold of it, turn the bucket with the water in it onto its side so that the ball rolled out. He would then put the bucket back up into a standing position and start the process all over again until someone took notice!

There are countless events that could be recounted like these but the most important was the love and the joy Harvey gave to Linda and Ralph. He was to play such an important part when visiting Ralph when he was in a care home in later life. That would never be forgotten. As far as Linda was concerned, the lady who came to her for counselling and subsequently gave her Harvey for much less than she paid for him, was a guardian angel to both her and Ralph – that act of kindness brought so much happiness and joy to them both.

Chapter 53

Marilyn Gaunt, formerly a researcher on "This is Your Life", was now well-known as a documentary filmmaker. She had produced many well-known and critically-acclaimed films such as "Women Behind the Veil", "Kelly and her Sisters", and "Class of '62", to name but a few. Marilyn kept in touch with Linda and Ralph over the years. Indeed, Marilyn filmed Linda and Ralph's wedding in 1987. She had also made an approach to Linda and Ralph back in 2002 to find out whether they would agree for her to periodically visit them at their home to film various aspects of their lives, culminating in a real-life documentary.

This was quite a difficult thing for Linda and Ralph to agree to because of the way that the film was made over a long period of time. It was incredibly invasive, showing the home situation, along with all the difficulties that Ralph was currently facing with his rapidly advancing Parkinson's, and Linda's stress at having to cope with her own disability whilst also supporting Ralph.

True to form, on the documentary, which was screened in 2004 on ITV, Alma and George made nothing but negative comments regarding Linda and Ralph's work for The Lin Berwick Trust. For example, George said that the home in Scotland would never happen and that they would never raise the money needed to complete the project and it would be a white elephant. Alma spoke about the stress levels for Ralph – the fact that he was tired, and that Linda was putting too many demands on him. She could not understand why they had to do all of this work.

George spoke about Linda's weight-gain and how that was making life difficult for Ralph. It was all incredibly negative and there wasn't one nice comment made about either Linda and Ralph's life together, or The Trust's achievements.

Meanwhile, Linda's claim for damages from the injuries she sustained with Go Airlines, was settled out of court. It totalled one-hundred-and-seventy-thousand pounds. Forty-thousand of which was for public humiliation, and one-hundred-and-thirty-thousand for care. Although that money was helpful to Linda, it proved to be grossly inadequate for the cost of the on-going care that was now required.

The documentary, which was eventually entitled, "Lin and Ralph: A Love Story", was extremely well-received. In fact, it came third in the Grierson Awards for documentaries, also known as the British Documentary Awards. The response concerning the film was positive, depending on which side of the fence that you came down on. People within the Methodist Church did not like the references made to the problems of Linda and Ralph's sexual relationship along with its associated problems concerning disability.

While all this was going on, Ralph's Parkinson's became progressively worse. One day whilst Linda was out with her carer, Liz, Ralph got it into his head that the polystyrene tiles on the suspended ceiling in the kitchen, needed to be washed and re-painted. Prior to this thought, Judy the cleaner, had just made the kitchen absolutely spotless.

Suddenly, Ralph climbed up onto the kitchen table and started to take the tiles off, one by one, and then number them, otherwise he felt that he wouldn't have remembered how to put them back correctly. He then lined all the tiles up against the skirting board on the floor in the hallway and the living room. He then got a wallpaper pasting table, some pots of paint and brushes, and leant them up against the microwave.

By now, all the loft insulation above the tiles was now exposed and the fibre was raining down into the whole kitchen. The fibre covered everything with a fine, black dust – the whole floor and every work surface. Ralph had managed to paint three tiles, before being so exhausted by his climbing up and down, that he slumped down and went sound asleep in the spare wheelchair in the kitchen.

When Linda and Liz returned, Liz couldn't believe what she was seeing and put Linda's hands over the work surfaces so that she could feel the mess for herself. On hearing the commotion, Ralph woke with a start.

Linda said to him, 'What the hell has happened here?'

He said, 'I just thought that the tiles needed painting.'

'Well what if you'd fallen over?' Linda asked.

Annoyed, Ralph said, 'Well I didn't, did I?'

Linda said, 'You know that you've been told by the doctors that you must not climb. This was quite a foolish thing to do when there was nobody around, wasn't it?'

Ralph said, 'You've always stopped me from doing things.'

'That's not fair,' protested Linda, 'I've never tried to stop you, I've only ever tried to encourage, but most of the time, you just can't be bothered. What I want to know is, what are you going to do about all this mess, especially as Judy has just cleaned the kitchen?'

Ralph made no comment. The trestle table was propped up against the microwave, with two pots of paint and brushes, and the tiles from the ceiling were still scattered all along the skirting boards of the hallway and the living room. Ralph made no further comments on the matter whatsoever.

Three days went by without any work being done by Ralph to improve the situation. Naturally, Liz spent hours cleaning up the kitchen. On the third day, Linda thought that enough time had elapsed to broach the subject again. She said, 'Ralph, what are you doing about the painting of the ceiling tiles and getting them back up?'

His response was, 'Absolutely nothing!'

Linda asked, 'Can you tell me the reason why?'

Ralph said, 'Because you have undermined my authority by telling me what to do.'

Linda said, 'Now you're just being bloody ridiculous. I haven't undermined your authority at all. All I've done, is to deal with the fallout, quite literally, of your efforts.'

Ralph said, 'Well, you can get someone else in to do it, because I'm not going to bother.' Linda telephoned a painter and decorator who came and painted all the tiles and put them all back. They looked better for the painting, but Linda didn't appreciate the bill at the end of it.

These outbursts of stubbornness were getting to be more frequent – Linda wasn't sure if Ralph was just being "bloody-minded" or if it was the result of the Parkinson's doing its horrible thing and now starting to affect his mind?

A few weeks later, Ralph fell out of bed and could not get himself back up. He refused to let Linda pull the bell-cord to summon the carer, so she struggled to help him for more than two hours. He was naked, and by now, extremely cold. Linda just couldn't pull him up off the floor because he weighed some eighteen-stone – it was just impossible for her.

Ralph said to Linda, 'If you call the carer, I'll never speak to you again. Then our relationship will be finished.'

Linda continued to try and help Ralph, but all that was happening was that both of them were becoming more and more exhausted. They were never going to succeed. So Linda had no choice but to call the carer. Together, Linda and the carer pulled and pushed Ralph to get him into a position so that he could fall onto the bed. He was absolutely freezing as it was in the autumn and he had the embarrassment of being naked. He was in bed for about half an hour and then, threw himself back onto the floor, saying, 'Now you can do all of that, all over again!'

Linda said, 'I can't Ralph, because the carer and I are both totally shattered.'

The carer immediately called the paramedics. They felt that Ralph should go into hospital because he had a urine infection. Yet again, Linda telephoned their good friend Stan Johnson, who told her not to worry and that he would wait for the ambulance to arrive at West Suffolk Hospital and then stay with Ralph until he was settled in.

Whilst in hospital, Ralph followed his usual pattern of non-cooperation. Linda would visit, six days out of seven. Every Friday his daughter Tina, would visit. She said to Linda, 'I don't know what we can do to help him? I'm at a loss, so it's down to you.'

Linda was getting so tired. She didn't know what was going to happen, not only from day to day, but literally, minute to minute. One day, Linda was told that Ralph's blood test results should be back within two days. When she went to the desk to speak to the Sister on duty, she was told, 'We don't speak to you, we speak to his daughter.'

Linda was furious and said, 'You will speak to me, because I am his wife, and his next of kin!

And if you persist with this, I will report you to the Matron.'

'Oh, please don't do that,' she said.

Eventually, the Matron came on the telephone and he humbly apologised saying, 'Of course, we will deal with you, but aren't you disabled?'

Linda said, 'Yes, I am disabled – I'm in a wheelchair and totally blind, but my brains are not in my backside and I have dealt with every single aspect of Ralph's care.'

Ralph was put on yet more antibiotics with the usual side-effects of diarrhoea and such like.

His health eventually improved a little and he was then able to return home.

Back at home, the situation was getting worse by the day and it was only a matter of time before the next crisis. It came in a most unexpected way. On the 1st December 2005, Linda awoke and started the process of getting Ralph to take his medication. They went through the usual routine with Linda pleading for him to take it and his refusal.

Linda was too tired for this daily drudgery. She just wanted to duck out for a while, but of course, she couldn't. She took her own water-retention medication and waited for it to take effect. It was usually something like a two-hour process before it totally went through her system so that she could get on with the rest of her day.

But, at seven-fifteen that morning, her brother John telephoned to say that Alma had been rushed to Addenbrookes Hospital. He said, 'I can't cope with all this, you will have to deal with it. You are much better at talking "medical" than me. You need to come now.'

Linda was frantic, saying, 'I can't come now because I've just taken medicine of my own which requires me to be near a toilet.'

There was almost an hour's journey just to go to the hospital from Sudbury to Cambridge, so Linda was unable to leave straight away. Fortunately, it was the week that her carer, Liz, was back with her so she had some good support.

When Linda, Ralph, and Liz arrived in Accident and Emergency at Addenbrookes Hospital, Alma had just been given a tracheotomy to help her breathe and she was drifting in and out of consciousness. Linda's father George, was also there with her brother John. John was in a total panic so Linda was left to speak to the doctors. It transpired that the doctors were trying to stabilise Alma so that she could have surgery. She'd had some extreme pains in her stomach during the night, but did not call for help.

The first time that George knew that something was wrong was when he went into the bedroom to ask what she wanted him to take out of the freezer for dinner that night. She was rolling around the bed in agony. George called John. John called the ambulance and the medical emergency began.

The doctors told Linda that Alma had got an infection in her bowel and that she was now suffering from Septicaemia, and that she was not expected to live. They would try to stabilise her enough to get her to theatre but the prognosis was bleak. If she should survive, she would need an ileostomy because there was a blockage in her bowel.

The doctors asked Linda her opinion on the situation and what she thought should be done. George and John said that they wanted her treated at all costs. But Linda said, 'I know that with Mum's heart-condition and how she feels about anything to do with the toilet, at eighty-two, I don't think that she will ever cope with this.'

The doctors said that they would know more once they could give her a CT scan. Linda was told that Alma would be going into intensive care and when she got there, Linda should hold her hand and talk to her, because even though she was unconscious, she would still be able to hear her. Linda used this special time to say how proud she was of her for the way that she had fought so hard to help her survive, how much she loved her, and how much she prayed that, when this was all over, she would be able to get to know Ralph better.

Linda said, 'I don't want to be at loggerheads with you, Mum. All I want is for us to have a happy time together.' Linda then called George over, explaining to him that although Alma could not speak, she could hear. So she said to him, 'Why don't you say something nice to Mum, Dad? She can hear you but she can't answer you.'

Linda put both their hands together. George sat motionless for a while then suddenly said, 'You were a bloody good cook, mate, and you kept the house beautifully clean.'

Linda was totally exasperated saying, 'Oh, for God's sake, Dad, why don't you tell her that you love her?'

He said, 'Of course I bloody love her. She knows that, don't you mate?'

Linda had been there from ten-fifteen in the morning and it was now six o'clock at night. John had made contact with his brother George, and George was on his way from Sweden where he was now living. Ralph was quite exhausted and needed to go home so whilst Linda was still with Alma, Liz took Linda's father, George back home to Haverhill in Suffolk.

Then she came back to the hospital to collect Linda and Ralph. Naturally, nobody really felt like eating – it had been such an emotional day. Doctors had told Linda and John that the surgery could not be done because Alma was far too ill and far too weak. It was now just a matter of time.

The brothers John and George stayed with Alma and in the morning Linda was about to come back to the hospital but John telephoned to say that they were turning Alma's life-support machine off. Her body had now become totally toxic with all the infection and there was no hope. Linda received a call from her nephew Paul, and it was decided that he would come over to Alma and George's home and cook a meal for everyone as they'd all just lived on sandwiches and cups of coffee for the last twenty-four hours.

Linda arranged for Paul to buy sirloin steaks for everyone and he prepared chips and salad. Linda's brother George's reaction was, 'We didn't want this bloody meal.'

Linda felt a little hurt because she had done it out of kindness for everyone and George senior would certainly want a meal. Linda thought it would be a nice time of togetherness in a very difficult situation. She certainly needed the fellowship. John Toosey, a member of The Lin Berwick Trust Team, drove Linda back home.

Now it was time to think about all the funeral arrangements.

Chapter 54

Alma's funeral had a lasting impact, but sadly for the wrong reasons. The Reverend Denis Duncan contacted the minister who was to officiate at the funeral and expressed a wish to attend in order to give Linda support, and to publicly pray about this amazing woman, Alma. The Reverend Denis Duncan was now in his late eighties, and had had a number of personal and emotional problems that had greatly influenced his thinking.

So, when he came to Alma's funeral, he started in his professional mode, but then quickly lapsed into an emotional state which was quite inappropriate for the occasion. He preached and prayed as though it were Linda in the coffin, and not her mother. He just got carried away with it all and didn't seem to know when to stop. Linda wanted to scream, 'Denis, for God's sake, what are you doing…Stop!'

She just didn't know how to sit there and listen to all this rubbish. Reverend Duncan should have been acknowledging Alma's achievements throughout her life but all he did was to constantly refer to Linda. Linda was terrified as to what her brothers George and John, and her father would say about it – it wasn't long before she found out!

Denis was not usually a smart dresser, but on this occasion he looked even worse. His shoes were dirty, and his clothing was unkempt, creased, and generally not looking at all smart. After the service, which had been lovely with its hymn-singing and music, Denis came over to Linda and it made her feel extremely agitated.

'Denis,' she said, 'What the hell were you thinking of up there? It was as though *I* was in the coffin!'

He couldn't see that he'd done anything wrong.

Linda said, 'It wasn't *me* in the coffin, but *Alma*? I cannot begin to imagine what untold damage you have done here today. I would not be surprised if my family never spoke to me again, let alone you?'

He still really couldn't see that he had done anything wrong, but the people around him told him that Linda was right and that her comments were fully justified. Reverend Duncan then said that although he couldn't see that he'd done anything wrong, he would still apologise.

Linda said, 'No, please don't. I don't want you to write to my family at this time after what has happened here today.' Naturally, when the family caught up with Linda, they were not best pleased. They were going to write to the Reverend Denis Duncan and tell him his fortune! Mercifully, they never did.

Linda was able to convince her brother George that she wasn't responsible for what the Reverend Duncan had done and she was convinced it was because Denis had been quite ill and indeed, he ended up in a psychiatric hospital some weeks later. It was a desperate situation for him to be in because in the past, he'd had such a wonderful mind and Linda had trusted him implicitly.

It seems strange, but at the point when Alma died, Linda felt a tremendous sense of relief as well as sadness. Alma had fought like a tigress on behalf of her daughter until Ralph came into Linda's life and she could never come to terms with Linda's happiness. It should have been something that they could have both cherished together but Alma could never let go.

She had a strangle-hold on Linda and Ralph's relationship that continued until the week of her death. It was such a shame because when her husband George had his first cancer, it was Ralph that offered to pay privately for the operation, and although George declined the offer and it was done on the NHS, George was utterly incredulous and never forgot that kindness offered by Linda and Ralph.

Nevertheless, at the time of George's operation, Ralph happily took Alma in to their home for a week so that she would not be on her own, due to her heart condition. Living with Linda and Ralph for that week, Alma began to realise just how much Linda and Ralph actually cared for each other. They took her out and about, meeting friends and sharing in every activity that she chose to join in with. She actually said to Linda, 'I can tell that he loves you.'

And Linda said, 'The feeling is mutual, Mum.'

Alma said, 'I'm jealous of the relationship that you and Ralph have, not just in your personal relationship, but because I would have wanted a husband who loved and cared for me like Ralph cares for you.'

Linda said, 'I realise that it has taken courage to admit that – well done. I feel really proud of you. Now that you have seen us together, let's hope that we can draw a line under all of the back-biting and begin again without so many recriminations.'

Alma agreed, but within two weeks, she was back complaining about all the same old rubbish that she'd moaned about before concerning Linda and Ralph. Sadly it seems, sometimes you really *can't* teach an old dog new tricks.

Chapter 55

The Lin Berwick Trust had good reason to be profoundly grateful to Scotland's National Lottery Heritage Fund. One morning, Linda received a telephone call from someone asking to speak to John Toosey. Linda explained that Mr Toosey wasn't there but she was the president of The Lin Berwick Trust so she could help. It was a young woman with a beautiful Scottish lilt to her voice and she said, 'I'm from the Lottery Fund, and I am calling to tell you that we have granted your application.'

Linda's bewildered reaction was, 'Pardon?'

The woman repeated, 'I am ringing to tell you that we have granted your application for the building of your holiday home for the disabled in Scotland.'

'That's amazing!' Linda exclaimed, excitedly. 'But can you tell me how much has been granted from our original application?'

'All of it!' She said, 'Two-hundred-and-ten-thousand, three-hundred-and-eighty-six pounds, and ten pence.'

Linda laughed, 'We mustn't forget the ten pence!'

Linda thanked the woman profusely and waited for Ralph to come back into the kitchen. He had just gone out to the tumble-dryer in the garage. As he came back through the kitchen door, Linda yelled excitedly, 'We've got it! We've got it!'

'What are you talking about?' Ralph asked, confused.

Linda said, '*We* have had our application for the remaining amount to build Denis Duncan House accepted – in full, namely the two-hundred-and-ten thousand, three-hundred-and eighty-six pounds, and ten pence! So, we can now finish the project!'

Ralph was utterly amazed, dropping down into the spare wheelchair in the kitchen. He asked Linda to tell him again what she had just said. So Linda repeated all the details once again about the telephone call. Linda eventually contacted John Toosey and his wife Miriam from The Lin Berwick Trust.

They immediately came round with a bottle of Champagne to share in the good news. The washing machine was going into a spin at the time – just like all of their heads! It was a moment of great joy. They could now plan for the opening, which was to be on the 6th April, 2006.

Fortunately, the Reverend Denis Duncan had now recovered from his mental breakdown and would take the service of Thanksgiving at St. Peter's Church in Direlton. There would also be a lovely afternoon tea for the supporters and people of the village of Direlton in Scotland. But the piece de resistance was to be that, as the people left the church service on the stroke of three o'clock, Angus, the Duke of Hamilton, and members of his old RAF squadron, would fly over the church and directly over Denis Duncan House, as it was to be known, trailing streams of coloured smoke, highlighting the name of The Lin Berwick Trust.

This was to be a most thrilling moment, greatly applauded by all in attendance. Linda and Ralph were to remain at Denis Duncan House for a few days to deal with press interviews and radio coverage, as well as talking to some groups of people and showing them around the house. They also used a little of the time to drink in the atmosphere of the area which was very beautiful, although April was not the best time to see Scotland.

Indeed, on the morning of the ceremony, when sound systems and a stage were erected at the front of the house, it was snowing and bitterly cold. Linda was very grateful for a thick suit made from Scottish wool which she thought was highly appropriate in the circumstances. Julie Cristin, a former trustee of The Lin Berwick Trust, wheeled Linda around Denis Duncan House and they prayed in every room, touching the walls and asking God to bless the house.

After all the activities of the afternoon, Linda's carer Liz, said to the Duchess of Hamilton, how much she had enjoyed the flypast and how much she would have loved to be in the plane when they turned them upside down in a roll. When Linda heard this, she said to Liz, 'You tell me that you would love to go in the plane and yet earlier today you were saying that you felt dizzy and unwell, so I don't know how you could even think of such a prospect?'

The Duchess of Hamilton said to Liz, 'Are you really sure you'd like to do that?'

Liz confirmed that she was. Within minutes, Liz was taken to one of the pilots and in no time at all, she was given a flying helmet, put in the plane, and taken up into the skies! The plane went over the house and could be heard as it flew around the surrounding area. On landing, Liz was ecstatic. She had experienced several various acrobatic manoeuvres.

Linda said to her, 'I'm glad that you're staying here for a few days to recover!' Liz spoke about this event whenever she got the chance.

On their return home to Suffolk, everything was quiet on the holiday-home building front for a while. For now, all Linda could do was concentrate on Ralphs's needs that were becoming more and more critical by the day, and concentrate on her own work where she was writing, lecturing, and giving interviews concerning aspects of disability.

She loved the interactions between students who were going to be doctors, nurses, and health care clinicians of various kinds. Some of them had relatives who were ill themselves so they knew what it was like to care for someone in a similar position. There was one such person Linda would never forget. Linda had gone to Suffolk University to give a talk about her life. She spoke about her husband Ralph and his Parkinson's and how his condition was deteriorating.

Fortunately, this was one time when Ralph did not attend with Linda. She spoke fervently about the situation and the ramifications for care needs. At the end of the class, a young woman came to her in floods of tears. She told Linda what a wonderful lecture it had been, but that Linda had just described what was going to happen to her father who had been diagnosed with Parkinson's just two days ago. She sobbed in Linda's arms.

Linda said to her, 'All you can do is to live for now. Make the most of every God-given moment, because none of us can know what will happen from minute to minute. Your role is to support your father, to give him the love and care that he needs, and to help him to enjoy the moments that he has left. That is all any of us can hope for.'

The tutor in the class said to Linda, 'I want to complement you on the beautiful way that you handled that situation with the student. Not many people would have dealt with it so well.'

Linda said, 'Well, I've been there, haven't I? And I've still got some difficult roads ahead which I know, won't be easy.'

Sometime later, the idea of a third holiday-home was broached. Linda thought that the Trust should make an approach to His Royal Highness The Prince of Wales, to ascertain whether a similar arrangement could be made such as the Duke and Duchess had offered at Direlton in Scotland. But for now, it was a case of just planting "seeds" to see what might come up. The Trust was still holding events to fundraise because the work was so crucial to the charity.

Linda's personal ambition was to build five holiday homes in total, situated in the North, the South, the East, and the West of Britain – with the possibility of a further home somewhere abroad.

It was important to remember that many people with profound disabilities needed specialist provision, such as a variable-height bed, a wheelchair-accessible shower, a toilet that washes and dries, or a bath that is able to raise to the height which is comfortable to the carer.

There were hardly any provisions suitable in London or anywhere else in Britain, discounting of course, the properties of The Lin Berwick Trust. This situation was a disgrace given the fact that there were more than a quarter-of-a-million profoundly disabled people in Britain at that time, and Linda felt that this had to change.

Chapter 56

Ralph was having more and more bouts of hospitalisation. Linda never knew when they were next going to strike. It was like living on a knife-edge. This particular bout of hospitalisation culminated in a seventeen-and-a-half-week stay. In that period, Ralph went from lucidity to being totally out of it, and having a diagnosis of Lewy Body Dementia in conjunction with his Parkinson's. Ralph's children, Tina and Paul, could not really believe what was happening.

Indeed, Paul's attitude was that Linda was a bit of a drama-queen. Linda said to Paul, 'In all the years that you have known me, have I ever spoken about my disabilities, or your father's, in a melodramatic, drama-queen-like way?'

Paul said, 'If I'm honest, no you haven't.'

Linda said, 'Well what makes you think I am going to start now? Look up the diagnosis of Lewy Body Dementia on the internet and read about the symptoms, and you will see that your father unfortunately ticks all the boxes. And furthermore, I think that you should talk to the consultant geriatrician who is looking after him, and hear it from someone else other than me.'

For now, Linda was coping with change on a daily basis. She would often visit Ralph on a freezing-cold, wet or snowy day, and on reaching the hospital, often found him unresponsive and generally uncommunicative, that is, until he unleashed a torrent of abuse saying, angrily, 'Why don't *you,* piss off and go back home!'

He was now at the point that he was refusing to do physiotherapy, take his drugs properly, or even wash. Linda went in to see him one day and she could smell his urine-covered body even before she reached his bedside. She was not going to have her darling Ralph treated like that. She went to the nursing station and spoke to them about it. The nurse's said, 'Unfortunately, it is against human rights legislation to try and force him to do anything.'

Linda said, 'So what do you do then?'

She replied, 'If we say to him, would you like a wash, Ralph? And he says no, then we have to walk away. We cannot force him.'

Linda said, 'Well, why do you ask him like that? You should just tell him that you are coming to give him a wash now. Don't ask him whether he would like one.'

The nurse's reaction was, 'Well, that's certainly a different approach. We could try that.'

When Linda met the nurse a few days later, the nurse said, 'He is certainly cooperating a little better since we tried your method.'

Linda had had many times when she'd had to use different strategies to get Ralph to respond. When he dug his heels in, nothing would shift him. It was the most frustrating thing to experience – Linda tearing her hair out, and Ralph just laughing.

Sometimes for no reason, Ralph would suddenly grab hold of one of the nurses in the night and not let her go. He was still quite a strong man, but when Parkinson's spasms got hold of his body, anything could happen. The nurses found this all quite distressing. On other occasions, he would empty his bedside locker, removing the contents, piece by piece, and dropping each one with a crash onto the floor.

Sometimes this was most annoying when Linda found out that he was deliberately smashing containers of Chanel toiletries and either breaking the bottles, or if the containers were not glass, emptying the contents all over the floor as well as himself.

All he would say was, 'At least I'll smell better now!' In that one statement, it was evident just how badly he felt about himself now.

Another time he managed to somehow climb over the bed support and drag himself naked across the floor, trying to get out of the ward. When the nurses questioned him as to what he was doing, he said that he had to get home to Linda and that she needed him and he must be there for her. Of course, Linda knew nothing of this until it was reported by the nurses the next day.

In fact, the nurses found the whole thing very sad but also amusing, because of his utter determination. The nurses told Linda that Ralph obviously loved her because she was the most important thing in his life. Now all his actions were being reported. Linda tried to tell Ralph that playing up like this was not doing his cause any good.

Ralph said, 'They're not reporting on me, are they? Tell me the truth – don't lie!'

Linda spoke to their friend, Stan Johnson, and asked him that when he visited Ralph in hospital, would he let Ralph know about the constant reporting by the nurses and doctors on his behaviour and the fact that it wasn't doing his cause any good at all. On one occasion, Ralph was taken to see the geriatrician in the hospital. On meeting the geriatrician, Ralph threw himself out of his wheelchair onto the floor in front of him.

The geriatrician decided that this might be a good position for him to work from and so promptly got onto the floor with Ralph. He started to ask Ralph various questions, whilst Ralph constantly rocked himself backwards and forwards, singing to himself, or making la la la noises to express the fact that he wasn't going to talk. Linda was summoned for a meeting with the geriatrician.

His response was, 'We don't know just how you have coped with this for so long. In fact, I'd go as far as to say, we think that you have been bloody marvellous.'

Linda admitted to the geriatrician that she was now at her wits' end, metaphorically on her knees, totally exhausted, and not knowing which way to turn, or what to do.

Ralph said to the nurses, 'When my wife comes in, I want to be in my wheelchair so that we can go to the hospital canteen and have a cup of tea and a private chat.'

Everyone thought that this was progress because he had made a request and he was seeking their cooperation. Stan had visited that day and taken Ralph to the canteen. Ralph had told Stan that he wanted to be put close to Linda when she arrived. People thought how nice this was, but Linda didn't want it because she knew that he would use this time to give her a lot of abuse. Her intuition proved to be correct.

When she arrived and was placed near to Ralph, he somehow got his body forward and grabbed hold of Linda's arm, tucking his head underneath it so that people could not hear what he was saying to her. He told Linda, 'I hate you because you're stopping me from coming home. It's my home and I'm going to be there, come what may, and I will do what I bloody-well like, and you won't be able to do anything about it.'

He then tried to swipe her across the face and generally lash out at her. This behaviour was so unlike her darling Ralph who had always been so loving and caring. It was like being with a totally different person – totally alien to what she'd known before. Linda felt so nervous that she asked people to move her away from him. She did not want to be lashed-out at.

The weeks were moving on and now Ralph was regarded as an NHS bed-blocker. So a meeting was held between Linda, Ralph, a social work team, and an occupational therapist to decide what should happen in the future. In Ralph's mind, there was no reason why he shouldn't return home, but Linda told the social work team that this was impossible. There wasn't the space to have powered wheelchairs, a manual hoist, and two carers because Ralph was so heavy to handle, especially at night when he was trying to get out of bed.

At times like that, he developed a super-human strength and would climb over anything to get out. Linda also had a problem because of his incontinence issues and constant diarrhoea. The smell of that would be unbearable for a blind person.

Back at home, Linda had a telephone call from the social worker, telling her how much Ralph wanted to be at home and that it was against his human rights to stop him.

Linda said, 'Well, what about *my* human rights? I think the best thing you can do is to come and visit my home and see what little space we have and how we have to manage.'

The social work team arrived to do an inspection. They agreed that the bathroom area was far too small for a powered wheelchair and there would not be enough bedroom space to house two additional carers, let alone cope with the costs involved. A further meeting was arranged between all the parties concerned and the social work team. Ralph was adamant that he was going home.

Linda said to him, 'Look Ralph, you've been in here for thirteen weeks and you are blocking a bed. At the moment, you are not physically capable of coming home because you now cannot weight-bear. When you first came in here, you were able to stand. What I would suggest is that we try to find a suitable care home so that you can be in a better place and it would free-up this hospital bed for someone else.'

'If you then improve to the extent that you can stand and go to the toilet on your own, then you can come home – that will be your goal. But they have assessed our home and they agree that two people in wheelchairs, one of whom is blind and needs a great deal of physical help, and the other with Parkinson's and other difficulties, would not have the space to move around freely, without the extra physical help required. So your role is to get well, because I want you back with me.'

Reluctantly, Ralph thought that this was the better option and he asked Linda to get it sorted. The social work team had already come to the meeting with a wad of papers telling Linda to sort out a suitable care home for Ralph. Typically, it was not printed in Braille, so in the first instance, Linda needed someone to read the different care home addresses out to her. There were fifty-three names on this list – just some of the many care homes in Suffolk.

Linda eliminated those that were too far away and visited some that were nearer. It was going to be difficult because of Ralph's diagnosis of Parkinson's with the added problem of Lewy Body Dementia which would inevitably get worse, but over a period of a couple of weeks, many homes were visited. Equally, many were eliminated, mostly because there were great slopes into the properties with rough ground to negotiate.

Also, if Linda was to be able to visit Ralph, the doors to the bedrooms had to be wide enough to take a wheelchair. Many were just standard doors so they were going to have a fight on their hands.

Linda was called back for another meeting and Ralph just lay in his bed, totally impassively. Stan came to the meeting to give both Linda and Ralph some support. Stan said later that the social workers' minds were already made up – they sat there with their heads pointed to the floor, not looking at the people concerned. The head social worker said to Linda, 'Is there anything you want to say?'

Linda said, 'You bet your sweet life there is.'

She recounted everything about the homes on the list, the problems with the ones that she had visited, and indeed, the only one that was really suitable for their needs, was St. Joseph's in their home town of Sudbury, although it was prohibitively expensive. Linda was told that the finance officer who made the decision as to where people could go was a very hard man and he didn't take no for an answer.

After Linda worked through the list, the social workers' eyes were no longer pointed at the floor but they were looking at Linda directly with their eyes wide open, agog at what she had managed to accrue in terms of information. The head social worker said, 'How did you do all this work?'

'With a great deal of difficulty,' Linda replied, 'Because I was unable to read the list. So I had to memorise every aspect of each home.'

The social worker said, 'Well, I admire the way that you are fighting for Ralph, but it won't be easy.'

The finance officer from Suffolk Social services telephoned Linda and told her that Ralph would be going to Hazel Court Care Home in Sudbury and that would be final.

'It isn't,' Linda said, 'Because, we would not get two wheelchairs into Ralphs's room there and were you to restrict my access to him that would be against our human rights. I will not leave a stone unturned, and if I have to, I will give it to every aspect of the media.'

Later, Linda had a further call saying that the access to Hazel Court had been checked out and it was indeed deemed unsuitable so the social services said that they would be willing to fund some of the extra cost for the larger, more accessible care home of St. Joseph's in Sudbury. The cost was nine-hundred pounds a week. The local authority would fund two weeks a month and the remaining two weeks would have to be funded by Linda and Ralph themselves. This would put an even more intolerable burden on care costs for Linda.

Thankfully, Ralph's pension from his old firm at Tate & Lyle Sugar was a great help. Sadly, it still didn't meet the costs together with everything that Ralph would need on a personal basis.

Eventually, that dreadful day dawned when Ralph would arrive at the care home. St. Joseph's had a rule that relatives could not visit for the first forty-eight hours in order to allow them to settle their new patients in. Linda sent a bouquet of a dozen red roses to Ralph along with a message sending him her love.

They were both in a highly-emotional state that day. Linda was tearful throughout the day, indeed, was tearful every time that she ever visited Ralph at St. Joseph's. Eventually, Linda received a telephone call from Ralph asking why she wasn't there. He said, 'I demand that you come!'

Linda said tearfully, 'I can't get anyone to bring me at the moment.' Even though Ralph's daughter, Tina, had in fact gone to the care home and then went back to Linda's home to sew some labels into his clothing. Linda said to her, 'Please, let me order a taxi so that I can get there.' But Tina refused.

Naturally, when Linda went to see Ralph, he was annoyed and very tearful. In fact, they both sobbed together. Ralph said, 'You should have been here with me. The only person I wanted to see was you and you couldn't be bothered to come.'

Linda said, 'Ralph, please don't say that. I tried desperately to get over to you but I was stopped by people who thought they knew better. I knew how much it would stress you for me not to be there but they refused to take me – including your daughter.'

Although Linda realised at the time, that Tina would have been hurting too.

Chapter 57

Ralph settled in to a reasonable routine at St. Joseph's. The staff were very kind for the most part, although sometimes the young carers didn't fully understand that Ralph was a very shy person and he didn't like "youngsters", as he put it, less than twenty years of age doing highly intimate and personal care for him. Linda visited some six days a week and everything was taking its toll. Ralph would ring Linda every morning and be on the phone for almost an hour.

Then, as soon as she replaced the receiver, he would call again, and again, repeating everything that he already said in the previous calls – this was obviously due to his dementia and the fact that he wanted Linda's undivided attention. In this regard, he would accuse Linda of all sorts of things, especially of her having an affair with a male friend who was taking her to concerts. On one particular occasion, when she visited Ralph, he again accused her of having an affair, so she asked him, 'And how do you make that out?'

'I can tell by the way that you look at him,' he said.

Linda asked, 'How is that then?'

'The very same way that you used to look at me,' he said.

Linda said, 'Listen, mate, You are stuck to me like shit to a blanket!'

His response was, 'Oh well, that's alright then.' And he never accused Linda of having an affair ever again.

One evening, Linda was scheduled to go to a concert at the Barbican in London, and asked the carers to remove Ralph's telephone to stop him from constantly calling. He quickly learnt that if Linda told him she was going out for the evening, he decided to "play up".

On one occasion, saying that he was tied up and couldn't get to Linda, and on another occasion, telling her for over an hour, that his computer did not work – he didn't have a computer! But Linda had to find ways to pacify him.

Ralph had gone on and on about the computer that would not work, 'You will have to fix it for me,' he said.

'Ok,' said Linda, 'You put your phone down, and when it's fixed, I'll call you back.'

Linda's carer asked what she would do now, as she had been party to this conversation.

Linda said, 'We'll just have a cup of coffee, and then I'll call him back.' Linda rang Ralph back and said, 'It's Ok, Ralph, I've fixed your computer. When you wake up in the morning, it will be ready for you to use, so you can rest now and have a good sleep.'

Ralph said, 'I *knew* you'd fix it for me!'

Linda thought, '*God forgive me, please.*' But there was nothing else she could do.

Ralph wanted to come home twice a week. But the community transport was often not able to help. In the end, Linda sold her beloved VW Passat Estate car and bought a second-hand Fiat Multipla with a hydraulic tailgate lift so that Ralph could drive his chair onto the platform and into the car by means of a winch. This worked incredibly well, but Linda really missed her lovely old car.

All this went well for a few weeks, with Ralph choosing what food he wished to eat and Linda's carer providing the food for them to share together. But then Ralph became more and more angry, as he realised just what he was missing in terms of family life at home. Ralph would suddenly start driving his powered wheelchair at full speed, eight miles per hour, down the hallway, and deliberately crashing into the doors, again and again, until he split the wood on the doors and the doorframes.

Then he would smash the chair into the walls, taking huge chunks of plaster out of them as he did so. Linda asked him to stop, but he would not. He said to her, 'Why should you be living here, living the life of Riley, while I am stuck over there, and yet *this* is my home too?'

Linda said, 'I can understand how you feel. I know that in your position, I would feel the same. But I am not living the life of Riley. I am still working, doing Braille transcriptions, lecturing and writing, and trying to make a living to help fund your care as well as mine, and to provide any extras that you may need.'

He would place his wheelchair menacingly between Linda and the door so that she could not get out. In the end, Linda had to say to him, 'If you persist on your one-man self-destruct campaign, then I will have to stop you coming home because I cannot cope with the way you are damaging the fabric of the house, and I am also feeling very nervous because you are driving your wheelchair at me, and I am terrified that you are going to split my legs open with the metal platforms on your chair. I do everything I can to help, and to try and make your life as pleasant as it can be, but you are never satisfied.'

Meanwhile, over the next couple of years, Linda's life was very stressful. But she still continued to work and to try and support both herself and Ralph, with care costs. Linda had an approach from New Suffolk College (later to become University of Suffolk) to make her a Fellow. This resulted in a presentation and a very pleasant dinner. It all seemed very strange without Ralph at her side to share it with.

Linda's life was still as busy as ever, with disappointments as well as victories. She was made redundant from the Disability Now Telephone Counselling Service which she had done single-handedly for eight-hours a week over some twenty-three years. This was another loss of earnings that she could not afford.

Then, Niagara Healthcare offered her a consultancy role in the company, talking to potential buyers of their products. Linda would often have clients visiting her home to try out the various pieces of equipment which had been supplied by Niagara.

Around three years earlier, Linda had made a personal approach to His Royal Highness The Prince of Wales, Duchy of Cornwall. It was evident that His Royal Highness probably didn't even see Linda's letter because, almost by return of post, Linda's request for help was dismissed. Not to be outdone, in 2010, John Toosey, from The Lin Berwick Trust, sent His Royal Highness photographs and a floor-plan of the recently-opened holiday home in Direlton, East Lothian.

Then, a response was almost immediate, but this time, for the right reasons. The Lin Berwick Trustees were invited to go to Cornwall for a meeting with the Duchy of Cornwall's Trustees. They were shown several pieces of land, and eventually one was selected, in a place called "No Man's Land", some two-and-a-quarter miles from Looe in Cornwall. The views were stunning, and the property that was to be built would be magnificent, and was to be officially opened in July, 2013.

Back in March 2010, It was Linda's sixtieth birthday. She decided to hold a celebratory dinner at the University of Suffolk, prepared by the Suffolk College Catering Division. It was a beautiful three-course meal, with wine, coffee and birthday cake for eighty-five people. The request was for no presents but, instead, to make a donation in honour of Linda's birthday to The Lin Berwick Trust.

Ralph was going to the dinner, being transported by Suffolk Community Transport because Linda needed her adapted vehicle for herself. Ralph had already said to Linda that he did not want to sit with her, but to sit with people he had not seen for some time. He sat with Jenny and Bruce Porter from Dorset, and Stan and Jonquil Johnson, because he knew that Stan and Bruce would talk boats to him, and he'd enjoy that.

Almost four-thousand pounds was raised for the charity that evening. Linda's brother, John, had a long-term drink problem. So, when he arrived at the dinner at six o'clock in the evening, he was already in an inebriated state. He approached Linda, punching her hard three times in the middle of her back which doubled her up in pain. He looked around at all the fancy arrangements and commented 'Thought you didn't have any bleedin' money, you lying cow?'

'John,' Linda said, 'I have been saving for this special day for more than three years so that I could give each of you a pleasant evening, and this is how you treat me?'

Then Linda's father arrived with her brother, George. Her father's reaction was, 'Blimey! It looks more like a bleedin' wedding!'

Linda said, 'Well I hope you will enjoy it, Dad?' But he was quite disparaging, wanting to know what the point of it all was?

There were some lovely moments with all the guests and Ralph went and sat with Linda once the meal was over. Sadly, this was to be the last ever occasion that Linda and Ralph were together in a social setting.

Chapter 58

It was New Year's Day, 2010. Linda had been ill all over the Christmas period with an extremely heavy cold and probable Flu. Suddenly, out of nowhere, like thunderbolts, she was in excruciating pain – she just collapsed onto the floor, so weak that she could barely move.

Paramedics were called to lift her back onto the bed, but she was so weak she couldn't even hold a glass to her lips in order to drink, but had to use a straw instead. Once the public holiday had finished, the doctor was called. Sometime earlier, Linda had heard a programme on Radio 4 called "Case Notes" with Dr Mark Porter.

It was on the subject of vitamin D deficiency. The more that Linda listened, the more she realised that she ticked all the boxes, because the description of people's pain and the way that it manifested itself, was identical to that which she was experiencing. She asked her GP whether she could have a vitamin D test.

The doctor reluctantly agreed. Normally, a person's vitamin D level should be around a figure of 75 or more, but Linda's was just 15! This is why she had been feeling ill for some considerable time. The pains struck her body indiscriminately, first the head, then the back, the stomach, knees, and anywhere else it took a fancy to. Firstly, Linda was given a specialised dose of vitamin D, made up by the hospital.

Once the problem was stabilised, she would take two vitamin D tablets daily, for the rest of her life. Once she was on the appropriate medication, the pain levels eased considerably. She thanked God for Doctor Mark Porter's programme, otherwise she may never have known – her pain and potential deformities would have progressed.

It was George senior's ninetieth birthday on January 16th of the same year. Linda had invited several family members and friends for a special afternoon tea to celebrate this event. Linda had also organised a beautiful birthday cake – it was a model of a vintage car, in keeping with his great age. No one told George that he was going out that afternoon, and Linda's brother, George, who had come over from Sweden specially for his father's birthday, stayed with him to make sure that he was smartly dressed for the surprise occasion.

George senior was absolutely blown away by the attention that he received, and he was so happy to see so many familiar people, many of whom he had not seen since Alma's funeral. He didn't normally show much emotion, but he shed plenty of tears on that day and said how happy he was that Linda had made the effort. Unfortunately, Linda was so weak with the vitamin D problem that she could only sit in her wheelchair for very short periods of time without resorting back to bed.

George kept saying to her, 'What's the bleedin' matter with you woman, can't you get out of bed?'

He just didn't understand how seriously ill Linda was, but true to form, she did not want to disappoint him. She wanted everyone to have a good time. Her brother John, was being his "extra-magnanimous" self, by giving away bottles of wine to everyone and loading his car up with anything left over, for himself, even though, Linda had told him that the wine was on a sale or return basis. He just saw this as a free-for-all, feeding his habit, which at that time, nobody realised was so serious. As always, Linda could not have achieved any of this if she hadn't had the help of her carers.

Linda's literary agent, Diana Tyler, the head of MBA Literary Agency, London, sent one of her acquaintances a book that Linda had written. She thought that it would make a very interesting television documentary. The film producer, Patrick Spence, was very enthusiastic about the book and the prospect of it being made into a film. A well-known scriptwriter was approached and a script was produced. It reached the final hurdle in the process of being made into a film on two separate occasions, but it was still a long way from being finalised.

Patrick Spence had requested a meeting with Ralph at the care home in connection with the proposed documentary. So, Ralph decided he would like a new suit for the occasion. Since his illness, he had never shown any interest in clothes, but for this, he wanted to look good and for Linda to push the boat out. Of course, with money being tight, all Linda thought was, '*Oh my God – more money that I haven't got!*'

A suit was made with a lovely shirt and pure silk tie. When people saw Ralph looking so immaculate, they couldn't believe it and wanted to know all about this film and who this producer was. All the people in the care home said that Ralph was strutting around in his wheelchair as though he were a king for the day. As far as Linda was concerned, he would always be king.

Linda explained to Patrick that Ralph's speech was now very difficult to understand and that he would have to give him plenty of time. Patrick wanted to interview both Linda and Ralph together. Ralph was more animated and more clearly spoken than he had been for years. Linda thought Patrick and Ralph really enjoyed meeting each other, but they would just have to see what the outcome would be.

Chapter 59

Linda visited Ralph in the care home and the meeting between them was quite difficult.

Ralph was still banging on about how he was coming home to *his* home, and the fact that Linda couldn't do anything about it. Ralph said, 'I, am going to make you feel, as guilty as hell.'

Linda said, 'Don't you think I feel that every *single* day?'

When he wanted to make definite points, his speech became relatively clear. Other times, he just mumbled, which was difficult for Linda to understand because she didn't have the "visual" clues. He kept saying to Linda, 'Why don't you wash your bloody ears out?'

Linda didn't realise that she had developed a problem with her hearing until it was tested a couple of years later. Ralph's anger really got to Linda that day and she started to cry, asking one of the carers to take her outside, because she just couldn't take any more of the criticism and the anger. She sat in the hallway of the care home and absolutely sobbed.

Whilst she was sitting there, her carer came in with her friend, Doctor Bevan. They could both see the stress that she was under and Doctor Bevan rushed into the care home and took Linda out of it immediately. He walked her around the gardens while she regained her composure, saying to him, 'I just couldn't take any more. It just breaks my heart when I am with him and he's going on about being in the care home.'

Doctor Bevan said, 'I don't know how you have held up for so long, and so well. I think you have been bloody marvellous.'

Linda felt that she couldn't just walk away from Ralph, so asked Doctor Bevan to take her back in to the care home. By now, Ralph had come out of his room and was looking for Linda, wondering where she had gone. Eventually, he saw her coming back into the home and said, 'I'm so sorry. I was out of order. I shouldn't have spoken to you and shouted at you like that – I'm just so frustrated.'

Frustrated or not, Linda had had enough. But she went back the next day, dreading that she would have to face the same kind of music.

Out of the blue, Ralph suddenly said, 'I've left it too late, haven't I?'

Linda said, 'What do you mean?'

'To end it,' Ralph said, 'I asked you to come with me so that we could "go" together because neither of us has a decent quality of life now. But you said that you felt you still had work to do.'

Linda said, 'I can't help you to end your life. All I would say is that I will support any decision you choose to make, and I will be there with you until the end. There is one simple way that you can achieve your wishes, and that is to close your mouth and refuse water, food, and medication. If you take that path, it won't be easy and the end also won't be particularly pleasant. But it's a choice that only you can make, and for a big man such as yourself, it will take time for your body to weaken.' After that conversation, Linda went home.

A few days went by, and Linda had a telephone call from the head of the care home who said, 'We have a problem here Lin. Ralph is refusing all his medication, water, and food.'

Linda replied, 'Oh, he's made his choice has he?'

The head of the care home said, 'So you know about this?'

Linda replied, 'What I know is that he doesn't have any quality of life now. He goes from one infection to another and the constant antibiotics have dire consequences for him with upset stomachs and the like.'

The head said, 'You realise that the GP will want to see you, and try to talk to Ralph.'

This meeting was duly arranged. The doctor asked Linda, 'What would tempt Ralph to eat?'

Linda replied, 'A crispy fried bacon sandwich with brown sauce.'

So, the doctor dangled this carrot to Ralph saying, 'You can, if you wish, Ralph, have a full English breakfast, or a crispy bacon sandwich?'

Ralph smiled at her, but stubbornly shook his head, with an emphatic, 'No!'

So Ralph started what was to be a two-week campaign. Linda visited every day, saying to Ralph, 'No one would blame you if you changed your mind,' But still the answer was no. Ralph had been in the care home since 2007, some four-

and-a-half years, yet nobody had thought to lower his bed so that Linda could reach him.

Suddenly, now that he was weaker, they thought to put his bed down, which made Linda feel furious because all she ever wanted to do was to hold his hand or give him a hug. Ralph asked for Harvey, their chocolate Cocker Spaniel, to be brought to him. Harvey was so pleased to see "his daddy". He jumped up onto Ralph's table top and lay on his chest, licking him all over. Ralph absolutely loved it.

All those who witnessed this encounter were very emotional. Each day that Linda visited they had prayer time together. Many of the staff asked if they could join in. Linda found their wish to be part of this process very touching. Every few days, Linda took in red roses.

Tina visited her father but found it incredibly difficult and on the day before he died, she visited and called Linda to say, 'Whatever happens now, you are going to have to deal with it. I can't cope any more – it's down to you.' Linda thought that it had always been down to her anyway.

Linda was called by the care home one Saturday morning, because they thought that the end was imminent for Ralph. When she arrived, she noticed that Ralph's hands were open normally. Due to Parkinson's, his fists had always been clenched tightly and he couldn't open his fingers. But this particular day, he was touching Linda's fingers, one by one, stroking them very gently.

He managed to speak the words, 'I love you,' but it took him some twenty minutes to do so. Linda said, 'I love you too my darling, and I always will.' She said to him again, 'You don't have to do this, no one is going to blame you if you change your mind.' Linda left that afternoon, totally broken-hearted.

The following day, she returned to the home, bringing fresh red roses. Her carer would not take her into the home—the thought of somebody dying was just too much for her—she wasn't even sympathetic towards Linda. Linda sat with a member of the care staff whom she knew very well and they both watched anxiously as Ralph's breathing was now very laboured and seemingly coming to the end but then suddenly, he would come to with a jolt and start breathing normally again.

The carer at the home said to Linda, 'Why don't you go home and we will call you when we think you will be needed. You need to rest, because you will have a hard task ahead of you?'

Linda rang for her carer to come back, but she would still not step into the care home, but waited outside for Linda to be brought out to her. They then went home and had their evening meal.

Linda's friend and secretary, Ruth, was about to collect Linda's incoming carer from Stansted Airport. She had travelled from Poland and would stay with Ruth until her shift started with Linda the following day – a Monday morning. Ruth called to say that her car was in trouble and she wanted to borrow Linda's car to collect the carer from the airport.

Linda said that it wouldn't be possible because she needed to be there for Ralph, therefore she would need her vehicle. Ruth said, 'If you want an excuse not to go back to the care home, this would be a good one.'

Linda replied, 'I don't need an excuse. I just want to be there. If you need to, get a taxi and I'll pay for it.' The care home called Linda, telling her that she should return immediately. When she got there, Ralph's breathing was very agitated. Linda said to Ralph, 'Hey, what's going on here then? It's Ok, I'm here now.'

Linda put her arm around Ralph and held him close. Fortunately the bed was on its lowest setting, but the positioning was absolutely backbreaking for Linda nevertheless, as she was to hold this position for the next couple of hours. The staff watched him very closely as they were all preparing for the end. At eleven twenty-five in the evening, the staff said to Linda, 'You have around five more minutes Lin, so say what you need to say, to Ralph.'

Linda said to Ralph, 'Ralph, you are going to see your Lord now, and when you get there, He is going to give you a most fantastic welcome old son.' Linda held Ralph close as he gave a loud exhalation of air from his lungs – and within a second, he was finally gone.

The strange thing was that as he passed, the roses that had been without fragrance all day, suddenly burst forth into a beautiful fragrance, so much so, that the carer said to Linda, 'Can you smell those roses?'

Linda said, 'That was Ralph giving me a sign that he was alright.'

Linda sat in the hallway of the home, feeling devastated and totally on her own, waiting for her carer to come and pick her up. When she arrived, not a word was spoken and Linda was doubled-up with the pain in her back because she had been cradling Ralph for most of the day.

On reaching home, Harvey was there to greet her. He seemed to know that something was wrong – he drew very close to her. Linda put her arm around him and said, 'Daddy's gone, Harv.' He whimpered, then came up to Linda and put his head into her lap and then lay down on the floor beside her.

The carer came through the hallway and said, matter-of-factly and unfeelingly 'Right, I'll get you to bed now.'

Linda said, 'No, not yet. I need a coffee and a Brandy, and while I'm drinking those I've got people that I must call. I'll give you a call when I need you.'

Linda called her around two in the morning and when she was put to bed, there wasn't a single friendly word, asking Linda if she was alright, or asking if perhaps Linda wanted her to stay with her for a while. It certainly showed Linda how *not* to care!

The next morning, Linda was like a zombie. The Polish carer came on duty and walked into the bathroom where Linda was, 'Why are you looking so sad?' She said to Linda.

'Well surely Ruth gave you the message?' said Linda, 'Ralph died last night.' The carer was utterly shocked.

Linda now had to carry out some of Ralph's last wishes that he had asked for over his last remaining weeks. He wanted his daughter, Tina, to have a special present from both him and Linda. He wanted every one of the carers who had helped him during his stay at St. Joseph's to have a gift from them both, and the carer who was with Linda on the day he died to have a special gift.

Also, he wanted Ruth and the carer who would be on duty on the day of his funeral, to also have a special gift – thirty-nine gifts in all! Linda went straight to John Hume, the Jeweller, who helped her to choose a lovely opal and diamond ring for Tina, Parker pens for all of the male carers, a silver cross for the young lady who was with Linda at the most difficult time, and gold or silver ear rings for all the female care staff.

It was Ralph's ambition to be late for his own funeral. He had always been such a stickler for timekeeping, but sadly, on the way to the church, there was a fatal accident involving a young boy who'd come off his bicycle and had been killed by a car. So in fact, the funeral cortege arrived more than half-an-hour late. Linda thought that Ralph would be giving a wry smile from on high!

The church was full of people who knew Linda and Ralph very well and some two-hundred and-fifty people were invited back to the church hall for a buffet lunch, provided by Linda and issued by Waitrose Hospitality. There was a team of people to supply hot food when it was needed, but of course, for many in Linda's family, the fact that there would be no alcohol, did not go down too well – especially for her brother, John.

John showed his disapproval in this matter even though he did not bother to attend. Linda's brother George said that he could not attend the funeral because he had visited his father just two-weeks before. Linda was absolutely disgusted at the response, but she knew in her heart that the actual service was beautiful.

Linda gave the eulogy and did some of the prayers and a reading with the Methodist Minister. It was Ralph's decision to go back to the church that he had come to love, and the church where he had committed his life to Christ in March, 1991.

Linda and Ralph's favourite music, Rachmaninoff's Second Piano Concerto (the music they fell in love to) was played at the service. Linda had said to the florist that she wanted Grand Prix red roses and Compassion red roses interlinked with greenery to be the full-length of Ralph's casket. She wanted it to be a true expression of the love that she felt for him.

The florist assured her that it would be and the flowers were brought in to Linda on the day of the funeral so that she could feel their beauty and intricate detail, along with their beautiful fragrance. Each member of the congregation was invited to take a candle and light it from a larger candle, then give their respects to Ralph and then place the candle in a large sand-tray with a black cloth covered in silver sequins. The overall effect of the flickering candles, reflecting in the sequinned-cloth and over the flowers gave a magnificent appearance, not just to Linda's flowers, but to all the others on display.

This may have been a closure for many people who knew Ralph, but to Linda, his life and what he stood for, would never be closed. She loved him with a passion and he knew just how much he was loved by her. They rejoiced in their life together and the life that they shared with others. It was so sad, that members of Linda's own family could not appreciate that fact. They didn't really get to know Ralph properly – it felt as though they didn't really want to. Linda was angered by the comments made by her family about Ralph.

They called him a malingerer, lazy, and attention-seeking. Little did anyone know that Ralph was quite seriously ill, even apart from his Parkinson's. He had Asbestosis in one lung, due to working with asbestos at Tate & Lyle. He had severe heart disease and kidney deterioration. Linda was so hurt when she read the autopsy report about Ralph's conditions that she sent each of her family members a copy with a note saying, 'When you read this, and see the suffering that Ralph went through, yet, up until the last few years of his life, cared for me beautifully, I hope you will feel suitably ashamed.'

Linda's brother George was the only person who humbly apologised and said that he had no idea what Ralph had been through.

Chapter 60

One month on from Ralph dying, Linda was asked to record an episode of BBC Radio 4's "No Triumph, No Tragedy" with the presenter, Peter White, who was himself totally blind.

Linda had met him many times but she felt that this was the best broadcast she had ever done. She had given several hundred interviews over the years to numerous radio and television stations, both throughout the UK and abroad, as well as frequent interviews for newspapers and magazines. It was particularly hard for her to speak about the relationship she'd had with Ralph and the circumstances surrounding his death.

In fact, she was very emotional during the interview with Peter White, especially as it was only one month on from his death when she recorded the episode. It would be broadcast six months later in September of 2011. Linda had advised the committee of The Lin Berwick Trust of the forthcoming broadcast, saying that she thought that the interview would have a big impact, so it would be advisable to have some up-to-date information if, on hearing it, people were to request details about the trust.

Certain members on the committee were quite disparaging, saying that they didn't think that it would have an impact – but how wrong they were! Six-and-a-half-thousand pounds was received by the trust as a result of the broadcast! Linda's response to the team was, 'I told you so!' Linda could just tell how good the interview was with Peter. He was extremely kind and sensitive.

This broadcast produced quite a lot of comments, all of them complimentary, except from Linda's brother, John. He said what a brilliant interview it was but then spoilt it by his rather rude and aggressive further comments, such as, 'You posh cow…trust you to do an interview like that,' and most sarcastically, 'Of course, *everyone* respects Dr Lin Berwick *MBE, don't* they?'

To this last most sarcastic comment, Linda replied, 'I'm afraid they do, John. Perhaps it's the way I've lived my life as opposed to yourself?'

He replied, 'You-smug-bastard!'

George senior was having more problems with his cancer and was having frequent hospitalisation and surgery. He was becoming very frail. John had taken on the role of looking after him, but unfortunately, it was not without strings. John constantly demanded money from his father, and even when his father obliged, it was never enough. He always wanted more, knowing that he'd had money when Alma died that he totally did not expect.

Linda's father said to her, 'I couldn't believe that we were married for sixty-three years, and I never knew anything about her bank accounts until I found the statements in her drawer after she died?'

George was furious that Alma had eighty-one-thousand pounds in her bank that he never knew about. And she hadn't made any arrangement as to what should happen to it, if she should either die, or not be in a position to deal with her own affairs.

George said, 'I cannot believe that she had eighty-one-thousand pounds – how did she get it?' Linda knew only too well, that the only way that she would have had such money, was to draw it from Linda's own account. However, she could not prove it because Alma went ballistic when Linda said that she wanted to have Braille bank statements.

Linda's father, George, was so enraged over this secret hoard, that he went straight out and bought a two and-a-half-litre Nissan Primera car – it was far too fast for him, and it proved to be his downfall, due to the fact that he hit another vehicle and the police said he should hand in his licence because of his age.

John continued to demand money from his father, saying that he needed to buy things like, a new wood-burner, or to carry out repairs to his home, a fresh second hand car or indeed, anything where George was expected to cough-up money for what turned out to be fictitious demands. John was using the money to feed his habit of alcohol, gambling, womanising, and to pay off debts that he'd accrued generally from a licentious lifestyle.

Unfortunately, John used to take money from his father's Post Office account, and as George became more frail mentally, John had a field day, taking full advantage. He went to the extent of withholding his father's main meal refusing to cook for him unless he was given more money. His father said to him, 'But I've given you more than fifty-pounds-a-week for cooking my meals?'

But John would not relent. So Linda spoke to her carers, and they agreed to take Linda over to her father, and cook him some steak and chips with salad, along with a dessert. George loved it, and he enjoyed the friendly attention that he was getting.

When he went back into hospital for more surgical intervention, John was there, shouting at George, and demanding money. George was getting weaker by the day and was finding it difficult to swallow. In fact, the situation got so bad with John demanding money from his father, that other patients reported John to the Ward Sister, even though Linda had previously asked him to stop demanding money from George. Linda had visited on this particular day.

When the Sister came over and said to Linda and John, 'If you don't stop this intimidating behaviour, you will be banned from the ward.' John walked off in a huff. The Sister then came over to Linda and said, 'My comment is not directed at you, my dear. All of us can see that you are a very caring and compassionate person. It's your brother who is the fly in the ointment.' Linda apologised profusely and said how embarrassing she found her brother's behaviour.

John kept insisting to the doctors that he wanted his father to come home. Of course George said that he wanted to be at home, but that wasn't the real reason why John wanted him there. So Linda made the necessary arrangements for a variable-height bed, incontinence protection and so on. George was brought home for what was a matter of hours and he was so ill and weak that he had to return straight back to hospital.

Sometime prior to this, George had given Linda his Post Office Savings Card along with the pin number. George said, 'I know you will take care of it, but I can't say the same for John.' When John realised that Linda had been given the card and the pin, he was furious. Linda said, 'I know what you've been doing – and you should be ashamed of yourself.'

But once George came home, John demanded to have the card back, because he said that he needed to buy food for his father. Linda said, 'Don't you dare take any more money out than you need because, both your brother George, and I, have got your number!'

His response was, 'He's got loads of bloody money, and he doesn't fucking need it, and I fucking do!'

Once George was rushed back into hospital, a meeting was requested between George's children and the geriatrician. John telephoned Linda and said, 'You don't need to attend, I am in control here, so keep out of the way.'

Then, Linda had a telephone call from the nurses on the ward. They told her that a meeting had been arranged for eleven in the morning and that they thought it was important that she was told, because they felt that she should be there. So, just before eleven, Linda arrived. John's reaction was one of absolute fury, 'What the fuck are you doing here,' he said, 'I told you, you weren't to come.'

Linda said, 'No one keeps me away from my father when it comes to what should be decided for him, so don't tell me I can't be here.'

John walked away down the corridor towards the geriatrician's office at great speed, and when the geriatrician opened the door, John said to him, whilst pointing at Linda, '*She* doesn't need to be here. I'm in control here, not *her.*'

Linda looked towards the geriatrician, and just shook her head. The geriatrician invited her in, much to John's annoyance.

In the geriatrician's office, John stood up in the meeting, and said about Linda, 'Don't take any notice about what she might want to say. I want you to give my father every conceivable antibiotic or drug to save him. I have done everything for him, so what I say, goes.'

The geriatrician let John have his tirade, then turning to Linda said, 'And what are your feelings about it all, my dear?'

'Well,' she said, 'I have observed him quite closely over the last few months and I believe that he has advanced Parkinson's with dementia.' John reacted angrily with, 'Because Ralph had Parkinson's, and everyone's got bloody Parkinson's!'

Linda said, 'That isn't the case at all.'

The geriatrician said to Linda, 'Could you tell me why you make that observation?'

Linda said, 'When he was at home and I visited him, I noticed that, as he walked, he was trying to "catch up" with his own feet. I also noticed that he was right-handed, but his left hand shook violently. He was having problems swallowing, and he could not manage to cut his food up so he often resorted to using his fingers to eat off the plate – something that he would never had done in the past.'

'I know you are in the business of curing people, but there is a sense when time catches up and one realises that to cure the person, is not going to be an option. So, I think that what should happen, is that you should ease his passage to the next world as comfortably as possible. And I want it to end for his sake.'

John stood up again and said, 'He hasn't got bloody Parkinson's, he's alright. She doesn't know what she's talking about.'

The geriatrician said, 'Actually, your sister knows exactly what she's talking about. Your father has advanced Parkinson's with advanced dementia and indeed, he is terminally ill, just having a matter of a few days to live.'

John was utterly shocked.

The geriatrician said, 'The problem is, we cannot ascertain your father's wishes. He is obviously too sick to go home.'

Linda said, 'Don't worry doctor, I will sort this out. My brother and I will visit Dad on Sunday, and I will find a way to get him to communicate his wishes.'

John was livid because he didn't want to do any of this. But, he went back to the hospital on the Sunday evening where he and Linda sat with their father. Linda said to George, 'Dad, I'm going to ask you some questions and I want you to help me by trying to communicate, either with a noise, a nod of your head, or, to speak if and when you feel that you can. John will write down your wishes for the doctors once we know them.'

Linda began by asking him if he wanted to go home? He shook his head with a "no". John was surprised by this and dutifully wrote down Linda's questions along with their father's answers.

Linda continued, 'Do you want to keep taking all this medication?' He shook his head again with another, "no" as Linda continued, 'Do you want the treatment to be stopped?'

George nodded in the affirmative. Linda said to him, 'Do you realise what that will mean?'

He nodded, with a 'yes,' again.

Linda said, 'So you have had enough?'

He nodded 'Yes.'

Linda said, 'Do you just want to have help with your pain, and slip peacefully away?'

'Yes,' he nodded.

Throughout the questioning, he kept hold of Linda's hand. He struggled to say to Linda, 'You're in pain, aren't you?'

Linda said, 'I'm always in pain, Dad, but it's fine.'

George said, 'I feel so guilty, because of you.'

Linda said, 'There is no need to feel guilty, and the buck stops here, right now. I have never blamed you or Mum because of my disabilities.'

George struggled to say, 'Yes, but it's my fault.'

Linda said, 'It isn't, and I love you.' He squeezed her fingers and they said goodbye. John and Linda went to the nursing station and handed in the piece of paper with the questions and answers. Within minutes of Linda reaching home, John telephoned her saying, 'I don't know how you did that today?'

Linda said, 'I don't know what you mean?'

'Well, talking to Dad like that,' he said.

Linda said, 'Well, was it wrong? Isn't it all about giving people a choice if it's humanly possible? It may not be our choice, but it is important that they are given it and we get to know their wishes.'

John said, 'Well, all I know is, I couldn't have done what you did. It was bloody marvellous.'

Linda said, 'So I'm not so bad after all?'

In the next few days, George became very weak. Linda called her brother, George, in Sweden, and he flew over on the 23rd of October. George Senior was told that he was coming. George got to the hospital and found that his father was coming towards the end so he said goodbye to him, and gave him a kiss. He died while George was halfway down the corridor towards the exit of the hospital. One of the doctors who was a Christian, rang Linda to tell her that her father had died.

Again, Linda felt sad because she had now missed the final partings of both her parents. However, she was relieved that her father was now at peace.

Linda was very grateful that her father had given her one of Alma's rings and he had also given her some of the money that he felt was owed to her from the whole mortgage and money situation that Alma and Linda had put together. He gave Linda ten-thousand pounds in recognition of what she'd lost. This was put towards her future care needs. Linda was grateful that her father had acknowledged that the way she'd been treated was desperately unfair, and he wanted to make amends.

Chapter 61

Linda's brother, John, wasted no time in getting things organised to suit himself. Within days of his father's death, he had organised one of his friends to make a bid for his father's home. All the furniture was cleared and he said that he'd given it all away to charity, but both Linda and George knew that that wouldn't be the case – he would have sold the leather furniture as quickly as humanly possible. He had taken the sideboard and corner units into his own home.

Most of Alma and George's personal possessions, including Alma's jewellery, were suddenly no longer in existence. Alma had wanted her jewellery to be given to Linda, but unfortunately John got his hands on it first! John had put six of Alma's rings into a wooden pot which George, not realising the significance, gave to Linda. Linda checked with a jeweller only to find that five of the good diamond rings had been swapped and replaced by John with cheap paste versions.

The final ring in the pot was of only a minimal value. Fortunately, Alma's favourite ring had already been given to Linda by her father just after she died. As far as John was concerned, all this was, "payback-time" for the way that his father had treated him all those years earlier – with his denigrating "shit-raker" comments.

John tried to exert his authority over everyone and everything, concerning his father's funeral arrangements. He contacted the minister of the Methodist Church that Alma had attended. He chose the hymns and the readings without any consultation with Linda or George. Linda had expressed that she would like to do a reading and speak at the service, but John told the minister that Linda wasn't capable of speaking, or doing a reading, because she would have to read it in Braille.

One of the hymns that John chose was, "Abide with Me", John loved this because of his connection with football, but Linda knew that her father hated it. George senior found the words very depressing. Linda rang the Methodist minister herself in her capacity as a local preacher. She asked him to come and see her so that she could explain to him the behaviour of her brother, John.

After their discussion, the Minister said that he could understand why Linda wanted to carry out her father's wishes, but because John was so aggressive, particularly in relation to her, he thought that in terms of the hymn, it would be better to let him have his way. Linda didn't agree, but went along with it for the sake of public relations. George, being in Sweden, was a little removed from the situation, so let John and Linda fight it out between themselves.

John was all set to make a speech on the day, but at the last moment, chickened-out, putting his thoughts down on paper and giving them to the Minister to read out instead. The service went without a hitch, but George felt that he did not wish to speak publicly. He was worried about breaking down in public, so Linda took the main speaking role. At the end of the service, the Minister came over to Linda and said, 'I owe you a profound apology.'

Linda was surprised. 'What for?'

'Your brother gave me the impression that you were not capable enough to be involved with the service, and that you didn't have the intelligence, and that it would all be too much for you to handle. I should have believed *you* when you told me what you had done as a local preacher. But unfortunately, your brother is very good at using his own "powers of persuasion".'

Linda said, 'Yes, I know, and that is his problem. He does not know the difference between reality, fantasy, and fiction, I'm sad to say.'

John was most upset that the bank froze his father George's bank accounts. He wanted to get his hands on his money as quickly as possible. Then, to his dismay, John found that Alma and George's lawyers had gone into administration, therefore, the matter of George's will would not be resolved quickly. John contacted Linda in a hysterical panic, and explained the situation saying, 'You have got to do something, and you've got to do it *now!*'

Linda said, 'I can't do anything about it. It's just got to take its course.'

John said, 'I know you could work your magic, but *I* could never be able to sort it out.'

Linda said, 'It's funny how you never give me any credit unless it's to your complete advantage. Your behaviour is absolutely disgusting.'

His expletives were *utterly* disgusting. Nevertheless, Linda asked her own solicitor to see what could be done. She also gave the solicitor dates when she felt that John would be using his father's Post Office card. The reality was, that

John had not informed the Post Office of his father's death, and was continuing to withdraw money every week on his dead father's behalf.

Much to John's annoyance, the solicitor demanded the Post Office card from him and informed the Post Office of George's death. Linda asked her solicitor to confront John over what he'd done and then ensure that the money was paid back to Linda and George because John had had more than his fair share.

John was livid. He told the solicitor that as the eldest son, he felt that he should take charge of Linda's percentage of George's estate because she was not capable of understanding and dealing with her own affairs. The solicitor said to John, 'Don't you dare talk to me about your sister in that way. She is one of the most highly capable people I have ever known, and she is certainly very capable of dealing with her own affairs – she does not need your greedy intervention.'

The solicitor said to Linda, 'In all my years as a solicitor dealing with testamentary affairs, I have never experienced such avaricious behaviour as I have received from your brother, John. I have told your brother that if he persists in this regard, implying that you are not capable, then I will go to the Court of Protection myself, and tell them that you most certainly are.'

Later that day, John called Linda, and heaped yet another torrent of abuse on her.

The share of George's estate was eventually divided up between all three siblings, less testamentary and funeral expenses. But John thought that he had the last laugh because when it came to the alteration of the headstone and the certificate that John held to put George's body alongside Alma's, he had decided that he would not share the cost of the contribution, so this had to be met by Linda and George alone – much to John's great glee. He really was a *despicable* individual. That was evident some years later when John died of dementia and the cost of his own funeral expenses was broached.

None of his children, or indeed, any of his family, made any contribution because they felt that they owed him nothing. As much as Linda tried to convince them otherwise, they would have none of it. So again, it was left to Linda and George to shoulder the responsibility, because as Linda said to George, 'Mum and Dad would expect us to bury their son.'

Much of the money that was left to Linda, apart from a ring that she purchased in memory of her father, was eventually swallowed up in care costs and now that it wasn't governed by sniping back-biting from John, Linda now had a much more peaceful relationship with her brother George, and his wife, who continue to live in Sweden. George and Linda could never understand the jealousy that John had towards them.

John wanted what they had worked hard for and he could never understand how his actions of leading such a selfish life, had not only affected his life, but everyone else's life that he touched. All of his children experienced rejection by him at one time or another, when he wanted to "move on" to pastures new and form other relationships having yet more children. So the resentment they felt was completely understandable and anyone who knew the situation could appreciate their lack of respect for him.

In relation to the feelings that Linda had for her family, particularly Alma and George, it was one of total admiration, particularly in relation to Alma – her total dedication to supporting Linda in her life had been exemplary. Alma gave her own life to support Linda's. Everything was fine for many years until Linda fell in love with Ralph.

This was something that Alma could not tolerate in any shape or form. She could not bear to think that Linda could love anyone more than her. However, for Linda, it had not been a case of loving Alma more or less than Ralph, as it should have been a happy, shared experience, and it was a profound tragedy that Alma could not come to terms with the fact that Linda had found love.

Linda, as Dr Lin Berwick MBE, continues to live her life as fully as she's able, despite the constraints of total blindness, partial deafness, and multiple physical disabilities. Linda continues to work as a writer, lecturer, broadcaster, and freelance journalist, and this is achieved by her wonderful support worker and amanuensis, Stephen Cottage, who continues to work tirelessly with her on all her projects. Linda is also indebted to Mary Spain for the way in which she has encouraged her with the reading of her scripts and for the wonderful literary advice that she has freely given in friendship.